SAMUEL JOHNSON
AND THE AGE OF TRAVEL

Samuel Johnson, L.L.D., from the original drawing in the possession of Mr. John Simco, taken from the life, a short time before his decease and etched by T. Trotter, probably the last portrait executed in Johnson's lifetime, appeared as the frontispiece of *The Beauties of Samuel Johnson* (1787). Courtesy of the Harvard College Library.

SAMUEL JOHNSON

AND THE
AGE OF TRAVEL

by

THOMAS M. CURLEY

Athens
THE UNIVERSITY OF GEORGIA
PRESS

Library of Congress Catalog Card Number: 74–30677
International Standard Book Number: 0–8203–0380–1

The University of Georgia Press, Athens 30602

Set in 11 on 14 pt. Janson type
Printed in the United States of America

For Ann

Wherein I spake of most disastrous chances,
Of moving accidents by flood and field,
Of hair-breadth 'scapes i' the imminent deadly breach,
Of being taken by the insolent foe
And sold to slavery, of my redemption thence
And portance in my travel's history;
Wherein of antres vast and deserts idle,
Rough quarries, rocks, and hills whose heads touch heaven,
It was my hint to speak, such was the process;
And of the Cannibals that each other eat,
The Anthropophagi, and men whose heads
Do grow beneath their shoulders. This to hear
Would Desdemona seriously incline.

Shakespeare, *Othello*

CONTENTS

ACKNOWLEDGMENTS

Whatever explorations and discoveries appear in the following pages owe much to the assistance and encouragement of friends, teachers, and family. I am grateful for the counsel offered by Bishop Hunt, Douglas Butturff, and Paul Hamill in the early stages of this undertaking. Joseph Yokelson and Donald Johnson read part of my manuscript and provided many helpful suggestions. My largest intellectual debt is to two devoted Johnsonians. Maurice J. Quinlan has been over the years a thoughtful mentor and a kind companion, who early introduced me to the riches of eighteenth-century literature and later urged me to investigate the subject of travel. For the past decade he has challenged and corrected me, and our shared literary voyaging into the past has profited me greatly. Walter Jackson Bate has been to me an inspiring teacher of Johnson's thought. His instruction and erudition have deeply influenced my understanding of the age of Johnson, and his supervision and support of my preliminary research have proved invaluable to me ever since.

For financial aid that enabled me to study in England and tour the Hebrides along Johnson's itinerary, I am indebted to the award of a Dexter Traveling Fellowship by Harvard University.

I am thankful for the generous help of numerous college librarians at home and abroad and wish to acknowledge the friendly assistance of Joyce Leung who eased the burdens that Johnson had associated with literary research: "A man will turn over half a library to make one book."

Finally, my greatest debt of gratitude begins and ends at home. What Johnson affirmed of all human effort, "whatever enlarges hope, will exalt courage," applies equally to the unwearied encouragement of my wife and parents. My wife has loyally dedicated the past five years to assisting me in this study, and to her I happily and gratefully dedicate this book.

INTRODUCTION

SAMUEL JOHNSON once remarked, "The eyes of the mind are like the eyes of the Body. They can see but at such a distance. But because we cannot see beyond this point, is there nothing beyond it?"[1] This statement is pertinent to a study of Johnson and his age of travel. He shared with his contemporaries a passion for investigating the new and the unknown embodied in the idea of travel. Travel was a national enthusiasm and a prime manifestation of that exuberant Georgian curiosity to survey and to study the expanding geographical frontiers of human knowledge. The eighteenth century ushered in a geographical revolution in exploration and discovery that colored Johnson's entire career. His writings proclaim a boundless curiosity about the globe and show a pervasive preoccupation with travel in every conceivable way. Travel remained for him a central vehicle and symbol of intellectual growth in his life, his morality, and his society. To examine his complex relationship to the subject is to illuminate a crucial concern of the man and the period. His biographers have all emphasized his fondness for a journey, and a few articles have analyzed his principles of touring. My attempt in this study is to explore his life and literary achievement in terms of the geographical movements and travel themes of his day.

Why, we might ask, was he so fascinated with travel? The cultural perspective of his age and his own moral vision of man best answer that question. The years spanning Johnson's life marked an era of unprecedented tourism and geographical discovery in English history. At the time Britons conquered Canada and half of India, lost control of North America but won dominion over the Pacific, sent embassies into China and adventurers into Africa, colonized Australia and traded everywhere else, and bequeathed to Victorians one of the most extensive empires ever known to man. Johnson could not but be interested in travel and geography during a period when

Englishmen emerged as the foremost tourists and explorers of Europe. Moreover, his philosophy of human nature made a study of the dynamics and procedures of travel imperative. His morality metaphorically elevates mankind to the plane of empirical explorers having to learn the art of living wisely from practicing the rules of traveling well. His literary criticism sets forth one of the most comprehensive theories of travel in his century to advertise the proper principles for conducting a journey on the road and in the moral pursuit of happiness. Under his pen, actual travel readily shaded into a symbolic journey of life and human growth in the disillusioning realities of the world. He could represent Susannah Thrale's modest jaunt to the Portland cliffs as a momentous moral adventure for all men to imitate: "Description is always fallacious, at least till you have seen realities, you cannot know it to be true, This observation might be extended to Life."[2] His metaphorical leap from real to symbolic travel is indicative of the close ties that existed between the study of geography and the precepts of morality in his writings.

He asked all men to make their lives a perpetual moral journey of empirical inquiry for testing unproven notions against true facts and arriving at valid conclusions about the human condition: " 'General principles must be had from books, which, however, must be brought to the test of real life'."[3] This observation could serve as a summary axiom not only of his ethical ideas but also of his two-fold intellectual debt to tradition and personal experience during his writing career. His mind was enriched by both a vast heritage of learning and an astute study of "the great book of mankind" before him. Though a bookish man who reverenced the legacy of past literature, he carefully attended to the realities of his modern world to validate or modify his great store of knowledge. Geography and travel afforded him a wealth of factual data about the human family to supplement and often challenge his ideas about mankind. A Renaissance guidebook admired by Johnson, James Howell's *Instructions for Forreine Travell*, had stressed the need for grounding traditional learning in an eyewitness survey of human diversity around

the globe: "*Books* also, and conversation with the *Dead* . . . edifie
infinitely; yet the study of living men, and a collation of his own
Optique observations and judgement with theirs, work much more
strongly, and where these meet (I meane the living and the dead)
they perfect."[4] Johnson carried out this recommendation and performed his empirical study of a worldwide humanity by traveling as
much as he could and by reading travel literature throughout his life.

His profound knowledge of geography embraced every region
of the globe and every major development in the history of exploration from Columbus's early feats to Cook's latest triumphs. He came
into close contact with many famous voyagers and travelers of his
century and defended the progress of geographical discovery for
the advancement of the arts and sciences: "The necessity of some
acquaintance with *geography* and *astronomy* will not be disputed.
If the pupil . . . is dedicated to any of the learned professions, it is
scarcely possible that he will not be obliged to apply himself . . . to
these studies, as no other branch of literature can be fully compre-
hended without them; . . . in a word, no studies afford more extensive,
more wonderful, or more pleasing scenes, and therefore there can
be no ideas impressed upon the soul, which can more conduce to its
future entertainment."[5] Geography was essential to human learning, and Johnson perfected his knowledge of the discipline by familiarizing himself with three centuries of travel literature. Reading
travel books remained one of his favorite pastimes and serious intellectual pursuits. His many writings on geographical literature display a solid grasp of various traditions of travel and promote improved literary standards in a genre that peculiarly appealed to
eighteenth-century readers. He spoke for many of his contemporaries when he praised the labors of travelers for both the instruction
and pleasure that their romantic reports gave a grateful public.

One measure of the immense popularity of travel literature is that
almost every important writer from Swift and Fielding to Smollett
and Sterne worked in the form or turned it to literary uses. Fiction
aped its conventions, and poetry absorbed its findings. Johnson's

labors in biography, history, and morality are an outstanding case in point. He plundered travel books for source material, published a distinguished travel book, and exploited the concept of travel in his moral essays and fables. When he prayed, or wrote, or talked, he organized his thoughts and dramatized all human endeavor by travel metaphors. The completion of the *Dictionary* reminded him of a "long and painful voyage round the world of the English language." The death of his wife left him appealing for grace in his earthly pilgrimage to "pass through things temporal as finally to gain ever-lasting happiness, and to pass by a holy and happy death, into the joy which thou hast prepared for those that love thee." His essays and poems transform the chaotic spectacle of human hopes and fears into an integrated Quixotic odyssey for self-fulfilment ultimately speeding his moral pilgrims on their progress to paradise. *Rasselas* is his classic expression of the journey theme permeating his writings. The creation of this masterpiece of moral analysis involved a complex synthesis of travel archetypes in history and literature that resulted in a unique interpretation of man's perennial quest for happiness. The tale brilliantly exemplifies that creative interaction between travel books and belles lettres so prevalent in eighteenth-century English literature.

Even more than writing about travel or reading travel books, Johnson dearly loved a ramble to invigorate the body and stimulate the mind: "Every new scene impresses new ideas, enriches the imagination, and enlarges the power of reason, by new topicks of comparison."[6] The fact that he never traveled more than five hundred miles from his beloved London has given rise to the erroneous notion of his contempt for touring. On the contrary, all his life he was planning distant expeditions around the world and actually executed tours of Great Britain, Wales, and France that reflected contemporary trends in geographical research. His major experiment in travel was his excursion to the Hebrides that inspired his masterful survey of cultural upheaval in *A Journey to the Western Islands of Scotland*. In one of the finest travel books of the century he appears as a scientific humanist of exploration, implementing investigative techniques that made his age a cosmopolitan era of remarkable geographical discovery. His travel book is unique among his works for documenting the intellectual process of a great thinker coming to grips with an unknown moral environment and forming conclusions about mankind from the immediate data of his Highland experience: "But now I am here, it will gratify me very little to return without seeing or doing my best to see what these places afford. I have a desire to instruct myself in the whole system of pastoral life, but I know not whether I shall be able to perfect the idea. However I have many pictures in my mind, which I could not have had without this Journey."[7] The Highland tour was meant to be a prelude to more ambitious travels abroad. Most readers are unaware of his keen curiosity to visit the most remote regions of the East and West. For many years he seems even to have considered a voyage to Iceland and other northern countries, but his explorations would carry him no farther than to the remote glens and gloomy isles of northern Britain. The failure to realize his numerous schemes of travel saddened his final years and made his life a personal case history of the vanity of human wishes.

Any appraisal of Johnson's varied interests in travel must take into account most aspects of his literary career and most of the revolutionary developments in Georgian exploration. His life and writings present a miniature history of geographical discovery that illustrates the cultural impact of a greatly broadened knowledge of the globe upon the minds and letters of contemporary Englishmen. He was a truly representative author caught up in the romance of eighteenth-century travel and intrigued by the influx of geographical information rapidly changing the Georgian world picture on all intellectual fronts. Reports of Australian cannibals, noble Pacific savages, Patagonian giants, African pygmies, and a Chinese culture antedating Noah's flood all offered new challenges to old assumptions about the nature of man and the formation of societies. Certainly the times aroused great geographical expectations when Bishop Berkeley could prophesy the rise of the United States and Samuel Johnson could hope for the spread of civilization around the world: " 'We have taught you, (said he,) and we'll do the same in time to all barbarous nations—to the Cherokees—and at last to the Ouran-Outangs.' "[8] The expanding frontiers of this richly diversified globe beckoned the Georgian pioneer, trader, missioner, and explorer with the irresistible promise of glory, adventure, and empire. Johnson usually applauded their enterprise, fully shared their curiosity, and always dreamed of joining their company.

I

JOHNSON'S LIFETIME
1709-1784
THE AGE OF TRAVEL

> It was a golden age, which united humanity and science, ex-
> empted men of liberal minds and education, employed in the
> noblest of all occupations, that of exploring the distant parts of
> the Globe, from being any longer degraded, and rated as little
> better than the Buccaneer, or pirate, because they had, till then,
> in manners been nearly similar.
>
> James Bruce, *Travels to Discover the Source of the Nile*

JOHNSON ALWAYS INSISTED that to know life well, one must see
it at first hand. He presided over an inquisitive age of travel and discovery distinguished by a spirit of restless inquiry in every corner
of the globe. The expanding British empire was broadening the Englishman's mind about the complex nature of his world and his fellow human beings. There was a growing awareness that new continents and advanced civilizations existed beyond European shores,
that religions were radically different and morality was not absolute,
and that social customs varied with race and environment. English
explorers were major catalysts of this contemporary geographical
revolution, which a vast store of travel books chronicled for a curious reading public. Travel literature had an immense impact on the
eighteenth-century arts and sciences; belles lettres fell under its influence as never before, and prose fiction was characterized by a
variety of journey plots and traveling protagonists. Johnson lived
in a time when history and literature were being dramatically shaped
by travel. His writing career and friendships with famous travelers
brilliantly mirror his geographical epoch.

To understand the rapid advances in eighteenth-century geography, we might follow Johnson's advice in *The Vanity of Human Wishes* and "Survey Mankind, from *China* to *Peru*" on the maps published before his birth in 1709. The empty spaces on early charts indicate European ignorance of nearly two-thirds of the earth. Some seventeenth-century cartographers had depicted America and Australia wider by almost half of their true size and Asia narrower by a fourth of its total land mass. The polar regions, Australasia, and Polynesia were virtually *terrae incognitae;* the interiors of Russia, Asia, Africa, India, and America were shrouded in mystery and ripe for future exploration. Near the end of the seventeenth century, Sir William Temple conceded the superiority of the moderns over the ancients in navigation but deplored the considerable deficiencies in geography: "Thus we are lame still in geography itself, which we might have expected to run up to so much greater perfection by the use of the compass; and it seems to have been little advanced these last hundred years."[1] To have surveyed mankind at the time of Johnson's birth would necessarily have resulted in overlooking vast areas and multitudes of humanity just when the scientific study of geography was dawning.

The consequences of this inadequate geographical knowledge upon contemporary attitudes toward mankind must have been immense. The failure to fully appreciate the diversity of foreign cultures made widespread generalizations about the moral uniformity of man easier to maintain. Johnson was but one of many in his age who believed that all men possessed basically the same rational nature, psychological code of behavior, religious and moral drives, and social instincts. The majority of famous English philosophers affirmed the existence of a homogeneous humanity, regardless of time or place. Hobbes assumed a "similitude of passions" among men, Locke postulated a universal pleasure-pain principle, Berkeley conceived a uniform working of the divine mind in nature, and even Hume the skeptic presupposed a "pre-established harmony" in human actions. To Hume, a denial of uniformity in human nature was self-confessed error: "Should a traveller . . . bring us an account of men, wholly different from any with whom we were ever acquainted . . . we should immediately . . . prove him a liar, with the same certainty as if he had stuffed his narrative with stories of centaurs and dragons, miracles and prodigies."[2] However, despite Hume's conviction, the eighteenth-century traveler would increasingly challenge such philosophical assumptions with forceful evidence of moral relativism around the world.

Centuries of geographical ignorance not only reinforced notions of moral uniformity but also strengthened English prejudices about foreign countries. Johnson was typically British in thinking that only Europe and the Mohammedan empire deserved being called civilized. Moreover, Europeans themselves were subjected to a rigid classification of national traits. From the time of the Renaissance, Spaniards were typed as grave, Germans were stolid, Italians were sensual, the French were frivolous, and the English were melancholy eccentrics. These stereotypes often survived in eighteenth-century literature, most notably in Goldsmith's *The Traveller* as well as in essays, plays, and novels portraying foreign personalities. In *Tom Jones* the Man of the Hill recognizes a uniform human nature cloaked under distinct national traits: "In *Spain* these are equipped with much Gravity; and in *Italy*, with vast Splendor. In *France*, a Knave is dressed like a Fop; and in the Northern Countries, like a Sloven. But Human Nature is every where the same, every where the Object of Detestation and Scorn."[3] So many travel books assumed these national stereotypes that in 1767 Samuel Paterson could burlesque the convention in his *Another Traveller!* and have his mock tourist replace objective inquiry on the Continent with mere presuppositions about Europe. Significantly, Paterson's satire suggests the growing reaction against national myths among the more enlightened tourists of the century.

Seventeenth-century guidebooks are an excellent index of English prejudices and tourist techniques prevailing before the rise of scientific travel in the next century. Jean Gailhard's *The Compleat*

Gentleman (1678) summarized the national types as follows: *"In Behaviour:* French courteous. Spaniard lordly. Italian amorous. German clownish."[4] Furthermore, Gailhard and fellow Renaissance commentators advocated a method of grand touring that served only to reinforce such generalizations. They asked tourists to accept these stereotypes beforehand, then superficially survey aristocratic sights tending to confirm their truth, and return home convinced of England's superiority over the Continent. Paradoxically, the grand tour was cried up as an educational experience and yet rested on preconceptions to be preserved abroad by a sufficiently generalized round of inquiries that would leave British prejudices untested and British patriotism intact. An outstanding example of a travel book based on unexamined generalizations is Gilbert Burnet's *Some Letters, containing an Account of . . . Switzerland, Italy, and Parts of Germany* (1686). Burnet was less concerned with geographical description than with political propaganda capitalizing on national stereotypes to advertise his Whig sentiments. Under his pen, countries become telling symbols of political conditions in England before the accession of William and Mary. Switzerland exemplifies rugged Protestant virtues whereas France and Italy represent Catholic corruption and tyranny. In the end, Germany and William of Orange offer the ideal pattern of Protestant moderation in religion and government for importation into England during the Glorious Revolution.

As Burnet's work testifies, the narrow geographical horizons of an earlier era fostered equally narrow generalizations about foreign cultures. At the beginning of the eighteenth century, Englishmen knew little more of the globe than their Elizabethan forebears did, and the excitement of opening up new frontiers increasingly colored the exuberant spirit of the age. The world lay all before them in beckoning splendor and portentous grandeur, and scientific travelers surveyed foreign shores with greater care and in ever greater numbers. The ancient fables of Cathay and *Terra Australis* now became realities of accurate empirical travel and tempted the contemporary imagination beyond European borders of experience: "When, after passing from *Europe*, we enter on the nearest part of *Africa*, do we not seem to be got into another World? Even the *Indians* themselves tho' not altogether so rude, can be accounted little better than Barbarians, when compared with our civiliz'd Nations. Who would have believ'd that beyond these, should be found a People powerful, well-govern'd, skilful in Arts, and addicted to the Sciences?"[5] With the passing years, Johnson and his age grew more intimately acquainted with Chinese mandarins, African hottentots, Indian maharajahs, Australian aborigines, and Polynesian islanders than ever before.

Blessed with peace at home, Europeans could shift their enterprising energies and martial ambitions to the work of exploring and colonizing the globe. French Jesuits surveyed China; Vitus Bering clarified the separation of Asia and America; Robert Clive made India a British province; James Bruce visited the source of the Nile; and English navigators ended conjectures about the unknown Pacific. At home the reliable maps of Herman Moll and Guillaume de Lisle, the perfection of the sextant by John Hadley, and the improvement of the marine chronometer by John Harrison went hand in hand with the most remarkable feat of all, the British exploration of the South Seas. The brilliant sailors and geographers of George III applied sophisticated techniques of scientific investigation to unveil the southern hemisphere and lay to rest the major remaining mysteries of the globe. John Byron, Samuel Wallis, and James Cook all brought glory to England by completing the mapping of all the earth's land masses and oceans. As the editor of Cook's last journal observed, "Before these voyages took place, nearly half the surface of the globe we inhabit was hid in obscurity and confusion. What is still wanting to complete our geography, may justly be termed the *minutiae* of that science."[6] When Johnson died in 1784, most of the blank spaces on early charts had been removed.

The progress of geographical discovery had been stimulated by the growth of the British empire. Pope's imperial prophecy in *Wind-*

sor Forest, "The time shall come, when free as Seas or Wind / Unbounded *Thames* shall flow for all Mankind," was a proper prelude to the unprecedented enlargement of the British domains in the western and southern hemispheres. Commercial expansion under the great chartered companies of England—East India, South Seas, Hudson's Bay, Royal African, and Levant—preceded political power and geographical exploration in those areas. During the Seven Years War (1756–1763), Chatham, the fierce imperialist, won from France complete supremacy over the seas and the world's trade. His victories in Quebec, Guadeloupe, Calcutta, Dakar, and Manila gave Britain control of North America, the Caribbean, India, the slave trade of Africa, and a South Pacific access to China. By the end of the century, England could boast of a virtually unrivaled hold over most of the non-European world as well as an unequaled mastery of geographical discovery in her remote possessions. The nation supported this aggressive imperialism although war-weariness, heavy taxes, and moral indignation over colonial exploitation created opposition among many of the Georgian writers. There was a growing body of anti-imperialistic literature, such as Abbé Raynal's *Histoire philosophique . . . du commerce des Européens dans les deux Indes* (1770), condemning encroachments abroad. Johnson himself strenuously objected to colonial policies on moral and legal grounds and yet felt a patriotic pride in the magnificence of the British Empire.

Johnson proudly addressed his king in glowing celebration of England's hegemony over the globe in 1766: "Your power is acknowledged by nations, whose names we know not yet how to write, and whose boundaries we cannot yet describe. But Your MAJESTY's lenity and benevolence give us reason to expect the time, when . . . multitudes, who now range the woods for prey, and live at the mercy of the winds and seasons, shall, by the paternal care of Your MAJESTY, enjoy the plenty of cultivated lands, the pleasures of society, the security of law, and the light of Revelation."[7] His Roman faith in a universal empire of law and Christianity, peace and letters, expressed the contemporary expansionist mood in its most humanitarian form.

But it was a faith qualified by serious doubts about the conduct of empire builders, who inevitably betrayed such civilizing goals to oppress backward cultures. Keenly aware of the sad history of European colonization, he shrugged at the price paid for geographical discovery: "It had been happy for the world, Sir, if your hero Gama, Prince Henry of Portugal, and Columbus had never been born."[8] Only if England fulfilled its moral responsibilities to the brotherhood of man, would she be worthy to assume imperial command "And o'er the globe extend your reign, / Unbounded masters of the main."[9]

The growth of the empire and geographical exploration encouraged a new cosmopolitanism in the period. Island bound and yet masters of the seas, Britons generally exhibited a curious blend of contemptuous insularity and sympathetic interest in the diverse human family. Johnson might write off China as uncivilized with something of an ancient Greek's pride in his Athens and distaste for the foreign *barbaroi*. However, Goldsmith could turn the tables on Johnson in *The Citizen of the World* and present a Chinese observer of European barbarity: "[Englishmen] are indeed ridiculous, yet every other nation in Europe is equally so; each laughs at each, and the Asiatic at all."[10] Secure in the knowledge of his homeland's preeminence among nations, the English traveler could afford to investigate other cultures more objectively and appreciatively than his seventeenth-century counterpart did. He was increasingly a scientific explorer, replacing the unenlightened techniques of early tourism with careful and comprehensive research of foreign phenomena. Notwithstanding his patriotism, he often repressed his English prejudices sufficiently to study other nations intensively and sympathetically for a more honest appraisal of people and places abroad. His boundless curiosity and emergent cosmopolitanism earned for his countrymen the title of Europe's citizens of the world. And his findings were offering new challenges to old assumptions of moral uniformity and national stereotypes.

The information of eighteenth-century travelers helped Europe to recognize the fact of moral relativism and cultural diversity around the world. Reports of utopian tribes, giants, pygmies, and other vagaries from the familiar norms of human nature raised doubts about the natural law and a universal code of ethics. Philosophical proponents of moral uniformity had to grant the existence of societies condoning rape, robbery, murder, promiscuity, polygamy, and mercy killing. Locke, for example, pointed out wide disparities in conduct to refute innate ideas. He praised modern navigation for disclosing "whole nations . . . amongst whom there was to be found no notion of a God, no religion."[11] His arguments made conscience a product of one's culture and helped to initiate a defense of relativism among later philosophers. Mandeville found no certainty in morality, and Hume saw the need for establishing new principles, discussed in his *Of the Standard of Taste* (1756), after realizing the discordant ethical and aesthetic values of mankind. No longer could any position possess quite the same absolute validity of reason as before, nor could Europe so easily boast a cultural superiority over other countries. The excellence of customs and conduct depended upon less normative common sense standards of virtue obtained by weighing the cumulative evidence of a diversified world. In Sicily, Patrick Brydone acknowledged that "beauty is a relative quality, and *To kalon* is no longer the same, no more in a physical than a moral sense, in any two parts of the globe."[12] In the Pacific, Captain Cook reported the promiscuity of Tahitians to determine "a question, which has been long debated in philosophy: Whether the shame attending certain actions . . . is implanted in Nature or superinduced by custom?"[13]

Greater familiarity with the Continent eroded conventional classifications of national types in Europe. Abraham Stanyan demonstrated the folly of stereotyping the Swiss in 1714; Lady Mary Wortley Montagu revised her homebred notions of the Viennese in 1718; Samuel Sharp found Savoyard mountaineers as polished as Parisian sophisticates in 1766; and Arthur Young questioned the whole theory of distinct national traits in 1792. Prejudices might persist even among these enlightened tourists, but their narratives manifest doubts about typing certain cultures and show a receptivity to unusual customs. As Arthur Young wrote of his erroneous preconceptions of the French, "I looked for great talkativeness, volatile spirits, and universal politeness. I think, on the contrary, they are not so talkative, have not equally good spirits, and are not a jot more polite."[14] National stereotypes were slowly yielding to an awareness of cultural complexities; the moral uniformity of man had to be proved, not assumed, by examining the facts of cultural diversity. As with Locke and Hume, so also with Pope and Johnson, the recognition of moral relativism was part of a continuing process of searching out universal laws of morality and psychology. This multifarious universe might be "A mighty maze! but not without a plan" of some sort—an intricate cosmos of variant values possessing some underlying principle of order after all.

In Johnson's view man was by nature geared to see and sift life's complexities in order to arrive at tested moral universals and tentative generalizations about mankind. According to his morality travel was a fundamental ethical duty that required all men to join in the Lockean search for factual truths illuminating the unity within diversity of human behavior. A disciple of John Locke, he followed *An Essay concerning Human Understanding* in treating conduct as a dynamic journey of psychological growth in life's realities. He inherited Locke's pervasive vision of man as a free and restless agent of empirical discovery, ever on the move from simple sensations to complex ideas and general axioms and ever on the rise from irrational goals and worldly ambitions to the stability of rational and religious truths: "The chief art of learning, as Locke has observed, is to attempt but little at a time. The widest excursions of the mind are made by short flights frequently repeated; and the most lofty fabricks of science are formed by the continued accumulation of single propositions" (*Rambler* 137). Like Locke and many other writers Johnson acknowledged moral relativism but carried on an inductive search for the uniform moral principles revealing the ultimate constitutional similarity of mankind. Imlac contrasts East and West in *Rasselas* before admitting their common unhappiness. Similarly, by travel and reading travel books, his creator was able to explore the different nations of the world and find "what will always be discover'd by a diligent and impartial Enquirer, that wherever Human Nature is to be found, there is a mixture of Vice and Virtue, a contest of Passion and Reason."[15]

"Deign on the passing world to turn thine eyes" was a basic Johnsonian injunction in all intellectual endeavors: Take to the road and study mankind objectively for the good of mind and soul. What he demanded of others, he practiced himself. He had surveyed mankind from China to Peru by means of travel literature and kept himself well informed about the human condition in every quarter of the globe. His preoccupation with geography embraced practically every major movement in contemporary exploration and colonization. He was a publicist of geographical discovery and mysterious cultures, a friend of eminent explorers and tourists, and an avid fan of voyages and travels. From his wide reading and varied contacts with travelers and navigators, he considerably enhanced his knowledge of foreign customs and societies to validate and sometimes revise his moral notions. What is more, his store of geographical learning is a valuable register of his well-traveled age.

Not surprisingly, his curiosity about the Continent was particularly acute. In his judgment, only Europe was truly civilized because of its inheritance of Christian revelation and classical learning. Hence, he studied its geography and history carefully and propagated its values in his writings. He read more travel literature on Europe than that of any other area, so much so that he wished to see fewer descriptions published. His familiarity with the history of English grand tourism alone ranged from the earliest accounts of Roger Ascham, Thomas Coryate, and James Howell to the more recent narratives of Joseph Addison, Tobias Smollett, and Philip Thicknesse. Some of his closest associates, like Charles Burney and Giuseppe Baretti, ranked among the notable Continental travelers of his day. The most famous grand tourist of all was his great biographer, that ever inquisitive James Boswell. Boswell's modern fame rests mainly on his *Life of Johnson*, but his initial notoriety stemmed from his travel book on Corsica and his account of Johnson's Highland tour. In fact he first became known to English society from his celebrated friendships with Voltaire, Rousseau, and Paoli on his European excursion (1764–1766) and subsequently earned a reputation as the propagandist of Corsican liberty. His journals preserve a brief exchange with perceptive companions who understood the restless nature of this indefatigable traveler: "I said, 'Then what country ought I to adopt?' She replied, 'Europe.' 'And who should be my wife?' Froment exclaimed, 'A post-wagon.'"[16] Johnson shared Boswell's passion for travel and interest in all things European. He would tour France himself in 1775, and, in testimony to his pride of European birth, always evaluated other countries by the Christian standard of European civilization.

Stabilized by the conviction of Europe's cultural superiority, his curiosity was at liberty to survey the most remote lands with considerable objectivity and sympathy. No area was more unlike Europe than the polar region to the north, and probably for that reason he was early intrigued by its geography. Iceland, Greenland, and Scandinavia had received growing attention because of their forbidding climate, Norse antiquities, and importance in explorations for a northern passage to India. Johnson studied polar geography intensively in exciting accounts of Arctic survival and abortive schemes for reaching the Indies by Thomas James, Henry Ellis, and Constantine Phipps. The missionary chronicles of Hans Egede and David Cranz acquainted him with the progress of Christianity in Greenland. Current scientific descriptions by Maupertuis, Erik Pontoppidan, and Niels Horrebov stimulated his imagination with reports of the incredibly destitute natural history of Lapland, Norway, and Iceland respectively. The historical studies of Robert Molesworth, William King, René Aubert de Vertot, Walter Harte, Paul Henry Mallet, and Nathaniel Wraxall kept him informed about the politics and antiquities of Denmark, Sweden, and other northern countries made famous by Charles XII and Peter the Great early in the century. Johnson's careful research in northern geography had a significant influence upon his writings on law and British antiquities and even gave rise to a Greenland tale in *Ramblers* 186 and 187.[17]

His curiosity was especially aroused by the generally terrible climatic conditions that made the people of these regions the most backward on earth. In his Greenland tale polar geography came to symbolize human frailty and mortality: "O life, . . . frail and uncertain! where shall wretched man find thy resemblance but in ice floating in the ocean?" The utterly barren Arctic landscape barely nourished human nature in the rawest form but provided an excellent testing ground for isolating the elemental psychological drives of humanity and proving the moral uniformity of man: "Yet learned curiosity is known to have found its way into those abodes of poverty and gloom: Lapland and Iceland have their historians, their criticks, and their poets; and love, that extends his dominion wherever humanity can be found, perhaps exerts the same power in the Greenlander's hut as in the palaces of eastern monarchs" (*Rambler* 186). To study the polar inhabitants was to discover the universal force of morality, the God-given distribution of basic human necessities to sustain life everywhere around the world, and the incomparable blessings of civilization for complete human fulfillment. The heroic work of Hans Egede and Moravian missionaries in converting and civilizing the Greenlanders powerfully moved a man who supported the pious aims of organizations like the Society in Scotland for Propagating Christian Knowledge and the English Society for Promoting Christian Knowledge.[18] The simple societies in Iceland and Norway offered a useful measure of innate human abilities and limitations and glimpsed the primitive practices and feudal customs that shaped the development of European civilization and English law. The northern countries taught Europeans to appreciate their advantages better and to understand better the origins of their social systems. They remained supreme examples of that wild state of nature which always made Johnson grateful for his London comforts and sympathetic to the plight of the poor savages. Consequently, they had an important place in his geographical inquiries and helped him to answer perhaps the central question in his morality: What is the nature and extent of true human happiness in this world?

Awed by the absolute bleakness of the Arctic, he was eager to survey the repellent scenery of the north on his own. Despite the perils of polar travel, he talked of touring Iceland midway in his writing career and later proposed to Boswell a trip to the Baltic countries in order to view glacial wonders, primitive manners, and Swedish monarchy. Unfortunately, he was destined to be only a reader of Arctic discoveries and left to his two acquaintances, Constantine Phipps and Joseph Banks, the labor of exploring the area. His friend, the lawyer Daines Barrington, persuaded the Royal Society to send Phipps into the Arctic in 1773 on a vain search for a northern passage to India. Johnson knew his northern geography well enough to predict that Barrington's theory of an ice-free polar ocean would prove incorrect: "They hope to find an open Ocean, but I suspect it is one mass of perpetual congelation."[19] Just a year before Phipps returned home in failure, Joseph Banks successfully surveyed Iceland and fulfilled Johnson's dreams of studying the impoverished inhabitants and the remarkable natural curiosities of the country. Banks would later be an influential advocate of Icelandic studies and political liberties and supported England's proposed annexation of the Danish colony in 1801 to improve the substandard life-style of the oppressed natives. Johnson generally approved of such civilizing aims and probably would have applauded both the liberation of Iceland and the discovery of the North Pole in the twentieth century. Yet he always feared the immoral consequences of European exploration even when humanitarian motives of reform governed political intervention abroad.

America was the geographical focal point of his misgivings about European exploration. Columbus "gave a new world to European curiosity and European cruelty" and prepared the way for a series of colonial atrocities and wars culminating in the tragic American revolution.[20] Johnson felt a growing aversion for the Western hemisphere after reading about its miserable colonial history in the voyage accounts of Columbus, Sir Walter Raleigh, and Lionel Wafer; the voluminous chronicles of Spanish, Portuguese, and English conquests by Garcilasso de la Vega, Giorlamo Benzoni, Joseph Lafitau, William Robertson, and Abbé Raynal; and the generally patriotic descriptions of British North America and the West Indies compiled by Richard Hakluyt and reported by Lewis Evans, William Johnson, Patrick Browne, Sir Hans Sloane, Thomas Thompson, and James Adair. The central importance of America in eighteenth-century politics caused Johnson to write considerably and scornfully about its troubled affairs throughout his career. One of his very earliest articles, the introduction to the *Debates in the Senate of Lilliput* (1738), had already deplored European imperialism in America even though there was ironic praise for the cultural and commercial benefits of geographical discovery. Fortunately, however, during this early phase of his career he could point to at least one great colonist in the person of James Edward Oglethorpe (1696–1785) who was indeed planting English civilization in Georgia according to the highest humanitarian principles.

General Oglethorpe obtained his charter for settling Georgia in 1732 and spent the next ten years of his life defending the infant colony against the neighboring Spaniards of Florida. He had the novel idea of establishing a pauper colony prohibiting slavery and, with the assistance of the Wesley brothers, transformed a wilderness of swamps and savannahs into a God-fearing society. London newspapers celebrated his exploits, and Pope enshrined his name in laudatory verse. Even Richard Savage, who had received financial help from Oglethorpe, commemorated the general's labors in a poem that Johnson highly esteemed: "Learn when *Despair* such sudden Bliss shall see / such Bliss must shine from *Oglethorpe* or Me!"[21] There is a tradition that Johnson's bankrupt brother, Nathaniel, planned to migrate to Georgia in the 1730s. Certainly the *Life of Savage* (1744) alludes to the settlement with a mixture of praise and regret over the depopulation of England: "The settlement of colonies in uninhabited countries, the establishment of those in security whose misfortunes have made their own country no longer pleasing or safe . . . cannot be considered without giving rise to a great number of pleasing ideas."[22] His first major poem, *London* (1738), characterizes Georgia as a worthy refuge for the poor and persecuted:

> Has heaven reserv'd, in pity to the poor,
> No pathless waste, or undiscover'd shore;
> No secret island in the boundless main?
> No peaceful desart yet unclaim'd by Spain?
> Quick let us rise, the happy seats explore,
> And bear oppression's insolence no more.
>
> (Ll. 170–175)

Oglethorpe returned the compliment by patronizing the poem in 1738 during a visit to England to recruit soldiers for a current war against Spaniards in Georgia. His enlightened policy of abolishing slavery and converting Indians in this pauper colony surely appealed to Johnson, who hated slavery and supported efforts to alleviate poverty and civilize the savage. Johnson's own black servant, Francis Barber, was a freed Jamaican slave, whom he personally educated and catechized at Gough Square. Years later, the general would seek Johnson's company and reminisce about his colonial experiences and Indian manners. Johnson, in turn, became so impressed with this gallant philanthropist that he considered writing his biography. There were ample materials for a stirring *Life* of Oglethorpe who had in his youth served under Prince Eugene in Eastern Europe; then campaigned for prison reforms and founded Georgia; later marched against the Highland uprising of 1745 and sat in Parliament promoting religious toleration in America; and finally ended his career as a celebrated member of Johnson's circle of friends. Boswell saw the potential for a great biography and urged the octogenarian general to furnish at least the bare outline of his long life: "Dr. Johnson would supply bones and sinews. 'He would be a good Doctor,' says the General, 'who would do that.' 'Well,' says I, 'he is a good Doctor,' at which he, the Doctor, laughed very heartily."[23] Johnson would never write that biography, but his admiration for this brave old soldier continued unabated to the end of his life.

To his sorrow, few American colonists shared Oglethorpe's humanitarian views. On the contrary, their rape of America had plunged Europe into three centuries of warfare in the Western hemisphere. Johnson's political writings in the late 1750s attack the Seven Years War and display unmitigated scorn for Chatham's imperialistic ambitions in the New World. He had not failed to appreciate the significance of such medical discoveries as quinine or the possibility of a powerful nation one day rising from the American wilderness: "Scarce anything is simply evil. . . . [There] is no reason to doubt that the time is approaching when the Americans shall in their turn have some influence on the affairs of mankind, for literature apparently gains ground among them. A library is established in Carolina; and some great electrical discoveries were made at Philadelphia."[24] The prospect of cultivating the rude America of Franklin and Oglethorpe had a strong appeal for this civilized man of civilizing ideas. But, as *Idler* 80 makes clear, Europeans quickly forgot their Christianity among the savages and fought over territories that legally belonged to the Indians. The evils of depopulation at home and tyranny abroad left him hostile to the Americans, who cried for liberty and yet kept slaves. His last political pamphlet, *Taxation No Tyranny* (1775), climaxed his increasing abhorrence of American hypocrisy and championed the cause of the British Empire against colonial struggles for freedom. For England at least had taken the first step in declaring slavery illegal at home in 1772 and, by her part in nurturing and protecting the colonies, had earned the tenuous right to regulate American affairs and control American trade.[25] As events turned out, the success of the American Revolution only reinforced his dark forebodings about the course of geographical discovery and colonization around the world.

Africa afforded him an equally disheartening glimpse of Europe's exploitation of backward races. His earliest condemnation of imperialism appears in *Lobo's Voyage to Abyssinia* (1735) and is directed against Portuguese missionaries "who might preach the Gospel with Swords in their Hands, and propagate by Desolation and Slaughter the true Worship of the God of Peace."[26] He had acquired considerable knowledge about the continent from a history of Portuguese imperialism by Manuel de Faria y Sousa; accounts of northern and western Africa by Lancelot Addison, John Windhus, and Michel Adanson; and numerous descriptions of Abyssinia by Job Ludolf, Michael Geddes, Charles Poncet, and several Portuguese Jesuits. His original interest in Africa centered on the ancient Christian country of Abyssinia but eventually broadened to include most of the known geography along the African coastline. Much of what he learned was put to brilliant use in his African tale, *Rasselas*, and stimulated his attack against Portuguese navigation in his *Introduction to the World Displayed* (1759). The fame of *Rasselas* alone earned him the sobriquet of "Abyssinia's Johnson" and a deserved reputation for being an authority on Africa in his lifetime.

Thus, when in 1773 James Bruce returned from Abyssinia amidst growing doubts about the veracity of his observations, Englishmen awaited Johnson's opinion of this discredited traveler. No doubt, Bruce was an honest man. If contributing no new discoveries himself, he helped to revive British interest in Africa. The Association for the Exploration of the Interior Parts of Africa was founded in 1788 and paved the way for the pioneering expeditions of Livingston, Burton, and Speke in the next century. However, Johnson's contemporaries unjustly suspected Bruce of lying about his amazing adventure and doubted his claim of having discovered the Abyssinian source of the Nile. A few celebrities did accept his findings. The Burney family befriended the haughty explorer and availed themselves of his information and illustrations of African artifacts for inclusion in Charles Burney's *History of Music*. Boswell defended his honesty in print though he considered the traveler a "flinty rock" for refusing to discuss his experiences openly. But

Johnson found him an "indistinct relater" of questionable adventures and apparent falsehoods. He knew that early Portuguese explorers had already claimed the discovery of the Nile's source and might well have rejected Bruce's pretensions to the same feat. Johnson's verdict helped to tarnish a reputation that would not be rehabilitated until the twentieth century. To compound the injury, *Lobo's Voyage to Abyssinia* was republished in 1789 as an antidote to the supposed lies that Bruce would propagate in his *Travels to Discover the Source of the Nile* (1790). So completely had Johnson's name become identified with Africa that his youthful translation of a travel book was allowed to challenge modern exploration.

Of all the global regions, only Asia Minor came close to competing with Europe in the possession of a civilization worthy of Johnson's esteem and closest scrutiny. His study of the Mohammedan Empire entailed research in many books: early English accounts by Richard Knolles and George Sandys; the Koran and two biographies of Mohammed by Humphry Prideaux and Jean Gagnier; Barthelemy Herbelot's *Bibliothèque orientale* and descriptions by Aaron Hill, Thomas Roe, and Thomas Shaw; and the most recent travel books by Richard Pococke, Alexander Russell, Frederick Norden, Lady Mary Wortley Montagu, and S. Lusignan. Johnson credited the Mohammedans with a truly advanced culture primarily because they acknowledged the Bible and Jesus Christ unlike other non-European nations and had developed a sophisticated literature and government influenced by revelation. Consequently, he always exhibited something of an Elizabethan's lively curiosity to visit Constantinople and examine personally Europe's only rival in power and learning. The oriental vogue stimulated by contemporary travel and Eastern tales like Antoine Galland's *Arabian Nights* (1704–1717) would have whetted his curiosity about Asia Minor all the more. There was a revolutionary contact between East and West during the period when Lady Mary Wortley Montagu could send Pope some specimens of Mohammedan poetry, introduce her countrymen to smallpox inoculation, and succumb to the spell of the

Orient: "I am almost of an opinion they have a right notion of life. They consume it in music, gardens, wines, and delicate eating, while we are tormenting our brains with some scheme of politics, or studying some science. . . . I had rather be a rich *effendi* with all his ignorance than Sir Isaac Newton with all his knowledge."[27]

This sense of culture shock pervades Johnson's oriental writings. The very tragic complication of his play *Irene* (1749) originates in a symbolic collision of East and West when his Greek heroine falls victim to a sultan's anti-Christian charms. His Persian tales exploit the exotic appeal of the East to inculcate a Western ethic. *Rasselas* itself communicates oriental romance and universal moral realities by comparing and contrasting the two great world cultures: "When I compared these men with the natives of our own kingdom, and those that surround us, they appeared almost another order of beings. . . . The Europeans, answered Imlac, are less unhappy than we, but they are not happy. Human life is every where a state in which much is to be endured, and little to be enjoyed."[28] The fact that the majority of Johnson's Eastern tales and geographical allusions in moral essays concern Asia Minor emphasizes his interest in the literary orientalism of his age. His reading included travel books on Greece that influenced the rise of that leavening spirit of Hellenism in Romantic literature. He was acquainted with the seminal antiquarian studies of Jacob Spon and George Wheler in the 1680s, the enthusiastic descriptions of classical and biblical ruins by Robert Wood and Alexander Drummond in the 1750s, and the nostalgic account of ancient Greece by Richard Chandler in 1776. The reports of these Grecian travelers combined with Winckelmann's research and the aesthetic theories of Lessing and James Stuart to help create the imaginative watershed, from which issued that momentous love affair with Hellas in the poetry of Keats, Shelley, and Byron.

India had an immense impact on the shift of European attention to the East, and its political importance to the British Empire guaranteed Johnson's fascination with the country. He followed its early colonial history in the chronicles of Jean Baptiste Tavernier, Manuel de Faria y Sousa, John Ovington, and John Fryer. Moreover, he probably read about the most recent political events in the narratives of two friends, Robert Orme's *History of the Military Transactions of the British Nation in Indostan* (1763–1778) and John Hoole's *The Present State of the East India Company's Affairs* (1772). His circle of acquaintances brought him into immediate contact with the affairs of this newest British colony. He became a friend of Warren Hastings in the late 1760s and ever after defended this great governor general of India despite growing opposition to his colonial administration. Other friends, like Robert Chambers and Chauncy Lawrence, relied on his recommendations to Hastings for career advancement abroad. Mindful of colonial abuses, the moralist worried about the conduct of such fortune hunters: "Whatever you do, I do not suspect you of pillaging or oppressing; and shall rejoice to see you return, with a body unbroken, and a mind uncorrupted."[29] He argued the merits of the caste system in the company of Charles Bourchier, governor of Madras, and praised the hospitality of that eminent empire builder, Sir Eyre Coote. A brilliant general instrumental in Lord Clive's conquest of India, Coote (1726–1783) assisted in the decisive victories over the French at Plassey and Wandewash by 1760 and later became the commander in chief of the colony. Briefly garrisoned in the Highlands in 1773, he entertained Johnson with a tour of Fort George and "with such elegance of conversation as left us no attention to the delicacies of his table."[30]

Johnson fully recognized the cultural importance of India to European letters. All his Indian and Persian tales were based on early historical research on the East that would lead to Nathaniel Halhed's *Code of Gentoo Laws* (1776), Charles Wilkins's *Bhagavad-gita* (1784), William Jones's *Institutes of Hindu Law* (1794), and a general renaissance in oriental studies affecting our civilization today.[31] Such a revolution in learning Johnson actively promoted in his letters to Hastings: "I shall hope that he who once intended to encrease the learning of his country by the introduction of the

Persian language, will examine nicely the Traditions and Histories of the East , that he will survey the remains of its ancient Edifices, and trace the vestiges of its ruined cities; and that at his return we shall know the arts and opinions of a Race of Men from whom very little has been hitherto derived."[32] If Hastings could not complete this grand design because of his administrative responsibilities, an admired member of the Literary Club, Sir William Jones, arrived in India to accomplish this scholarly undertaking in the very year of Johnson's death.

As the principal founder of the Asiatic Society of Bengal, Jones (1746–1794) would through his writings revolutionize Indian studies and establish the science of comparative linguistics. His mastery of Sanskrit would unlock the intellectual riches of the *Vedas* and Hindu history, literature, and law to the Western world. His ten presidential discourses for the Asiatic Society gave impetus to others to carry on the devoted labors of his short-lived career in the study of oriental languages and civilizations. His theory of an Indo-European family of languages would challenge centuries of European idolatry for the Graeco-Roman heritage: "The *Sanscrit* language, whatever be its antiquity, is of a wonderful structure; more perfect than the *Greek*, more copious than the *Latin*, and more exquisitely refined than either, yet bearing to both of them a stronger affinity, both in the roots of verbs and in the forms of grammar, than could possibly have been produced by accident."[33] Johnson himself had perceived affinities within certain European languages and supported linguistic research during his career. Had he lived, he would have been the first to approve the new developments and appreciate their significance in the intellectual history of the human race.

China played an equally important part in the contemporary cultural revolution, and Johnson had helped to introduce his countrymen to the wisdom and history of this remote nation. His early review of Jean Baptiste Du Halde's *Description of the Empire of China* for the *Gentleman's Magazine* (1742) distinguished him as one of the first English publicists of the most comprehensive accounts of Asia that existed until the mid-nineteenth century. Moreover, a letter on this work possibly written in part by Johnson appeared in the same magazine in 1738 and conventionally idealized the Chinese to satirize European statecraft. But the long review of 1742 tempered the adulation found even in Du Halde's compilation with a more balanced appreciation of Chinese virtues. There is a careful enumeration of the travelers' credentials and Du Halde's encyclopedic topics to demonstrate the incomparable authenticity and scope of the treatise. Johnson praises the wall of China and the incredible longevity of the Chinese government. Admiration colors his comments on Chinese morality and social moderation in a brief but very sympathetic biography of Confucius: "His whole Doctrine tends to the Propagation of Virtue, and the Restitution of Human Nature to its original Perfection, and it is related that his Precepts always received Illustration from his Example, and that in all Conditions of Life, he took Care to prove by his Conduct, that he required no more from others, than he thought it his own Duty to perform."[34] Yet for all his early interest in Chinese philosophy, Johnson seems to have considered the people a weak and timid race and never granted the Asian culture an equal status with the learning and literature of the West. He would continue to advertise the Chinese in a few later writings and through his patronage of William Chambers's *Designs of Chinese Buildings* (1757). Nevertheless, the nation as a whole was little more than semi-barbarian in his eyes: "I consider them as great, or wise, only in comparison with the nations that surround them; and have no intention to place them in competition either with the ancients or with the moderns of this part of the world."[35]

Probably what most intrigued him about China was its development of advanced arts and sciences independent of any Western influence. To better understand this mysterious culture, he read widely in descriptions of China and neighboring countries. In addition to the studies of China by Du Halde and Chambers, he was familiar with Sir John Mandeville's fabulous medieval *Travels* and John Bell's recent and reliable *Travels from St. Petersburgh, in Russia, to divers Parts of Asia* (1763). He also knew Engelbert Kaempfer's *History of Japan* (1727) and consulted accounts of Russia and Central Asia by John Perry, Jonas Hanway, and Jean Chappe d'Auteroche. *Rasselas* pays tribute to the Chinese wall as the world's greatest wonder, and his assistance in editing Chambers's architectual treatise indicates a concern for acquainting the public with the glories of the Far East. Chambers (1726–1796) would long remain a close friend and later used his firsthand knowledge of China to advance his career and write a second book, *A Dissertation on Oriental Gardening* (1772). He became the architect of Asian landscapes in Kew Gardens and a significant force in spreading an enthusiasm for Chinese art and crafts among his countrymen. Johnson refused to idolize the culture but did express a wish to visit the empire of China in later life. His age obviously stood in his way, but another member of the Literary Club would accomplish an important expedition into China. George Macartney (1737–1806) had earned by his diplomatic services in Russia and the West Indies the royal privilege of attempting to open up political relations between England and China. Johnson pronounced this cultivated earl "in some degree a literary man" and would have envied him the opportunity of leading a major English embassy to Peking in 1792.[36] However, if Johnson had survived to see this undertaking, he might have predicted the unfortunate consequences of British interference in the East in nineteenth-century politics. Ironically, his own small role in publicizing the Chinese added to the growing interest in Asia that preceded the aggressive imperialism of the Victorians.

No area of the globe was more important to British exploration than the South Pacific. Here was the scene of the century's greatest triumphs of scientific discovery. Polynesia and Antarctica entered the European consciousness for the first time and filled the major remaining vacuum in geographical knowledge. Despite Johnson's contempt for the crimes often committed by Pacific discoverers, the heroic dimension of their achievements could not have been missed by a writer who so warmly praised the curiosity of travelers: "Curiosity is, in great and generous minds, the first passion and the last. . . . When Jason, in Valerius Flaccus, would incline the young prince Acastus to accompany him in the first essay of navigation, he disperses his apprehensions of danger by representations of the new tracts of earth and heaven which the expedition would spread before their eyes; and tells him with what grief he will hear, at their return, of the countries which they shall have seen, and the toils which they have surmounted."[37] Not only did Johnson read and write extensively about the entire history of Pacific exploration, but he also associated with many of the principal figures responsible for unveiling the southern hemisphere in his time. His connection with South Sea discovery constitutes an important, if little known, episode of his career and encompasses virtually all the century's maritime feats initiated by Dampier and completed by Cook.

Not all the motives behind Pacific exploration pleased Johnson. While he advocated progress in geography and trade, he realized that securing a Pacific access to the wealth of the East had already led to colonial warfare and exploitation of natives. He was shocked by the flagrant piracy of early South Sea voyages recounted in Hakluyt's collection of travels; laudatory biographies of Sir Francis Drake; and the narratives of Sir John Narborough, William Dampier, and George Shelvocke. Dampier, for example, began his naval career as a buccaneer but after several celebrated voyages in the Pacific established himself as the father of scientific exploration and later colonization in Australasia. Dedicated to the Royal Society, his *New Voyage Round the World* (1697) helped to set a precedent for future expeditions by adopting the geographical principles of that scientific body "for the advancement of Knowledge" in natural history and navigation. This seminal work, which Coleridge considered one of the finest travel books ever written, may have provided both Swift and Defoe with a model to imitate in their voyage tales. Certainly a comparison of *Gulliver's Travels* with the voyage account of "Cousin *Dampier*" greatly illuminates Swift's subtle and pervasive attack against scientific travel. Even the Yahoos of Swift's grotesque world have much in common with the benighted Australian aborigines of Dampier's New Holland: "And setting aside their Humane Shape, they differ but little from Brutes. . . . Their Eye-lids are always half closed, to keep the Flies out of their Eyes. . . . And therefore they cannot see far, unless they hold up their Heads, as if they were looking at somewhat over them."[38] Dampier's account may have provoked Swift's satire, but its positive influence upon later scientific research in the Pacific can scarcely be exaggerated.

George Anson reiterated Dampier's appeal for more professional standards of exploration. His celebrated privateering expedition against Spain (1740–1744) kept interest in the Pacific alive and demonstrated by the loss of numerous ships and sailors the dire need for improvements in navigation, maritime hygiene, and geographical investigation. The voyage uncovered no new discoveries but did offer Englishmen the exciting romance of great adventures, great treasure, and great trials. Anson's description of sailing the horn is a good example of the heroic exploits that so attracted Johnson and Coleridge: "As . . . we presumed we had nothing now before us but an open sea, till we arrived on those opulent coasts, where all our hopes and wishes centered, we could not help flattering . . . our imaginations in those romantick schemes, which the fancied possession of the *Chilian* gold and *Peruvian* silver might be conceived to inspire. . . . Thus animated by these delusions, we travers'd these memorable Streights, ignorant . . . that this day of our passage was the last chearful day that the greatest part of us would ever live to enjoy."[39] A Johnsonian essay or a Coleridgean poem on the delusive voyage of life could hardly have made the point better.

Johnson could claim some part in assisting Anson's designs. His patriotic biographies of Drake and Blake were published on the eve of the commodore's departure in 1740 to arouse public support for current naval operations against Spain by glorifying the past exploits of two famous English sailors. A decade later Johnson was promoting a maritime invention aimed at lessening the kind of navigational problems graphically reported in Anson's *Voyage Round the World* (1748). In a letter partially ghost-written by Johnson, Anson was asked to give his support to Zachariah Williams's scheme for determining the longitude because the seasoned navigator was now the First Lord of the Admiralty who knew "not only by theory, but by long hazardous experience, how much would be added by this improvement to the safety of navigation."[40] Unfortunately the petitions to Anson and the Admiralty Board proved abortive, and Johnson's somber *Account of an Attempt to Ascertain the Longitude at Sea* (1755) documented Williams's successive failures to win acceptance for his findings. Anson's neglect might have soured Johnson's apparent respect for the man. Although Johnson afterwards visited the old sailor at his estate, he repaid Anson's hospitality with a satiric poem and would one day denounce his Pacific voyage in print. The former supporter of Anson's undertaking became its angry critic but would live to see techniques for navigational calculations vastly improved by John Harrison's invention of a more accurate marine chronometer that aided Cook in his Antarctic expedition.

The accession of George III marked a turning point in Pacific exploration. His valiant sailors—John Byron, surveyor of Falkland's islands (1764-1766); Samuel Wallis and Philip Carteret, discoverers of Tahiti in the South Pacific (1766-1768); and, above all, James Cook, explorer of Australasia, the South Pole, and Hawaii (1768-1779)—extended the domains of the British Empire into the southern hemisphere. Their geographical inquiries ended the old myths of Patagonian giants and an idyllic southern continent and inspired the dream of a Polynesian paradise that would haunt Europeans ever after: "[The Tahitians] have no project which is to be pursued from day to day, the subject of unremitted anxiety and solicitude. ... Yet if we admit that they are upon the whole happier than we, we must admit that the child is happier than the man, and we are losers by the perfection of our nature, the increase of our knowledge, and the enlargement of our views."[41] Johnson's published response to the early phase of this Pacific navigation appeared in his *Thoughts on the Late Transactions respecting Falkland's Islands* (1771). This political pamphlet attacks the past history of European piracy in the South Seas to prevent another imperialistic war with Spain. His anger was not directed against geographical discovery as such but against maritime rivalries that could have precipitated a murderous Seven Years War in the southern hemisphere. Abstracted from their political context the remarkable advances in Pacific geography stirred his curiosity to read all the official accounts of the current voyages edited by his close friends John Hawkesworth and John Douglas. The comprehensive research that went into writing his pamphlet would in itself have prepared him to appreciate the monumental significance of Cook's return from Australia in the same year.

On his first voyage (1768–1771) Cook completed the charting of East Australia, New Guinea, and New Zealand and laid the foundation for English colonization there. Two scientists known to Johnson, James Ferguson and Sir John Pringle, had originally encouraged the Royal Society's support of this expedition for the purpose of observing the transit of Venus to gauge the earth's distance from the sun. Consequently Cook's voyage was distinctively scientific in nature and depended upon the expertise of trained scientists on board for gathering accurate and comprehensive data. Cook himself was a cool, fact-minded man, possessing a genius for navigation and displaying the cautious perseverance and disciplined curiosity that Johnson associated with the best travelers. His skeptical turn of mind enabled him to study Polynesians without awe, describe kangaroos without embellishment, and document cannibalism without moral commentary. His firm command of self and crew preserved his ship from disaster even when the hull seemed hopelessly shattered on the Great Barrier Reef: "We all knew that our boats were not capable of carrying us all on shore, and that when the dreadful crisis should arrive, . . . a contest for preference would probably ensue, that would increase even the horrors of shipwreck,

... yet we knew that if any should be left on board to perish in the waves, they would probably suffer less ... than those who should get on shores, ... condemned to languish out the remainder of life in a desolate wilderness, ... cut off from all commerce with mankind, except the naked savages, who prowled the desert, and who perhaps were some of the most rude and uncivilized upon the earth."[42] Fortunately for posterity, Cook survived his adventures and safely returned to England an eminent botanist who became intimately associated with Johnson and his interest in the Pacific.

Sir Joseph Banks (1743–1820) had early dedicated his life to botanical research and, through his connections with the Admiralty, received permission to accompany Cook on a grand tour of the Pacific. He contributed to the success of the expedition by reporting on a variety of natural and human phenomena and by securing friendly relations with the natives. Upon his return, the public lionized him even more than Cook. Johnson commemorated his first visit to Banks in 1772 with some Latin verses on Cook's goat and left wishing that an epic poem would celebrate the heroic voyage. There was even a passing thought of his joining Cook's second voyage (1772–1775) since at the time Banks was actively recruiting men of learning for the Antarctic cruise. However, disagreements with the Admiralty prevented Banks from going, and old age kept Johnson at home. In any case the idea of pursuing research in natural history at sea was not wholly pleasing to Johnson, who preferred to study native manners and detested sailing all his life. He decided to tour the Hebrides instead in the very year that Cook was heading for the New Hebrides after crossing the Antarctic circle for the first time. In the Highlands Johnson perhaps soothed his sense of a lost opportunity by relating Banks's Pacific adventures and illustrating the traits of the newly discovered kangaroo for his astonished hosts: "He stood erect, put out his hands like feelers, and, gathering up the tails of his huge brown coat so as to resemble the pouch of the animal, made two or three vigorous bounds across the room."[43] His friendship with Banks grew over the years. He would second Banks's nomination for membership in the Literary Club just four days after the botanist's election to the presidency of the Royal Society in 1778. Banks used his presidential post to champion colonization in Australia and exploration in Africa, Iceland, and India. Appropriately, this famous naturalist-explorer would ask to be a pallbearer at Johnson's funeral out of respect to the memory of a man who shared his curiosity about the Pacific.

Johnson never met Captain Cook. That honor was reserved for Boswell in 1776. After three interviews with the navigator, Boswell petitioned Royal Society Fellows for permission to join the third Pacific voyage (1776–1780). His conversations with Cook are a revealing memorial of those sturdy qualities of mind and that love of truth which made this courageous sailor the greatest scientific explorer in England's naval history: "Only I must observe that he candidly confessed to me that he and his companions who visited the South Sea Islands could not be certain of any information they got, . . . except as to objects falling under the observation of the senses, their knowledge of the language was so imperfect [that] . . . anything which they learnt about religion, government, or traditions might be quite erroneous. He gave me a distinct account of a New Zealander eating human flesh in his presence and in that of many more on board, so that the fact of cannibals is now certainly known. We talked of having some men of inquiry left for three years at each of the islands . . . so as to learn the language . . . and bring home a full account of all that can be known of people in a state so different from ours."[44] Boswell then retailed these sentiments as his own in Johnson's company and found that the moralist agreed with Cook's critical appraisal of the voyages. Precisely because Johnson was as scrupulous as Cook about accurate findings, he objected to Boswell's plans for a Pacific expedition. Johnson criticized the voyagers for their ignorance of native languages that hampered reliable research in anthropology and natural history (only one new insect and animal sighted). What, after all, could savages teach Boswell or any other civilized traveler about religion, philosophy, and all else most necessary to man? "Fanciful people may talk of a mythology being amongst them; but it must be invention. They have once had religion, which has been gradually debased."[45]

Johnson was no enthusiast of the noble savage. He accepted the Genesis account of the dispersal of the original human family around the globe and the consequent debasement of the original body of inspired truths given man by God. Adam's descendants in the West preserved the Hebraic traditions, but the nations to the East, including the Polynesians, gradually lost sight of their primordial origins and religious heritage. The Bible was the ultimate authority for his faith not only in the brotherhood of man but also in the superiority of Western civilization. Hence, when Cook's navigators introduced Omai the Tahitian to England after the second voyage, Johnson stoutly resisted the primitivism of fellow Londoners. Omai might beat a crestfallen Baretti at chess, but Omai learned his manners from Europeans. The unhappy consequences of Pacific exploration must have made Johnson glad that he and Boswell never sailed the South Seas. Captain Wallis brought syphilis to Tahiti, Cook would be killed by Hawaiians in 1779, and Omai would return home too spoiled by Englishmen for a useful life in the islands. The tragedy of the Pacific voyages was vividly brought home to Johnson as he toured a ship commanded by Charles Burney's son on the last of Cook's expeditions: "I have seen Captain Burney and his cargo. You may remember I thought Banks had not gained much by circumnavigating the world."[46] The penetration of the Southern hemisphere had produced the greatest discoveries since the time of Columbus, but, at the end of his life, Johnson had good reason to mourn the corrupt tendency of maritime exploration and colonial exploitation.

Whatever his reservations about colonial abuses, his curiosity about the world was clearly insatiable and fundamental to his career. The inclusive range of his geographical studies spanned the East and West to the extreme polar reaches of the globe. His cosmopolitan interests were in keeping with an era of geographical discovery when travelers emerged as culture heroes in fiction and travel literature had an unprecedented popularity with readers. So pervasive was the impulse to travel that Sterne repeated the biblical curse, "Make them like unto a wheel," to characterize his rambling generation of topographers and tourists eager to examine life everywhere to better understand its meaning for man. The modern bibliography, Edward Cox's *A Reference Guide to the Literature of Travel* (1935), lists thousands of voyages and travels flooding eighteenth-century bookstalls. Twentieth-century scholarship has only just begun to deal with these voluminous writings so important to Georgian literature: Philip Gove's *The Imaginary Voyage in Prose Fiction* (1961) and Percy Adams's *Travelers and Travel Liars* (1962) are excellent surveys of geographical fiction and phenomena; a few books have examined further aspects of travel, such as the grand tour, navigation, antiquarian research, and nature study. But a comprehensive investigation has yet to appear. In isolating Johnson's representative interest in the subject, the present study can suggest many areas for future inquiry.

The vogue of travel literature was firmly established in the beginning of the century; probably peaked in the 1720s and 1730s; and declined only when travel books often degenerated to simple guidebooks in the second quarter of the nineteenth century.[47] Travel books offered the twin appeal of comic book fantasy and scientific facts conducive to an overwhelming popularity with the literate masses. An empire-building age relished the unfolding prose chronicle of Britain's expanding domains abroad, and the highest royal circles devoured this favorite literary fare. When Johnson's *Journey to the Western Islands of Scotland* appeared, there was regal acknowledgment to comfort its proud author: "You must not tell any body but Mr Thrale that the King fell to reading the book as soon as he got it, when any thing struck him, he read aloud to the Queen, and the Queen would not stay to get the King's book, but borrowed Dr Hunter's."[48] Writers of professional and amateur status heeded the public demand for more descriptions. At a time when a successful play might guarantee an author instant fame and fortune, the publication of a travel book could at least strengthen his pretensions to literature and learning. The consequent outpouring of narratives became one of the cliché jokes among literary circles. Travelers were made uncomfortably aware that the era's compulsion to ramble caused a concomitant drive to produce too many accounts ranging from the sublime to the ridiculous, the pretentious, false, and repetitious. Some had a high literary quality, and many contributed worldwide data to the Baconian advancement of learning. As one publisher claimed, "The Advantage of keeping judicious and accurate Journals ... are so many and great, in the Improvement of Geography, Hydrography, Natural and Moral History, Antiquity, Trade, Empire, etc. that few Books can compare with them either for Profit or Pleasure."[49]

When genuine travel books were not forthcoming, unscrupulous writers foisted bogus description on an unsuspecting public. Incredible as it may seem now, Johnson noticed that *Gulliver's Travels* sometimes gained "belief from the most obstinate Incredulity."[50] Swift's fiction was apparent to all except the most obtuse, but in other cases the line between truth and falsehood was less easy to draw. Novels like *A Sentimental Journey* and *Humphry Clinker* occasionally appeared in lists of bona fide travel books, and the apocryphal travels of Misson, Leguat, Correal, and Defoe were widely considered authentic. Defoe especially made travel literature his stock in trade by producing the best reliable survey of Great Britain and a succession of voyage fictions in *Robinson Crusoe*, *Captain Singleton*, and a *New Voyage Round the World*. Another charlatan, George Psalmanazar, fooled readers of his *New Description of Formosa* for fifty years before repenting his sins in print and winning Johnson's esteem for piety and honesty. The number of hoaxes weakened the reputation of honest travelers but also indicates the ease with which real travel books could shade into fiction and prove an inspiration for English poetry and prose.

As never before, prose fiction exploited travel as a narrative vehicle for presenting a character's psychological growth in picaresque social survey, grand touring, a rake's progress, or an imaginary voyage. Among the major English writers, Swift, Defoe, Smollett, and Sterne actually adopted the format of travel books in their masterpieces while Johnson, Fielding, and Goldsmith made a journey their characteristic plot. Satirists frequently employed the geographical perspective of foreign customs to inculcate neglected universals of proper conduct at home. If travel books habitually compared cultural differences to prove man's moral uniformity, then too comic tales of travel contrasted variant social systems to teach the uniform absurdity within diversity of mankind. The exposure of domestic vices in foreign settings or, conversely, the deflation of domestic values by critical foreign observers left readers of *Gulliver's Travels* and the *Citizen of the World* with a heightened awareness of true virtue on a global scale. Belles lettres glorified Polynesian islanders, Chinese mandarins, noble American savages, and oriental sages to shake less enlightened Europeans out of their moral lethargy and cultural complacency. By juxtaposing foreign manners with cherished domestic values, Rasselas, Matthew Bramble, and Yorick came to learn the valuable lesson of Gulliver's voyages: "Undoubtedly philosophers are in the right when they tell us, that nothing is great or little otherwise than by comparison."[51] The global estimate of virtue was a new and important way for travelers in life and literature to judge correctly the merit of their homebred ideals and native civilization.

The current geographical revolution helped to establish the traveler as a dominant presence in prose fiction. So often the Georgian protagonist is cast as a modern tourist renewing the age-old quest of Ulysses, Mr. Christian, and Don Quixote in the contemporary scene. Historical and literary traditions combined to make him an archetypal wanderer following contemporary tourist conventions while re-creating the journey patterns formulated chiefly by Homer, the Bible, and Cervantes. He surveyed humanity from China to Peru in the guise of a modern traveler on an updated odyssey, pilgrimage, and Quixotic quest through life. For Johnson, the application of these journey archetypes to human behavior amounted to a fixation of his literary sensibility. He saw life in terms of a journey and portrayed man in his morality as a composite Quixote-Ulysses-pilgrim in search of meaning and certitude in a chaotic universe. In his best work the mythic variations of the journey theme come together to define the moral psychology of the modern hero in all of us:

> Then say how hope and fear, desire and hate,
> O'erspread with snares the clouded maze of fate,
> Where wav'ring man, betray'd by vent'rous pride,
> To tread the dreary paths without a guide.

Such was the moral problem, the possibilities and limitations of the modern quest for happiness, that the great moralist set before him to analyze and resolve. A religious pilgrim at heart, the Johnsonian traveler possessed an irrepressible Ulyssean instinct to wander through a world that Quixote found wanting in ultimate fulfillment.

Johnson shared with other writers a vision of man, the tireless traveler, seeking knowledge of self and society in the footsteps of famous wanderers in literature. Ulysses was renowned as the great classical exemplar of travel from the time of Strabo's *Geography*: "The wars of Troy, and the travels of Ulysses, have furnished almost all succeeding poets with incidents, characters, and sentiments" (*Rambler* 121). When Pope's *Dunciad* satirized the modern tourist —"All Classic learning lost on Classic Ground"—the portrait was intended to parody the *Odyssey* adventures. Prose fiction embodied the *Odyssey* archetype in the form of restless heroes, curious to survey the manners of many men in journeys of moral discovery. The telling epigraph of *Tom Jones*, *Mores hominum multorum vidit*, excerpts the Horatian motto for Ulysses in *Ars Poetica* to signal Fielding's production of a comic odyssey based in England. Moreover, the preface to *Joseph Andrews* defines novels as the eighteenth-century prose epics. The Homeric terrors of Neptune's realm and the resilient curiosity of Ulysses passed on to the seaborne Crusoes, Gullivers, and Roderick Randoms of fiction, so often shipwrecked themselves by hostile forces in nature and society on new islands of experience. An *Odyssey* metaphor summarized the perils of the human journey in *Rasselas:* "The world . . . you will find a sea foaming with tempests, and boiling with whirlpools: you will be sometimes overwhelmed by waves of violence, and sometimes dashed against the rocks of treachery. Amidst wrongs and frauds, competitions and anxieties, you will wish a thousand times for these seats of quiet."[52] The sea of life with its Scylla and Charybdis of human calamities remained a native element of English literature, and the search for an Ithaca of happiness was a prime aspiration of the English hero.

In what was yet a predominantly Christian literature, the religious pilgrim archetype permeated the journey plots of even the most ostensibly secular stories. Characters as different as Rasselas, Tom Jones, Robinson Crusoe, and the Vicar of Wakefield all deserve their critically ordained title of Christian heroes on a latter-day *Pilgrim's Progress.*[53] Their travels all reenact a *Paradise Lost* in a moral wilderness of worldly evils and human limitations and sometimes happily terminate in an earthly *Paradise Regained.* They physically and psychologically participate in a process of departure, discovery, and return to havens of happiness basic to the biblical interpretation of human history: "And thus is Mans whole Life a Pilgrimage from God as Cains, or from himselfe as Abels, and all the Saints which confessed themselves Pilgrims on the earth, and to seeke another Country, that is a heavenly."[54] So Samuel Purchas wrote in his seventeenth-century collection of travels and could have affirmed of many Georgian protagonists.

The high-minded pilgrims of eighteenth-century fiction had a Ulyssean curiosity to study mankind, but often they displayed the impractical idealism of the Don Quixote archetype. Johnson spoke for numerous contemporary writers when he described *Don Quixote* as a modern classic "to which a mind of the greatest powers may be indebted without disgrace."[55] Cervantes's genial balancing of a fool-hero's illusions against the corrupt realities of a knave-society had stimulated many English imitations. Quixotic antiromance pervades

Fielding's novels and Johnson's tales and accounts for the unheroic treatment of modernity in *David Simple*, *Sir Launcelot Greaves*, *The Female Quixote*, and *The Spiritual Quixote*. In these and many other works the Don Quixote archetype introduced a disillusioning series of frustrated hopes and ideals that obstructed the normally successful course of prose odysseys and pilgrimages in the period.

By assimilating any of the three archetypes in their tales, authors conveyed what may be literature's most basic plot: the mythic journey of the everyman hero traveling from happy innocence into maturing experience on a downward path through underworlds of evil and despair for his growth in wisdom and final ascent to some good.[56] What Thoreau predicated of all travel certainly applies to the mythic dimensions of eighteenth-century journey plots: "The traveller must be born again on the road, and earn a passport from the elements. . . . He shall experience at last that old threat of his mother fulfilled, that he shall be skinned alive. His sores shall gradually deepen themselves that they may heal inwardly, . . . and at night weariness must be his pillow, that so he may acquire experience against his rainy days."[57] When a Georgian protagonist toured England or the globe, his itinerary circumscribed the whole life's journey.

His travels were symbolic of man's learning experience and aging process. In novels his adventures generally conformed to a common sequence of birth, maturation, enlightenment or conversion, death or imprisonment, and final bliss frequently achieved. His journey expressed the ancient migratory restlessness of man, dissatisfied with his original state and curious to explore himself, the world, and the ultimate meaning of existence in an alien environment nourishing new revelations of truth. Homer and the Bible offered Georgian writers the classical and Christian interpretations of this perennial quest. Cervantes, in turn, made the quest mock-heroic for our unheroic times and conducted his romancing knight-errant through a disillusioning life experience to his death as an unfulfilled anti-hero. Depending upon the archetype dominant in a story, the Georgian protagonist attained his heaven on earth only when Quixotic illusions departed and Ulyssean persistence carried him through. Rasselas and Gulliver failed their quests by succumbing to Quixote's impossible desires and diseased imagination. But the majority of wanderers, from Crusoe to Yorick, reached their destinations by steadfastly accommodating the world's limitations to their prudent vision of life's possibilities.

The eighteenth-century heritage of geographical discovery and travel themes had its literary florescence in the succeeding age of the Romantics. Alexander von Humboldt's *Kosmos* harmonized the geographical data of previous explorers into a coherent scientific theory demonstrating the unity of the cosmos through the interplay of natural laws. Analogously, Romantic poets wrought an imaginative synthesis of earlier geographical findings and themes to create a rich variety of natural and supernatural journeys exploring the transcendent harmony of a discordant universe. The gradual dissolution of many traditional values led writers to renovate the quest of Ulysses, Mr. Christian, and Don Quixote in an uneasy search, sometimes as cursed as Cain's, for new truths and spiritual regeneration. Keats echoed Ulysses' travels in his tribute to Chapman's Homer in order to capture for all time the romance of discovery: "Much have I travell'd in the realms of gold, / And many goodly states and kingdoms seen. . . ." Wordsworth was perpetually the pilgrim of spiritual revelations as he wandered in *The Prelude* through a world that Quixote found deficient in ideals: "This semi-Quixote, I to him have given / A substance, fancied him a living man." Blake and Shelley portrayed the perennial human quest for personal and social rebirth while Byron unfolded the universal fate of the fallen man doomed to the bittersweet life of exile from Eden: "Flung from the rock, on Ocean's foam to sail / Where'er the surge may sweep, the tempest's breath prevail."

The Romantics were devotees of travel literature. William Cowper expressed the gratitude of his contemporaries and succeeding poets for the pleasures imparted by voyages and travels in *The Task:*

He travels and expatiates as the bee
From flower to flower, so he from land to land;
The manners, customs, policy of all
Pay contribution to the store he gleans;
And sucks intelligence in every clime,
And spreads the honey of his deep research
At his return—a rich repast for me.

The New England wilderness would evoke that incomparable nature travelogue of *Walden*, and the varied wonders of the world would inspire the Romantic poets. Who was ever more a fan of travel books than Coleridge? Where else is there a better travel poem than *The Rime of the Ancient Mariner?* Anticipating Humboldt's achievement in geography, Coleridge synthesized and transformed the history of Pacific exploration into a magical poem that is the cosmic harmony which it proclaims. The mariner is the archetypal pilgrim-Ulysses of Quixotic travel who sails the sinister oceans of Dampier, Anson, and Cook to sound the depths of human evil and chart the purgatorial course of human salvation.[58] In a very real sense he remains the culminating symbol of eighteenth-century travel in English literature.

The Romantics inherited another geographical legacy from the previous era. Georgian travelers laid the foundation for an appreciation of foreign cultures, sublime landscapes, and the joyful escapism of a ramble that distinguished early nineteenth-century tourism. Their residual English pride gave them the necessary security to add foreign values to their cherished national life-style and bask in sublime emotions without unduly disturbing their celebrated self-composure. Thus, Boswell was "fully able to enter into the ideas of the brave people" of Corsica, and Sterne already exhibited the subjective enthusiasm of later tourists. The Romantics would convert this latent cosmopolitanism into a completely liberating imaginative empathy with foreign scenes in travel. As William Hazlitt confessed, "We are not the same but another, and perhaps more enviable individual, the time we are all out of our own country."[59]

The eighteenth century was preparing for an unparalleled receptivity to the fascinating diversity of the globe. British partiality might aggrandize Johnson's love of homeland, "For any thing I see, a foreigner's a fool," but never completely blinded him to foreign achievements around the world. While Boswell went celebrity-hunting abroad, Johnson held court at home to a veritable United Nations of personalities. The moralist numbered among his acquaintances Paoli the Corsican, Solander the Swede, Baretti the Italian, the American William Samuel Johnson, Omai the Tahitian, the Jamaican Francis Barber, the Bohemian Joseph Ritter, the Irishman Thomas Campbell, the Cambrian Joseph Cradock, and a host of Scots. The gallery of nationalities at his door speaks volumes about an era of cosmopolitanism, travel, and social interaction among the middle classes. A civilized society allowed Johnson a glimpse of King Louis and Antoinette at court instead of at war and permitted Boswell to visit Rousseau, Voltaire, Condillac, and the pope on the same grand tour. As Georgian geographical vistas expanded, the world became a little smaller and less intolerant of national differences.

The age rightly bears the name of Johnson. His mind was attuned to the geographical developments and cultural changes of the period and regaled in its dynamic thrust for the new and the provable on all intellectual fronts. His debt to Georgian travel deserves the fullest exploration since his literary achievements, studies, and pastimes were so intimately tied up with this national preoccupation. His was a moral vision of man's restless and inquiring nature that fully suited the exuberant spirit of his imperial era. His writings reflect the contemporary geographical revolution and insist on the importance of exploring the totality of human existence at first hand. If a bookish man, he grounded his learning in the empirical truths of the globe to obtain an accurate appraisal of the human condition: "Books without the knowledge of life are useless . . . for what should books teach but the art of *living?*"[60] Appropriately, at the dawn of modern aviation, one of his final gestures in 1784 was a subscription to the first aerial balloon in England: "I subscribed a few days ago to a new ballon, which is to carry five hundred weight, and with which some daring adventurer is expected to mount, and bring down the state of regions yet unexplored. . . . I wish well to such soaring curiosity."[61] Such soaring curiosity, prophetic of the coming revolution in travel, inspirited Johnson and Georgian England.

Rowlandson's Johnson and Boswell *Setting Out from Edinburgh*. Courtesy of the Harvard College Library.

2

JOHNSON AND THE TRADITION OF TRAVEL LITERATURE

Nothing perhaps more evidently proves the greatness of the
mind of man, and the immortality to which it aspires, than not
finding ourselves contented or satisfied in one place, but pro-
curing the gratification of our desires, which are inclined to a
diversity of objects, by rambling about the world.
Richard Twiss, *Travels through Portugal and Spain*

ONE OF THE FAVORITE pastimes that our age shares with the eighteenth century is a middle-class enthusiasm for travel. In Johnson's
era Englishmen toured the city and country in unprecedented numbers and became justly renowned as Europe's restless citizens of the
world. Compared to our modern conveniences, traveling conditions
were extremely poor then. Without our high-speed thoroughfares
and air lanes, tourists had to be a hardy breed in order to cope
with inadequate roads, unreadable signposts, inhospitable inns, faulty
coach springs, and the inevitable turnpike toll and passport duty.
Nevertheless, not even the dangers of highwaymen or hostile foreigners ever greatly daunted Englishmen from riding the roads or
writing up their narratives of travel and spreading their influence
around the globe. The literary result of their worldwide wander-
ings was the flourishing genre of travel literature in England, a body
of writings that immensely influenced contemporary thought and
letters.

Unlike our mediocre guidebooks, Georgian voyages and travels
were expected to be serious intellectual documents with important
information to contribute to the advancement of the arts and sci-

ences. Travel books constituted the second most popular reading matter of the period and had an impact, proportionate to their popularity, upon the development of geography, philosophy, belles lettres, economics, and history. A journalist like Johnson could not afford to ignore their appeal and happily spent a considerable part of his career reading and reviewing them in magazines and periodicals: "One part of mankind is naturally curious to learn the sentiments, manners, and condition of the rest; and every mind that has leisure or power to extend its views, must be desirous of knowing in what proportion Providence has distributed the blessings of nature or the advantages of art, among the several nations of the earth. This general desire procures readers to every book from which it can expect gratification."[1] In a geographical epoch that first demonstrated the arrangement and shape of the earth's lands and seas, he was quick to recognize the commanding position of travelers in his literary milieu. The climate of public opinion and economic circumstances consistently favored the traveler's enterprises. Peace and the wider circulation of wealth, a gradually improved system of roads and canals, and the expansion of colonial territories made travel a national pastime in the armchair or on the road. Every major author from Addison to Boswell traveled and published his travels or at least used travel books for literary purposes. As the presiding Cham of English literature, Johnson could not help but be interested in the current vogue of travel.

His writing career began with the translation of a travel book and almost ended with the publication of his own splendid account of the Highlands in *A Journey to the Western Islands of Scotland*. During his middle years he produced numerous articles and essays on the subject and seriously meditated several journeys that would occur in his old age. All his biographers stressed his love of travel that motivated his tours of England, Wales, and France. The controlling theme of his morality revolves around the dynamic concept of travel to such a degree that the journey patterns in his fiction are indistinguishable from the touring habits of his life. The Rambler's fondness for rambling profoundly influenced the tendency of his reading, writing, and thinking throughout his lifetime. Both his theory of travel and literary uses of a journey illuminate his restless personality and artistic strategies for creating fiction. Thanks to the distinguished scholarship of Walter Jackson Bate, James Clifford, and many other Johnsonians, attention has shifted away from Boswell's great *Life of Johnson* to a serious appreciation of the moralist's achievement in and of itself. An investigation of his diverse preoccupations with travel can only enhance our knowledge of the man's multifold talents.

As Paul Fussell has remarked, the outgoing thrust of travel and discovery expressed a Lockean drive for empirical inquiry basic to the inquisitive mood of the eighteenth century.[2] The general acceptance of an empirical epistemology helped to establish travel as a principal manifestation of man's sequential confrontation with fact in life and literature. Johnson placed such an empirical emphasis on travel and considered a journey, whether in *A Journey to the Western Islands of Scotland* or in *Rasselas*, as an unfolding education in the realities of a complex moral world: "The use of travelling is to regulate imagination by reality, and instead of thinking how things may be, to see them as they are."[3] From a Lockean standpoint, both Georgian tourists and traveling protagonists repeatedly participated in epistemological tests to correct their tentative ideas and ideals by facing the illuminating facts about man, nature, and society. Their journeys were often a veritable *Paradise Lost* of empirical inquiry resulting in a passage from parochial innocence into a maturing knowledge of life's limitations for their growth in experiential wisdom about the world.[4]

With a common emphasis upon the developing self in nature and society, travel books and belles lettres had close literary ties in the period. For travel books possessed the very stuff of romance—the perilous journey to strange lands followed by intrigues, captivities, escapes, and discoveries educating the traveler—conducive to adaptation in novels. Johnson's description of the contents of travel books could pass as a summary of events in most Georgian prose fiction: "Curiosity is seldom so powerfully excited, or so amply gratified, as by faithful Relations of Voyages and Travels. The different Appearances of Nature, and the various Customs of Men, the gradual Discovery of the World, and the Accidents and Hardships of a naval Life, all concur to fill the Mind with Expectation and with Wonder; . . . the Student follows the Traveller from Country to Country, and retains the Situation of Places by recounting his Adventures."[5] The obvious narrative similarities between real and fictional travels were fully exploited by authors. Novelists from Defoe to Sterne habitually imitated the format of travel books to plot the development of characters, the sequence of incidents, and the evolution of themes.

At the dawn of the modern novel in the seventeeth century, allegorists were already applying travel book techniques to tales of Christian pilgrimage. Bunyan's Mr. Christian is a modern tourist consulting his holy guidebook for directions out of his spiritual wilderness: "I looked, and saw him open the Book, and Read therein; and as he read he wept and trembled, and . . . brake out with a lamentable cry; saying, *What shall I do?*"[6] Ten years before *The Pilgrim's Progress* appeared, Simon Patrick's *Parable of the Pilgrim* (1667) equated the Bible with a pilgrim's travel book that described heavenly Jerusalem according to the conventional topics of the genre: "And then turning over several leaves that treated of this Country: he shewed him such an exact Description of the Situation and Nature of the place, of the Quality of the Inhabitants, of the imployments wherein they are ingaged, of the Fruits of the Soil, of the Way that led to it, of the Travels of several Persons that had gone thither . . . (all servants of Jesus)."[7] In the eighteenth century, travel book conventions and journey plots would magnificently fructify in such tales as *Gulliver's Travels*, *Robinson Crusoe*, *A Sentimental Journey*, *Humphrey Clinker*, *Rasselas*, and other sophisticated ancestors of the allegorical pilgrimage in literature. The circle of interrelatedness was complete when in 1773 John Hawkesworth could edit Cook's voyages with the novel in mind as a model. He defended his use of a single first-person narrator and a chronological arrangement of adventures by appealing to Richardson's *Pamela*. The new format would help readers of his travel book enjoy the imaginative pleasures experienced "by those who feel themselves strongly interested even for Pamela, the imaginary heroine of a novel."[8]

The intimate relationship that existed between novels and travel books extended to other literary forms. Voyages and travels also influenced such descriptive "survey" poetry as Thomson's *Seasons* and Goldsmith's *The Traveller;* oriental romances like *Rasselas* and oriental plays like *Irene;* and numerous geographical satires ranging from *Gulliver's Travels* to *The Citizen of the World.* Johnson was expressing a prevailing sentiment among literary circles when he welcomed the poetic inspiration coming from the "unclassic ground" of the New World. His review of James Grainger's *Sugar Cane* in 1764 calls for an even more extensive use of geographical discoveries in literature: "It is, indeed, a little extraordinary how regions so poetically striking and so well known to the merchant, have been so little visited by the muse."[9] His own life and writings bear striking witness to the literary and cultural importance of travel literature in his century. Few authors read more widely in travel books, wrote more wisely about them, or made them serve more ends in morality and fiction than he. The incredible range and amount of his reading take in virtually the entire history of travel literature up to his own time. Outside of the innumerable narratives that he reviewed for the Harleian library catalog, his conversations and literary canon testify to his familiarity with well over a hundred voyages and travels.[10] From the evidence of his omnivorous reading habits in his diaries, he certainly read many more descriptions that remain unrecorded. When alone or bored with friends, he picked up any available account and, sometimes skipping over every other page, read far into the night for entertainment. Moreover, he often borrowed other travel reports from friends to supplement his library holdings.

By the end of his life he had acquired a vast knowledge of geography from journals, treatises, diaries, logs, letters, memoirs, chronicles, topographical surveys, atlases, and descriptions of domestic, Continental, and remote regions. All these diverse forms of writing are today classified under the category of travel literature. Many of the narratives read by him had distinctive outlooks and styles and yet generally adhered to the established conventions of the genre. Some had primarily a political (James Boswell's *Account of Corsica*), antiquarian (Richard Pococke's *Description of the East*), or historical (Du Halde's *Description of the Empire of China*) emphasis. Others promoted the Baconian advancement of the sciences in natural history (Griffith Hughes's *Natural History of Barbados*), cartology (Lewis Evans's *Geographical . . . Map of the Middle British Colonies in America*), or navigational techniques (George Anson's *Voyage Round the World*). From the time of his boyhood he delighted in ancient and modern geographies, topographical dictionaries, and atlases. At Oxford he probably read Laurence Echard's geographical digest, *The Gazetteer's or Newsman's Interpreter* (1695), and Joseph Harris's *Description and Use of the Globes* (1703) and pursued his studies at a time when the famous Edmund Halley served as the Savilian professor of geometry and astronomy. In his lifetime he also consulted Renaissance atlases and treatises on geography by Abraham Ortelius, George Abbot, Sir Walter Raleigh, Edward Brerewood, Peter Heylin, Lucas de Linda, and Bernard Varenius. When he was an old man, he versified the measurements in Thomas Templeman's *New Survey of the Globe* (1729) to alleviate boredom and anxiety. At home and abroad he might read the ancient geographies of Strabo, Ptolemy, Pliny, and Pomponius Mela for his amusement.

As his study of the ancient geographers implies, travel literature had a long and illustrious history reaching back to Xenophon's *Anabasis* and Herodotus's *History*. Its usual format in the eighteenth century was a journey narrative with a chronological presentation of facts and reflections often organized around codified topics of inquiry. Johnson considered the genre a subspecies of history and an essential branch of learning. He ranked the science of geography below only theology and morality and far above belles lettres in its importance to man. In his judgment travel books had a great intellectual value in documenting the cultural history of mankind and served the higher ends of morality and theology by reporting information about human limitations and aspirations everywhere on the earth. They also possessed a great imaginative value by recounting exciting adventures grounded in fact. Indeed their combination of geographical romance and reality made them safer reading than the pure make-believe of fiction. Along with his contemporaries, Johnson might occasionally group them with "works of mere amusement." Travel books could be studied at leisure with profit and pleasure without requiring the mental exertion needed to follow abstruse theological or philosophical arguments. Hence, he would have agreed with Isaac Watts about lumping "*history, poesy, travels, books of diversion or amusement*" all together except for one important qualification.[11] Unlike belles lettres, travel books presented a true history of human life unattainable in the falsehood of fiction. Precisely because they recorded authentic wonders of the globe, their imaginative and intellectual appeal made them second only to religious writings in popularity with Georgian readers.

The number of travel books issuing from presses underscores their overwhelming popularity in the eighteenth century. Between 1660 and 1800 eight encyclopedic collections and forty-five smaller compilations appeared in England. Besides the major works, there were thousands of individual accounts and miscellanies of local tours, distant expeditions, and Continental travels. If we include publications from the Continent, the number of all European collections of voyages and travels would alone amount to well over a hundred voluminous productions in several editions and translations.[12] Johnson's principal publishers, Cave, Newbery, and Strahan, all cashed in on the lucrative market for travel literature and advertised many compilations of their own. The century had caught what Johnson termed "the modern infection of travel" and left few Englishmen immune. What specifically so fascinated Johnson about the genre? First of all, travel books intellectually and imaginatively stimulated his mind and provided necessary data for reaching valid conclusions about human nature. Therefore, "an inquiry into the state of foreign countries was an object that seems at all times to have interested Johnson."[13] His theory of education in his preface to Dodsley's *Preceptor* (1748) made an expert knowledge of geography a prerequisite for learning all the other arts and sciences. Full mental and moral growth depended upon a lively curiosity to study human manners and the history of the world's societies: "A generous and elevated Mind is distinguished by nothing more certainly than an eminent degree of Curiosity, nor is that Curiosity ever more agreeably or usefully employ'd, than in examining the Laws and Customs of Foreign Nations."[14] Curiosity implied an active intelligence, and one's intelligence could reap important benefits from the geographical investigation of man's various accomplishments around the globe.

Aside from its intellectual and moral usefulness, travel literature was an excellent source of entertainment. Descriptions offered sedentary readers the vicarious experience of travel and allowed the restless "imagination to wander over the lakes and mountains" of foreign lands that rivaled the romantic realms of fiction.[15] They had a strong imaginative appeal for Johnson, who welcomed the chance to escape into the romance of true adventures, exotic landscapes, and mysterious cultures. In his time travelers began consciously to exploit the romantic elements inherent in the genre so as to engage the reader's imagination in the vicarious experience of travel. Giuseppe Baretti wanted readers of his *Journey from London to Genoa* (1770) "to . . . see what I saw, hear what I heard, feel what I felt, and even think and fancy whatever I thought and fancied myself."[16] As Baretti recognized, travel books were a literature of process with an obvious potential for creating an imaginative bond between the reader's mind and the places observed through the medium of the author's subjective flow of impressions. Patrick Brydone went so far as to identify this imaginative effect with the intimate diary style of travel books like his own *Tour through Sicily and Malta* (1773): "Few things I believe in writing [are] more difficult than thus 's'emparer de l'imagination,' to seize, to make ourselves masters of the reader's imagination, to carry it along with us in every scene, and make it in a manner congenial with our own, every prospect opening upon him with the same light, and arising in the same colours, and at the same instant too, as upon us."[17] Novelists and nature poets drew on the travel book style to achieve a comparable emotional empathy and imaginative immediacy. Sterne's *A Sentimental Journey* and Wordsworth's *Prelude* are outstanding examples of writings evoking our imaginative identification with the flowing sights and sensations through the medium of the traveler's personality and his peripatetic mode of inquiry.

Johnson fully responded to the romance of travel literature. Along with his contemporaries, he was fond of regarding it as a modern substitute for medieval romances of chivalry. Many a traveler in his fiction, such as Will Marvel and Euryalus, are likened to knight-errants of the road, and his writings on travel defend the romantic quality of the form: "Many relations of travelers have been slighted as fabulous, till more frequent voyages have confirmed their veracity" (*Idler* 87). Doubtless, his taste for travel literature had its roots in the dual imaginative and intellectual pleasures imparted by a genre merging romance and historical veracity. An early notice of Du Halde's *Description of the Empire of China* in the *Gentleman's Magazine* (1738) contains a psychological analysis of these two pleasures that foreshadows Johnson's remarks on voyages and travels in *Idlers* 87 and 97: "As the Satisfaction found in reading Descriptions of distant Countries arises from a Comparison which every reader naturally makes . . . between the Countries with which he is acquainted, and that which the Author displays to his Imagination; so it varies according to the Likeness or Dissimilitude of the Manners of the two Nations. Any Custom or Law unheard and unthought of before, strikes us with that *surprize* which is the effect of Novelty; but a Practice conformable to our own pleases us, because it flatters our Self-love, by showing us that our Opinions are approved by the general Concurrence of Mankind."[18] Thus, travel books aroused the imagination and reason by presenting new wonders and universal truths familiar at home. Because they united fantasy and fact, they fulfilled an ideal, which, according to Jean Hagstrum, became a touchstone of the finest writing in Johnson's literary criticism: they approximated the remote and familiarized the wonderful.[19] Reading them appeased the mental hunger of the imagination and curiosity for romantic adventures and stimulating realities about the human family.

The consequent popularity of travel literature explains Johnson's steady professional interest in the subject as a journalist and moralist. His first major literary venture in prose was a translation of a travel book, *Father Lobo's Voyage to Abyssinia* (1735). He first read the work during his residence at Oxford and later translated it rapidly at the prodding of Edmund Hector and Thomas Warren's to help destitute Birmingham printer. There were probably other motives besides charity that caused him to launch his literary career with the publication of a travel book. He might reasonably have expected some profit and renown from a public fond of voyages and travels. His translation had a triple romantic, political, and scientific appeal; it carefully described a mysterious Portuguese colony with an ancient Christian heritage at a time when England was allied with Portugal. The Royal Society had already found its accurate findings of enough significance to warrant an English translation of extracts in 1669. Its *Short Relation of the River Nile* concentrates solely on scientific information and employs a simpler, more matter-of-fact style than Johnson's version exhibits. Joachim Le Grand later published a complete French translation from the Portuguese original, *Relation historique d'Abissinie du P. Jerome Lobo* (1728), and added fifteen dissertations mainly on religious issues. The new religious emphasis must have enhanced the value of the book for Johnson. For when he worked from the French version, he greatly abridged Lobo's adventures but preserved almost all of Le Grand's dissertations disputing the Protestant character of Abyssinian Christianity.

At this stage in his life Johnson's sympathies were staunchly Protestant. An anti-Catholic bias is evident not only in his prefatory attack against Portuguese Jesuits but also in his telling emendations of Le Grand's text. There are wholesale deletions of complimentary Roman Catholic references, ceremonies, and lists of clergy.[20] While his criticism of Catholicism softened considerably in later life, his antipathy to the cruel imperialistic policies adopted by the Portuguese never waned. His translation expresses other attitudes prophetic of his later interests in travel. There is a concern for transmitting "every thing either useful or entertaining" in his narrative, whether it be scientific data, historical traditions, religious rites, political customs, verifiable marvels, or geographical truths. Although his style seemed unusually plain to Boswell and Hawkins, he did actually introduce some elegance and order to the French version of the travel book. The multiple voyages that open the original account seem more like a single unified expedition in Johnson's work. The tighter narrative that appeared in the English translation would have important consequences for the plotting of *Rasselas*, which assimilated the simplified journey of *Lobo's Voyage* and many of its elegant passages. As events turned out, this travel book brought him no immediate literary acclaim but would have a long-range effect, far greater than his biographers suspected, upon the creation of his fiction.

His translation of *Lobo's Voyage* marked the opening phase of a literary career almost continually involved with travel literature thereafter. During his early search for fame and fortune in Grubstreet, he probably contemplated a translation of Giorlamo Benzoni's *Historia del Mondo Nuovo* and a compilation of voyages and travels.[21] His hackwork for the *Gentleman's Magazine* included exciting naval biographies of Sir Francis Drake and Robert Blake (1740), thoughtful reviews of Claude Marie Guyon's *Histoire des Amazones*

(1741) and Du Halde's *Description of the Empire of China* (1742), and possibly a few more articles on travel during the years of Edward Cave's management of the magazine. In the early 1740s he might also have served as a reviewer of foreign books occasionally dealing with geography and seems to have been a major contributor to the Foreign History section of that periodical. For the *Literary Magazine* in 1756 and 1757 he reviewed several descriptions by Jonas Hanway, Patrick Browne, Alexander Russell, William Borlase, Lewis Evans, Johann Keysler, John Armstrong, and probably other travelers such as General William Johnson. Three more pieces of great importance in a study of Johnson's views on travel appeared between 1759 and 1760: his *Introduction to the World Displayed* and *Idlers* 87 and 97. In 1764 his critiques of Grainger's *Sugar Cane* and Goldsmith's *The Traveller* in the *Critical Review* suggested some literary uses of travel. Seven years later he composed his masterful pamphlet on Pacific exploration in his *Thoughts on the Late Transactions respecting Falkland's Islands*. There were also his elegant prefaces written for geographical treatises by Richard Rolt, Alexander Macbean, and George Adams. Finally in 1775 he climaxed his literary adventures with geography by publishing his own superb travel book, *A Journey to the Western Islands of Scotland*. Taken together, all these writings comprise the central core of his thinking about voyages and travels.

Besides articles and books directly concerned with the subject, his efforts in satire, morality, biography, and history often depended upon travel books. Voyages and travels made as many contributions to contemporary literature as to geography, and Johnson's writings are a good case in point. The psychological analysis of the imaginative and intellectual pleasures derived from travel accounts in the 1738 notice of Du Halde's *Description of the Empire of China* is an excellent explanation of the emotional effects evoked by geographical satire. According to this anonymous essay, the reader's comparison of new and familiar ideas in travel books arouses both surprise and recognition of universal moral truths in his mind. The same rationale applies to satires like *Gulliver's Travels* and Johnson's introduction to the *Debates in the Senate of Lilliput* (1738). Readers of such works are similarly encouraged to compare foreign and domestic manners, the new and the known, and experience both surprise and recognition from finding that strange vices abroad are flagrant abuses at home. Geographical fiction was designed to stimulate a comparative process of moral discovery in the reader's mind. Thus in Johnson's *Debates*, Gulliver's grandson presents in travel book fashion the Lilliputian "History . . . Laws and Customs of the Inhabitants, . . . Works of Art, and Productions of Nature" to acquaint English readers with their national vices and parliamentary debates in a thinly disguised foreign setting. Later, in *Idler* 87, Johnson invited readers to make a geographical comparison of English women and their rebellious comrades in arms, the Amazons. Travel books inspired this geographical satire. Abbé Guyon's *Histoire des Amazones* (1740) and C. M. de la Condamine's *Relation abrégée d'un voyage fait dans l'interieur de l'Amérique Méridionale* (1745) supplied the pertinent information for writing the essay. In fact, Johnson's early review of Guyon's account (1741) had adumbrated his mocking study of modern Amazons in describing how the legendary "Ladies lost the Pleasure of governing, forgot their military Exercises, and fell back into their original Subordination" under male authority.[22]

For Johnson's essays, however, travel literature served numerous literary ends other than satire. A wealth of geographical allusions, from Muscovite marriage customs to Peruvian mining operations, enriched his moral discussion and furnished geographically accurate settings for all his oriental tales. Occasionally, as is the case in *Adventurer* 67, his global awareness of the human condition among savage and civilized races provided the necessary empirical evidence of universal moral truths: "But a survey of the various nations that inhabit the earth will inform us, that life may be supported with less assistance, and that the dexterity, which practice enforced by necessity produces, is able to effect much by very scanty means. The nations of Mexico and Peru erected cities and temples without the use of iron; and at this day the rude Indian supplies himself with all the necessaries of life: sent like the rest of mankind naked into the world, . . . he is to provide by his own labour for his own support." Elsewhere in his writings, travel books documented biographical and historical studies.

His early *Life of Drake* (1740) eulogizes the great English navigator and Elizabethan patriotism for the express purpose of stimulating courage among his Georgian readers during a current war with Spain. The work contains only a few original remarks on the noble savage and the virtue of heroic enterprise, which are his definitive statements on the subjects to be repeated in later moral essays. Most of the biography is a distillation of three voyage accounts: a collection of Elizabethan narratives published by Nicholas Bourne (1652–1653); Nathaniel Crouch's *The English Hero* (1687); and the previously undocumented source of Richard Hakluyt's *Two Famous Voyages . . . by Sir Francis Drake and M. Thomas Candish* (1600).[23] Johnson chose to paraphrase these sources directly in order to communicate effective seventeenth-century propaganda against the Spanish and Dutch and champion the growth of the eighteenth-century British Empire. When he next wrote about war with Spain in his *Thoughts on the Late Transactions respecting Falkland's Islands* (1771), the jingoistic theme of his early biography had given way to pacific and anti-imperialistic sentiments opposing colonial warfare by England. No longer are English sailors and "the reign of Elizabeth, the favourite period of English greatness" so blindly extolled. Instead there is a penetrating analysis of the greed and pride that drove Europeans to aggression and internecine bloodshed. What remains the same in this later political pamphlet is his debt to voyage accounts for evidence to support the government's stand against another Spanish war. The English ministry supplied him with a veritable history of the South Pacific in the narratives of Thomas Cavendish, Sir Richard Hawkins, Sebald de Wert, John Strong, John Narborough, William Dampier, Amedée-François Frézier,

George Anson, John Byron, and John Macbride. These sources constituted a complete chronicle of Pacific navigation up to the most recent discoveries in the area. Therefore, Johnson's perspective on the present conflict in the southern hemisphere was just about as thoroughly authoritative as possible in the period.

Travel books provided historical documentation for other works. They illustrated word usage in his *Dictionary* and contributed practically the entire text of his *Introduction to the World Displayed* (1759). The *Introduction* was written for John Newbery's inexpensive collection of travels and surveys the early history of navigation from Noah's Ark to Columbus's discovery of America. The essay conformed to an editorial convention observed by most compilers of travel books, that of prefacing collections with a summary of maritime exploration. Although Johnson incorporated some original anti-imperialistic remarks, the work is mainly one continued paraphrase of two geographical treatises by Joseph Lafitau and Manuel de Faria y Sousa and a third unmentioned source, *The History of Navigation*, probably written by John Locke. [24] Johnson's derivative preface is another testimony to his knowledge of geography and readiness to use travel literature for his own purposes in literary creation. Furthermore his services for John Newbery possibly included editorial guidance in the selection of narratives for *The World Displayed* since many of his favorite travel books by George Sandys, Richard Pococke, Johann Keysler, and others appear in this collection. There may be some truth to the claim made in the Philadelphia edition of *The World Displayed* (1795) that Johnson was one of its original editors.

This introduction, his *Life of Drake*, and two other surveys of modern navigation in his *Introduction to the Political State of Great Britain* (1756) and *Observations on the State of Affairs in 1756* together constitute a miniature history of exploration and colonization. As such, they offer a useful historical perspective for studying his ideas about travel literature and the traditions of travel that inspired them. From these writings we learn that he equated the major political movements of modern Europe with the shifting balance of maritime power held first by Spain, then by Holland, and finally by France and England. From the time of the Renaissance to his own age of Georgian empire, "the sea was considered as the wealthy element; and, by degrees, a new kind of sovereignty arose, called naval dominion."[25] The Renaissance race for naval dominion had been spurred by romantic dreams of discovering a fabled Cathay in the east, an Atlantis in the west, a Terra Australis in the south, and an easy passage to India in the north. To Johnson's dismay, less romantic aims soon intervened, and the "desire of riches and of dominion" replaced the worthier goals of geographical discovery and missionary activity around the globe.[26] His study of Portuguese navigation in the *Introduction to the World Displayed* bitterly reviews the earliest European atrocities among the savages, denied their right to civilization and religion by their depraved Christian oppressors. His two essays on the political affairs of England in 1756 complement his denunciation of the Iberian conquistadores with a trenchant critique of later colonial abuses by adventurers from Holland, France, and England. His writings always insist on the need to explore and civilize the world rather than exploit backward races and corrupt national morality at home. He had the compassionate conscience of a moralist repelled by the sordid history of colonial warfare.

Although he deplored the cruelties initiated by Renaissance explorers, he enjoyed reading about Renaissance discoveries in a body of travel literature that is unsurpassed in heroic quality and epic scope. The Iberians had their Camöens and Cortes, and the Elizabethans and Jacobeans could take pride in the first English collections of voyages and travels by Richard Eden, Richard Hakluyt, and Samuel Purchas. Many of the early British narratives exhibit a patriotic breadth of vision, a romantic color and gusto, unrivaled in later travel literature. Voyage accounts had the rough and ready simplicity of hardy sailors writing their diaries, logs, and letters for practical reasons rather than literary fame. Journey accounts showed a greater diversity in style, ranging from the elegant to the mundane. However, a simple style generally remained the accepted norm for writers of travel books well into the eighteenth century. Johnson's *Life of Drake* exemplifies most of the heroic qualities and patriotic spirit that distinguished Elizabethan narratives and permeated his sources. Based as it is on Renaissance voyage accounts, his biography capitalizes on the glories of England's past naval triumphs for sheer propaganda purposes. Not only did he carefully follow his sources to achieve this end, but he also magnified their emotional impact by introducing a more elegant style and minimizing scientific inquiries and other details that might distract attention away from Sir Francis Drake.

As a result of his unwavering focus on Drake, the biography artfully transforms the navigator into a national symbol of heroic adventure to be emulated by all Britons. Johnson captures the Elizabethan romance of discovery in his description of Drake's first sight of the Pacific. The passage conveys the heroic excitement later expressed in Keats's famous image of discovery in the sonnet on Chapman's Homer: "This prospect exciting Drake's natural curiosity, and ardour for adventures and discoveries, he lifted up his hands to God, and implored his blessing upon the resolution, which he then formed, of sailing in an English ship on that sea."[27] Such was the patriotic sense of a great national destiny inspiriting the best works of Elizabethan travel literature. While stressing this spirit, the biography also contains Johnson's most considered views on the noble savage. Although Boswell's *Life* portrays the moralist as an opponent of the popular contemporary cult of primitivism, the *Life of Drake* presents a much more balanced attitude to the noble savage concept. An abhorrence of primitive ignorance and squalor is qualified by generous praise of primitive simplicity, strength, native intelligence, and benevolence far surpassing the depravity of European oppressors. However, his final judgment on the subject is unqualified. He thoroughly endorses the incomparable blessings of civilization and revealed religion. According to his Christian conviction of moral uniformity, God created all men equal in their natural endowments but not in their advantages. For only the civilized man had the material and religious opportunities to pursue a fully human life.

As his *Introduction to the Political State of Great Britain* emphasizes, the seventeenth century witnessed the emergence of the British Empire as the naval strength of other countries waned: "Our princes seem to have considered themselves as entitled by their right of prior seizure to the northern parts of America, . . . and we accordingly made our principal settlements within the limits of our own discoveries, and, by degrees, planted the eastern coast from Newfoundland to Georgia."[28] As England expanded abroad, its travel literature multiplied under the encouragement of the Royal Society and its scientific program for collecting geographical data. Samuel Purchas had already sounded the Baconian note for empirical research in *Purchas His Pilgrimes* (1625). His preface announces that "his Pilgrimes minister individuall and sensible materials . . . to those universall Speculators for their Theoreticall structures."[29] Royal Society Fellows carried on the Baconian advancement of the Nova Philosophia in geography by advertising more efficient methods to achieve a worldwide accumulation of scientific facts. The *Philosophical Transactions* not only reported geographical findings but also published articles explaining proper techniques of investigation. In 1666, for example, Robert Boyle's "General Heads for a Natural History of a Country" and Laurence Rooke's "Directions for Seamen bound for long Voyages" recommended a more systematic format and approach to inquiry in travel books. They asked travelers to use a comprehensive checklist of topics in natural history, geography, and anthropology in the interests of thorough research. The changes promoted by the Royal Society would be fully implemented in the eighteenth century.

The Restoration's stress on a more codified study of the globe left travel literature with a much more rigid organization than ever before. The new scientist-traveler was expected to record information on every conceivable subject and employ specified topics and subtopics in his narrative. He had to cover a country's size, situation, waters, minerals, plants, animals, and inhabitants and deal with each of them under a detailed series of headings. What travel books gained in scientific accuracy and comprehensiveness, they lost to less enlightened Renaissance descriptions in exuberance and individuality. As much hampered as helped by the restrictions of form, a great writer of travels had to rise above the rigorous conventions of the genre to set his work apart from the common run of narratives. Johnson did so in his account of the Hebrides. Boswell, Sterne, and Smollett also faced the problem of standardization and happily found various solutions suited to their unique personalities.

Otherwise, there could be a monotonous sameness in travel books to cause even an avid reader like Johnson to complain of boredom with repetitious narratives: "There can be little entertainment in such books; one set of Savages is like another."[30] He had another complaint relating to the genre. Eighteenth-century thinkers had a habit of using the evidence of travel literature to prove any political, religious, or moral theory, often of a dangerously unorthodox turn. Such evidence could be untrustworthy because of the conflicting nature of reports in different narratives: " 'That puts me in mind of Montesquieu, who is really a fellow of genius too in many respects; whenever he wants to support a strange opinion, he quotes you the practice of Japan or of some other distant country, of which he knows nothing.' "[31] Yet, Johnson himself showed a penchant for using geographical proof to support his orthodox views on morality, religion, and society. In an era when many philosophers, from Hobbes and Locke to Shaftesbury and Rousseau, made geographical discoveries a platform for philosophical discoveries, hardly any writer could refrain from quoting the data of voyages and travels.

If travel books often exhibited a tedious uniformity in format, so too English navigation between 1660 and 1760 tended to display a barren uniformity of purpose. Sailors kept mostly to the beaten tracks of maritime trade and naval warfare in the Atlantic without making notable discoveries. Johnson's *Observations on the State of*

Affairs in 1756 denounces the misuse of European navies for colonial wars instead of peaceful exploration and likens the American conflict to the brawling of two thieves over ill-gotten foreign spoils. When in 1763 the Peace of Paris decided the imperial contest in Britain's favor, an unparalleled period of geographical discovery commenced in England to match her new global supremacy. Previously, English voyages had been mainly haphazard buccaneering expeditions bent on piracy and plunder rather than on serious exploration. A few early navigators and geographers had proposed sending "skilful *Painters, Naturalists,* and *Mechanists,* under publick *Stipends*" on ships to improve geographical research.[32] At the beginning of his career Johnson himself appealed for more sophisticated scientific investigation: "What may not be expected from the united Labours of Travellers . . . not intent, like Merchants, only on the Acts of Commerce, the Value of Commodities, and the Probabilities of Gain, nor engaged, like Military Officers, in the Care of subsisting Armies, securing Passes, obviating Stratagems, and defeating Opposition, but vacant to every Object of Curiosity, and at Leisure for the most minute Remarks."[33] However, not until the momentous Pacific voyages sponsored by George III did the professionals supersede the amateurs in exploration. Captain Cook sailed with botanists, astronomers, and artists on his first two voyages and was government-financed for all three. Cook's discoveries represented the fruition of scientific travel promoted by the Royal Society ever since the Restoration.

While navigators and explorers roamed the most distant seas and lands, grand tourists were crowding the Continent in growing numbers from the time of the Renaissance. With regard to the grand tour, Johnson sided with such conservative educators as Roger Ascham, Bishop Hall, and John Locke in opposing the fashion of sending callow youth abroad before their college training and growing up were completed. He feared for the moral state of inexperienced travelers exposed to temptations and corruptions on the Continent. Yet his theory of travel literature has a humanist emphasis upon the moral, spiritual, and cultural goals of travel derived from Renaissance treatises on grand touring. As with other types of travel literature, grand tour accounts resist tidy classification either by form, content, or style. However, there are some perceptible trends in subject matter changing from period to period. According to George Parks, tourist narratives fall into three large groups: those written before 1620 stressing the study of foreign governments for training in a public career; those appearing between 1620 and 1670 emphasizing moral improvement and the fine arts; and those published after 1670 concerned with scientific inquiry as well as the older humanist studies of foreign manners, statecraft, and art.[34] The style of early tourists ranged from the stately periods of George Sandys and the breezy sentences of Thomas Coryate to the scientific simplicity of John Ray and the gentle elegance of Joseph Addison. The subjects surveyed tended to be more cultural and ethical than scientific in nature at least until the Restoration. Moreover, an appreciation for the sublime beauties of Alpine landscapes and Gothic architecture would not become generally popular until midway in the eighteenth century.

Unlike many eighteenth-century descriptions of remote places, early accounts of the Continent often lacked a codified format but did deal with certain routine topics of their own. Most tourists rambled casually through such urban scenes of foreign society as courts and cathedrals, treasuries and monasteries, palaces and castles, harbors and inns, antiquities and ruins, and manors and manners. A Renaissance tract on grand touring, *Profitable Instructions* (1613), outlined a program of study as detailed and comprehensive as the codified topics of scientific inquiry later advocated by the Royal Society. The work recommends an impossible tripartite examination of a country's geography, people, and government under a proliferating series of subtopics.[35] By following this endless checklist of subjects, the traveler could accomplish a complete investigation of a nation's topography, history, and culture and earn the right to call his Continental jaunt a truly grand tour of great intellectual

discovery. After the Restoration, the grand tour steadily degenerated from a serious educational experience into a short vacation-
exercise abroad for acquiring social polish, gathering specimens for a
virtuoso's collection of curiosities, basking in scenic splendors, succumbing to immorality, or simply wasting time. The grand tour
would become the jest of Georgian satirists and the delight of Georgian adventurers like Boswell who found maturity and notoriety on
the Continent. Yet, however adulterated by later fashions, it would
keep alive the old Renaissance ideal of studying men and manners.
As John Evelyn noted, "It is written of Ulysses that he saw many
cities, but withall his Remarks of men's Manners and Customs,
was ever preferred to his counting Steeples, and making Tours:
It is the Ethical and Morall part of Travel, which embellisheth a
Gentleman."[36]

Johnson's theory about the uses of travel and travel books assumes
an intimate knowledge of the history and changing conventions of
geographical literature. Two traditions of travel, comprising the
Renaissance moral ideals of the grand tour and the eighteenth-
century methods of scientific inquiry, converge in his theory. Except for his views on style his philosophy of travel is largely an inheritance of both geographical traditions wrought into a harmonious
whole. Always a man whose thinking bestrode two world views of
Renaissance moral verities and modern empirical values, his theory
contains the best of old and new ideas about travel. Renaissance
guidebooks inspired his overriding ethical outlook on the proper
concerns and purpose of travel. His principles emphasize a humanist
study of men and manners, rather than nature or artifacts, for the
purpose of clarifying the true state of human nature and the intellectual history of mankind. Boswell wisely associated Johnson's
dominant interest in manners with Renaissance concepts of tourism.
For the biographer directly alluded to the Renaissance guidebook,
Profitable Instructions, when describing the moralist's fundamental
preoccupation in travel: "He was of Lord Essex's opinion, who
advises his kinsman Roger Earl of Rutland, 'rather to go an hundred

miles to speak with one wise man than five miles to see a fair town.' "[37]

By concentrating on the distinctly human phenomena of men and societies, travelers best served the public interest and their personal development morally and intellectually. Their findings in sociology and anthropology added to the sum total of European knowledge about the quality of human life and learning for the advancement of civilization at home. Johnson's fascination with foreign manners was the uncompromising priority of a moralist committed in his life's work to analyzing human aspirations and promoting social progress. His reviews of travel books as different as Du Halde's *Description of China* and Alexander Russell's *Natural History of Aleppo* always stress cultural information rather than technical and scientific data. When travelers set aside the study of manners to inquire "after those things by which the greatest part of mankind is little affected," Johnson usually registered a negative critical verdict on their re-search.[38] Only a careful attention to the cultural diversity and moral uniformity of mankind fully satisfied his expectations concerning travel literature. Mrs. Thrale recognized the favorite geographical interest of her friend: "*My* great delight like yours would be to see how Life is carried on in other Countries, how various Climates produce various Effects, and how different Notions of Religion & Government operate upon the human Manners & the human Mind."[39]

Fortunately, the specific Renaissance source for the humanist tenets of his theory can be identified. First printed in 1642, James Howell's *Instructions for Forreine Travell* is one of the earliest English guidebooks on grand touring and was probably the single most important influence upon Johnson's philosophy of travel. Better known for his gossipy correspondence in *Epistolae Ho-Elianae*, Howell (1594–1666) had learned the rules of tourism from his experience as a foreign diplomat and clerk of the Privy Council under Charles I. His guidebook proclaims his Royalist sympathies to church and crown, a political position that led to his imprisonment during the Civil War. Yet, such sympathies would have strongly appealed to a Stuart loyalist like Johnson. Certainly the emphatic moral and religious tone of the guidebook proved very attractive to him since the work was quoted from memory in the *Life of Browne*, used for moral illustration in *Rambler* 169, and, as we shall see, paraphrased throughout his major statement on travel in *Idler* 97.[40] Because the views of the two writers are so alike, a summary of Howell's ideas is an excellent introduction to Johnson's theory and practice of travel in his life and writings.

First of all, Howell stressed the study of manners for a tourist's moral and spiritual enrichment. The acquisition of humanistic wisdom is "the prime use of Peregrination, which therefore may be not improperly called a *moving Academy*, or the true *Peripatique School:* This made Ulisses to be cryed up so much amongst the Greeks for their greatest wise man, because he had *Travelled* through many strange Countreys, and observed the manners of divers Nations, having seen, as it was said and sung of him, more *Cities* than there were *Houses* in *Athens*."[41] The allusions to Plato, Aristotle, and Homer suggest Howell's admixture of philosophical, scientific, and humanistic principles in his guidebook. They are also meant to remind readers of the close ties between grand touring and the Renaissance training of princes. For Plato taught the prince of Syracuse, Aristotle tutored Alexander the Great, and Homer recounted the education of a Greek prince. Johnson was mindful of this tradition in *Rasselas* and depicted the education of an Abyssinian prince by his philosophical tutor, Imlac, on a moral grand tour through the Orient. According to Howell, the method most conducive to acquiring wisdom for the good of self and society is to study the foreign country and language beforehand, visit courts and scholars abroad for the most valuable information, and shed all national prejudices so as to become a receptive and knowledgeable citizen of the world. All these directives were adopted by Johnson, who not only supported the same moral aims, careful preparation, and cosmopolitan outlook but even echoed Howell's language in his remarks.

As early as his preface to *Lobo's Voyage* in 1735, Johnson re-iterated Howell's assumption of the divinely ordained equality of men and nations everywhere: "*The Earth is the Lords, and all the corners thereof, he created the Mountaines of Wales, as well as the Wildes of Kent; the rugged Alpes, as well as the Fertile plains of Compagnia,* . . . and to . . . deride a Countrey for the barrenesse thereof, is tacitly to taxe God Almighty of *Improvidence* and *Partiality.* . . . For . . . herein Nature may seeme to recompense the hard condition of a Countrey the other way" (pp. 29–30). Howell's faith in the global equality of the human condition underlies Johnson's comments on the geographical compensations of countries in *Lobo's Voyage:* "The reader will here find no regions cursed with irremediable barrenness, or blessed with spontaneous fecundity; no perpetual gloom or unceasing sunshine. . . . He will discover . . . that the Creator doth not appear partial in his distributions, but has balanced in most countries their particular inconveniences by particular favours."[42] *Rasselas*, in turn, would transform this principle into a moral statement about life's uniform unhappiness: " 'The Europeans, answered Imlac, are less unhappy than we, but they are not happy. Human life is every where a state in which much is to be endured, and little to be enjoyed.' "[43] Finally, Goldsmith's *The Traveller* (1764) would repeat the lessons of *Rasselas* and carry on the tradition of a global equality in the lot of mankind:

> And yet, perhaps, if countries we compare,
> And estimate the blessings which they share,
> Though patriots flatter, still shall wisdom find
> An equal portion dealt to all mankind:
> As different good, by Art or Nature given,
> To different nations makes their blessings even.
>
> (Ll. 75–80)

Idler 97 is Johnson's most important essay on travel and paraphrases Howell's key chapters 14 through 17 of the *Instructions* to reaffirm the Renaissance moral ideal of examining manners: "He that would travel for the entertainment of others, should remember that the great object of remark is human life." Most of the principles expressed in this moral essay originated in Howell's guidebook. As we shall see, the way that Johnson composed *Idler* 97, by an editorial revision of an admired text preserved in his memory and adapted to suit his sentiments and style, was characteristic of his technique of creation in literary productions like *Rasselas*. This imitative technique was not far removed from his habit of freely paraphrasing and quoting passages from works in magazine reviews during his years as a journalist under Edward Cave. *Idler* 97 is a product of paraphrase and opens with a criticism of useless travel books adapted from Howell's attack against hasty tourists: "He that enters a town at night and surveys it in the morning, and then hastens away to another place, . . . guesses at the manners of the inhabitants by the entertainment which his inn has afforded him" and, therefore, can report nothing worthwhile in shutting himself off from the sights of the trip. In chapters 14 and 15 of the guidebook, Howell had similarly scorned the habits of such trifling tourists who learn nothing valuable in their haste "and as *Jonas* in the *Whales* belly *travelled much*, but *saw little*, . . . and after a long *perreration* to and fro; . . . returne as wise as they went, because their Soules were so ill lodged, and shut up in such stupid bodies" (pp. 67–68).

Where Howell next proposes an ideal "medium" in deportment between Spanish gravity and French levity, Johnson next advocates an ideal middle style in travel books between labored minuteness and empty generality. *Idler* 97 criticizes those tedious tourists who survey Italian palaces, "hear masses in magnificent churches, . . . recount the number of the pillars," and record in boring detail the architecture of "every edifice, sacred and civil." Their information is useless to readers. Similarly, Howell had enumerated an equivalent series of Italian sights without any educational value: "To see the *Treasurie of Saint Mark, and the Arsenal of Venice;* . . . The proud Palaces in and about Genoua, whereof there are two hundred . . . and not one of the same forme of building; To see *Saint Peter's*

Church, the *Vatican*, and other magnificent structures in *Rome;* . . . All this is but vanity and Superficiall Knowledge, unlesse the inward man be bettered hereby" (p. 71).

Having dealt with the worst types of tourists, Howell then concludes his discussion by noting the great ethical and social ends of travel: "Moreover, one should . . . bring something home, that may accrue to the publique benefit and advantage of his Countrey. . . . Therefore he should pry into the *Policy* and municipall Lawes of other States . . . and by collation thereof with that of his own, Examine well whether any wholesome constitution or custome may be applyable to the frame of his owne Countrey. . . . At his returne home, hee will blesse God, and love England better ever after" (pp. 72–74). Johnson closes his essay with almost exactly the same advice but in a tidier style and a less religious tone: "He only is a useful traveller who brings home something by which his country may be benefited; who procures some supply of want or some mitigation of evil, which may enable his readers to compare their condition with that of others, to improve it whenever it is worse, and whenever it is better to enjoy it." Johnson's dependence upon *Instructions for Forreine Travell* in *Idler* 97 directly links his theory of travel to the moral and civic ends of Renaissance grand touring. His paraphrase of Howell's ideas to compose the essay has an important bearing on the creation of *Rasselas* just a year before since the tale was produced in part by a similar process of imitation and had embodied Howell's principles in its journey plot.[44]

More than one tradition of travel had influenced Johnson's philosophy of travel. Besides his adherence to Renaissance modes on tourism emphasizing the moral study of manners, he also advocated modern principles of scientific inquiry to ensure accuracy in the examination of human life. Opposing the vulgar errors of ancient credulity, he allied himself with the moderns in geography: "The information we have from modern travellers is much more authentick than what we had from ancient geographers; ancient travellers guessed; modern travellers measure."[45] He demanded a careful in-

vestigation of the most minute facts in a country's common life to
document generalizations about the cultural state of mankind. His
writings on travel literature endorse a Baconian distrust of the falsifying imagination, a Lockean insistence on eyewitness verification,
and a skepticism worthy of Hume with regard to fraudulent Man-
devillian descriptions filled more with tall tales than true facts.
His preface to *Lobo's Voyage* and review of Du Halde's *Description of China* defend the aims of the new science in travel. They recommend a professional study of geography by conscientious observers of foreign manners. Travelers must therefore trust to "their
own Eyes" rather than "uncertain Informations," avoid all "Suspicion of Falsehood" and mercenary motives in exploration, strive for
complete and objective findings, and learn native languages well to
penetrate the deepest secrets of a nation's cultural affairs.[46]

Most of these guidelines for disinterested scientific research would
be realized in the great Pacific voyages of English navigators in the
second half of the century. Yet, so scrupulous was he about full
and precise geographical data, that even Cook's professedly scientific expeditions failed to satisfy his high standards of research.
We have already noted Johnson's criticism of Cook's ventures; the
Pacific explorers failed to learn the Tahitian dialects and inadequately studied Polynesian manners. Cook's sailors were only guessing, and the fact-minded moralist detested unfounded opinions.[47]
In lieu of the detailed evidence that Johnson desired, guessing led
to inexcusable errors and omissions. With his skeptical and empirical
turn of mind, he was naturally receptive to the scientific techniques
of travel encouraged by the Royal Society since the late seventeenth
century. He advised the use of a codified format in travel books
for the sake of systematic geographical observation. He urged Warren Hastings to thoroughly research the Indian culture by employing the exhaustive checklist of topics embracing history, religion,
antiquities, arts, manufactures, and natural history. Again, in *Idler*
97, there is mention of the conventional subjects of scientific inquiry
to guarantee a comprehensive examination of human life: "Every

nation has something peculiar in its manufactures, its works of genius, its medicines, its agriculture, its customs, and its policy." To know a people well, a tourist had to survey every facet of the national life-style. Ultimately, Johnson's theory synthesized modern scientific methods and Renaissance moral aims, the former subservient to the latter, to promote a reliable study of the human family. Like most of his thought, his philosophy of travel was a Georgian compromise of ethical and empirical traditions welded into a critical unity of purpose.

In matters of style Johnson departed from previous standards and supported the growing mid-century vogue for polished writing in travel literature. A simple style had long been the accepted norm for descriptions and had the blessing of the Royal Society since clarity ensured accuracy and unpremeditated writing implied honesty in reports. The usually plain style of narratives did result in a racy individuality, spontaneity, and authenticity not often matched in the more elegant travel books appearing later. Nevertheless, a skilled rhetorician like Johnson naturally reacted against the heritage of artless descriptions: "Those whose lot it is to ramble can seldom write, and those who know how to write very seldom ramble."[48] His own *Journey to the Western Islands of Scotland* is one of the most eloquent geographical documents produced in the period. Moreover, he praised the cultivated travelers of his century, such as Addison, Burney, and Boswell, capable of combining elegance and truth in their narratives. Fielding himself complained of the "heap of dulness" in the poorly written accounts of previous travelers.[49] However, the taste for elegance could be abused when mid-century compilers of travels like Smollett and John Hawkesworth felt free to tamper with an explorer's original journals, condense and strip them of technicalities, and even mix separate accounts without warning for the sake of "improved" readability.

Johnson strongly opposed such editorial abuses. Authenticity was obviously more important to him than the quality of writing. His advocacy of an elegant style was meant to give travel books a literary respectability already possessed by the established genres of history and belles lettres. To assist this end, his essays and reviews promulgated numerous literary criteria for the traveler's consideration. Descriptions should exhibit a clearly defined organization without unnecessary digressions, an admixture of facts and reflections, a polished presentation of observations neither too minute nor too general, and a care for variety and novelty in reporting findings. When travel books lacked variety in their coverage and novelty in their subject matter, they failed to entertain and instruct readers: "The traveller who tells, in a pompous folio, that he saw the Pantheon at Rome, and the Medicean Venus at Florence; the natural historian who, describing the productions of a narrow island, recounts all that it has in common with every other part of the world; the collector of antiquities, that accounts every thing a curiosity which the ruins of Herculaneum happen to emit, though an instrument already shewn in a thousand repositories, or a cup common to the ancients, the moderns, and all mankind, may be justly censured as the persecutors of students, and the thieves of that time which never can be restored" (*Idler* 94). All these criteria of style Johnson implemented in his travel book and demanded of other travelers.

According to Boswell's *Life*, Johnson selected six travel books and ranged them on an ascending scale of literary value.[50] By comparing his evaluation with the actual contents of the works, we shall find that his critical judgments assumed all the principles of his theory of travel. He placed Richard Pococke's *Description of the East* (1743) lowest on the scale probably because of its poor style and emphasis upon ancient architecture, a subject that he considered less important than the manners of foreign people. Higher on the scale are three accounts of Continental travel by Richard Twiss (1775), H. de Blainville (1743), and Johann Keysler (1756), all of whom blended a study of foreign manners with a variety of observations on natural history, scenery, and artifacts. Furthermore, Twiss's *Travels through Portugal and Spain* could claim the added virtue of novelty in dealing with two countries off the beaten track

of the English grand tour in the eighteenth century. Yet, on Johnson's critical scale, these three books lie below Addison's elegant
Remarks on Several Parts of Italy (1705) because of their dull style.
Addison had surveyed the classic grounds of Italy, so venerated by
eighteenth-century Englishmen, "with the eyes of a poet." He won
a reputation for his supposedly innovative technique of interweaving
translations from the classics in his nostalgic descriptions of Roman
ruins. His aesthetic tastes were distinctly classical in his preference
for ancient Roman architecture over more modern designs. Johnson, however, faulted him on his ignorance of Italian and consequent
inability to report any new information in a travel book which
"might have been written at home."[51]

Therefore, highest on the critical scale was Patrick Brydone's
Tour through Sicily and Malta (1773), an excellent work that fulfilled all the moral, scientific, and literary principles of Johnson's
theory of travel. Only Brydone's anti-Mosaical remarks on the
earth's geological age seem to have offended the religiously orthodox
moralist. Otherwise, the travel book met his critical specifications.
The *Tour* possessed variety and novelty in its colorful description
of two little-known countries and stressed the study of native manners according to the codified topics of scientific research. A Fellow
of the Royal Society, Brydone (1736–1818) was an elegant stylist
who imposed a thematic unity on his rambling journey narrative by
concentrating on the significance of Mount Etna in the natural and
social history of the islands. Mount Etna is both a metaphorical
"phoenix able to destroy and create at will" and an intriguing scientific phenomenon for geological analysis, barometrical measure-
ment, and electrical experimentation.[52] He was a highly literate tourist concerned with imparting the vicarious experience of travel and
an elegiac vision of Etna's destructive power over the lives of the
people. His artistic and scientific survey of an unfamiliar Mediterranean culture deservedly won Johnson's highest approval. By any-
body's standards Brydone's *Tour* ranks with some of the best travel
literature of the century. The year 1773 was not a very notable one

for English literature, but this travel book was as distinguished a register as any of a well-traveled age and a great moment in English exploration when Johnson, Cook, Phipps, and Bruce were touring the expanding domains of the British Empire.

As in no other time before or since the Renaissance, the romance of travel captured the public's imagination and permeated English literature. Johnson's writings are an irrefutable testimony to the impact of travel and geographical discovery on his contemporaries. The vogue of travel literature colored his career as a journalist and moralist and evoked from his pen one of the most complete theories of travel in the century. Combining the best of old and new ideas, his philosophy of travel was aimed at improving the standards and status of a genre that so importantly contributed to the increase of human knowledge. Reading travel books was second only to the actual experience of travel in enriching the mind, invigorating the imagination, and improving society. For as James Howell affirmed, "*Books* also and conversation with the *Dead* . . . edifie infinitely; yet the study of living men, and a collation of his own *Optique* observations and judgement with theirs, work much more strongly" (p. 13). Johnson would take this lesson to heart in his later years. In his case, a lifelong love of travel literature concealed a larger passion to travel himself and bring his eye and mind to bear upon the totality of human experience.

3

HABITS OF TRAVEL IN
WALES AND FRANCE
WITH THE THRALES

Be not solitary, be not idle.
　　　　　　　Robert Burton, *The Anatomy of Melancholy*

ALL HIS LIFE Johnson wanted to tour the farthest reaches of the globe. However, years of poverty and struggle in Grubstreet confined him to the role of an armchair traveler delighting in the narratives of more fortunate wanderers. When a government pension and friendship with the Thrales freed him from financial worries in the 1760s, this established writer embarked upon a new career of exhilarating travel through Great Britain and France. His extensive touring in later life clearly refutes Thomas Macaulay's notorious opinion, still widespread in some quarters today, that "of foreign travel and of history he spoke with the fierce and boisterous contempt of ignorance."[1] On the contrary, Johnson had few equals in his appreciation of travel for stimulating the mind, exercising the body, and reviving the despondent spirit. He knew from the teachings of James Howell and John Locke that any ramble had an inestimable moral and intellectual significance. Something about the vitality and joy of a journey answered the innermost psychological needs of this unsettled man, who believed with Tristram Shandy that "so much of motion is so much of life, and so much of joy—and that to stand still, or get on but slowly, is death and the devil!"[2]

Perhaps Macaulay's capacious memory for once forgot that it was Johnson's destiny as a native of Staffordshire to possess a passion to travel wherever his means and health permitted. As Defoe reported in his survey of Great Britain, "the people of this county have been particularly famous, and more than any other county of England, for good footmanship, and there have been, and still are among them, some of the fleetest runners in England . . . exercising themselves to it from their child-hood."[3] During his childhood Johnson was smart enough to do his footwork astride the backs of duller pupils, carrying him to grammar school for the promise of help in their lessons. Otherwise, handicapped by poor eyesight, he once had to crawl on all fours to feel his way home from Dame Oliver's school. The situation changed little in his maturity when he needed the assistance of friends like Boswell and the Thrales, with better eyes and more money, to set his tours in motion. Perhaps his omnivorous reading in his father's bookshop first acquainted him with his principal mentor in matters of travel, Howell's *Instructions for Forreine Travell*. Certainly, Howell's emphasis upon the peculiar necessity for English travel would have appealed to a provincial youth: "Amongst other people of the Earth, *Islanders* seeme to stand in most need of Forraine *Travell*, for they being cut off (as it were) from the rest of the Citizens of the World, have not those obvious accesses . . . to mingle with those more refined Nations, whom Learning and Knowledge did first Urbanize and polish."[4] The ambition of shedding some rustic insularity was, in fact, a powerful incentive behind Johnson's wanderlust in later life.

Already during his poor but promising years at Oxford, his mind ranged far beyond the Lichfield common and Pembroke quadrangle. Outside the happy valley of his confining undergraduate studies, there lay a golden world of foreign learning: " 'Well, I have a mind to see what is done in other places of learning. I'll go and visit the Universities abroad. I'll go to France and Italy. I'll go to Padua.' "[5] Unfortunately, those early dreams of grand touring never materialized during a long lean period of hackwriting for Edward Cave, supporting a family, and composing the *Dictionary*. When fame finally came to him in his fiftieth year, he fictionalized his frustrations in Omar of *Idler* 101, who, despite a "desire of seeing distant countries," had also to confess at the age of fifty that he "always resided in the same city." Only the last twenty-five years of Johnson's life would begin to redress his thwarted ambitions with an unprecedented outburst of travel beyond the pale of London. Even then, he tended to write as a disillusioned Imlac in *Rasselas*, grateful for his new friendship with the Thrales and new opportunities to travel soothing his past disappointments: "Life has upon the whole fallen short, very short, of my early expectation, but the acquisition of such a Friendship, at an age when new Friendships are seldom acquired, is something better than the general course of things gives Man a right to expect."[6] Nonetheless, if sharing Imlac's sense of sorrow, he would partially realize young Rasselas's dreams of travel in his old age.

Boswell documents the moralist's inquisitive spirit: "He talked with an uncommon animation of travelling into distant countries; that the mind was enlarged by it, and that an acquisition of dignity of character was derived from it."[7] For these reasons Johnson considered undertaking major expeditions into the North through Iceland, Poland, and Baltic regions; into the Near and Far East through Egypt, India, and China; and even around the uncharted Pacific with Captain Cook. Only savage Africa and America were missing from his proposed global itinerary since their lack of civilization repelled a man most curious about foreign manners and societies: "In America there is little to be observed except natural curiosities."[8] To participate at least vicariously in the experience of travel, he read widely in travel literature and gathered around him many eminent travelers of his day. His associates in the Literary Club alone included such notables as "Corsica" Boswell; William Jones, the orientalist; Lord Charlemont, the grand tourist of Egypt and Greece; George Macartney, the Sino-Russian diplomat; Robert Chambers, the Indian judge; and Joseph Banks, the Pacific explorer and sponsor of Australian colonization. He rubbed shoulders with celebrated Continental tourists like Henry Swinburne, Giuseppe Baretti, Samuel Sharp, Richard Twiss, Richard Chandler, Nathaniel

Wraxall, and William Fullarton. He conversed with famous and infamous travelers alike from "Abyssinia" Bruce and the pseudo-Formosan Psalmanazar to the Corsican General Paoli and the American agents, Benjamin Franklin and Arthur Lee. Doubtless, what he wrote of the Elizabethan era applied equally to his own, that "one of the entertainments at great tables seems to have been the discourse of a traveller."[9]

An impressive group of explorers whetted his curiosity to travel without fully satisfying it. As James Howell had inculcated, nothing substituted for the actual experience: "And although one should reade all the Topographers . . . and mingle Discourse with the most exact observers . . . Yet one's own *Ocular* view, and personall conversation will . . . enable him to discourse more knowingly and confidently and with a kind of *Authority* thereof" (pp. 12–13). Significantly, when news of the government pension reached Johnson in 1762, his first thoughts turned to the abortive schemes of travel in his youth: "Had this happened twenty years ago, I should have gone to Constantinople to learn Arabick, as Pococke did."[10] The next year marked his meeting with Boswell, who not only instigated many of Johnson's rambles but left invaluable records of his theory and practice of travel in the *Life* and *Tour to the Hebrides*. By 1765 Johnson had befriended the Thrales and found in these generous companions a further stimulus to travel. Thereafter, some of his most carefree moments would come from touring England, Scotland, Wales, and France: "Is not mine a kind of life turned upside down? Fixed to a spot when I was young, and roving the world when others are contriving to sit still, I am wholly unsettled. I am a kind of ship with a wide sail, and without an anchor."[11] The topsy-turvy course of his career, with its early hopes and late fulfillments, concluded with an old man's amazing energy to take to the road and study mankind at first hand.

However belated, his trips represented the vindication of a life-long moral imperative to confront life directly for personal growth and social progress: "Deign on the passing world to turn thine eyes, /

And pause awhile from letters, to be wise." As with his views on travel literature, his habits of travel reflect a combination of old and new traditions of tourism found in the respective writings of Howell and Locke. Howell's ethical ideals were Johnson's humanist priorities on a journey; the great object of remark was human life. To study mankind in the original amounted to an essential duty in forming one's mind and character and improving society at home. The *Instructions for Forreine Travell* lists many of these ends as follows: "Amongst those many advantages, which conduce to enrich the mind with variety of knowledge, to rectify and ascertain the Iudgment, and to . . . build one up to the highest story of perfection, *Peregrination . . .* is none of the least. But to bee a Sedentary *Traveller* only, . . . to run over and traverse the world by *Hearesay*, and traditional relation, with other mens eyes, . . . leaveth but weak and distrustful notions behind it; in regard the *Eare* is not so authentique a witnesse as the *Eye*" (p. 11). Howell's Renaissance concern for developing right reason became Johnson's eighteenth-century interest in contributing empirical data to the intellect according to Lockean theory: "he must mingle with the world that desires to be useful. Every new scene impresses new ideas, enriches the imagination, and enlarges the power of reason, by new topics of comparison."[12] If the passage compresses Howell's sentiments, its terminology suggests the faculty psychology of Locke.

Johnson followed Renaissance precepts in attaching a prime ethical significance to travel. A study of foreign manners promoted individual virtue and the public welfare. Always a moral traveler he stressed the need to research the various societies of the world in the interests of a summary appraisal of man's achievements and setbacks, his complex nature and purpose for being. By knowing the human condition better, a tourist might learn more tolerance for cultural diversity and more compassion for a weak and suffering humanity. In the process he might contribute useful discoveries in the arts and sciences for the benefit of his countrymen. So Johnson wrote to George Staunton en route to America: "I do not doubt but you will be able to add much to knowledge, and, perhaps, to medicine. Wild nations trust to simples; and, perhaps, the Peruvian bark is not the only specifick which those extensive regions may afford us."[13] Johnson regarded the study of nature as subservient to the exploration of cultures. He philosophically affirmed the moral uniformity of mankind and looked for the discoverable universals in conduct on trips and in travel books. However, what most intrigued him and his fellow tourists were the "petty differences" and unusual practices in foreign societies. Henry Fielding subscribed to uniformitarian ideas in his novels but preferred to see the variety of human cultures in his travels: "If the customs and manners of men were every where the same, there would be no office so dull as that of a traveller."[14] Although human nature was uniform, customs perceptibly varied to the delight of curious observers. In Johnson's age and in all ages the romance of travel depended upon finding the strange and exciting discriminations in national character and natural phenomena.

Ironically, despite their cosmopolitan sense of human equality, Englishmen were notorious for emphasizing human differences to the prejudice of other nations. Howell had already noticed the British penchant "to undervalue and vilify other Countreys, for which I have heard them often censured" (p. 29). Unfortunately neither Howell nor Johnson was free of the English insularity that they both deprecated. The *Instructions for Forreine Travell* only grudgingly concedes civilization to the Mohammedan Empire and to nowhere else in the non-European world. Asia Minor alone was worth seeing "If my *Travellers* curiosity hath a further extent, and that Europe cannot bound the largenes of his desires, but that he hath a disposition to see the *Turks* dominions, which next to *Christendome* are fittest to be known, in regard He is the sole Earthly potentat, and fatallest foe of the Crosse of Christ" (p. 82). Johnson remembered this lesson and similarly relegated four-fifths of the world to a hopeless state of savagery: "Yes, Sir; there are two objects of curiosity,—the Christian world, and the Mohametan world. All the rest may be considered as barbarous."[15] All men might be created equal, but the European, and especially the Briton, possessed the clear cultural advantage. His pronounced patriotism matched Howell's own love of homeland "For the *free condition of the subject*, and *equall participation of the Wealth of the Land*, for the *unparalleled accomodation of lodging*, and *security of Travell*, for . . . the *rare fertility of Shoare and Sea*, . . . above all; for the *moderation and decency in celebrating the true Service of God*" (p. 75). Perhaps more than anything else, Howell's proud and pious outlook on his country made Johnson his admirer and pupil.

The Georgian tourist would gradually modify his chauvinistic attitude toward foreigners through a more objective study of mankind. Nevertheless, he had valid grounds for lauding his nation's virtues. The reports of Continental travelers testify to the relative lack of liberty and prosperity among middle classes abroad. Untroubled by courts of inquisition and *lettres de cachet*, Englishmen enjoyed an incomparable freedom of movement and economic well-being allowing them to be the most active, if most contemptuous, travelers in Europe. Of all the seventeenth-century tourists, Howell had claimed that "the major part of them were English," and during Johnson's lifetime, English travel flourished all the more. Traveling conditions improved despite continuing inadequacies to annoy and endanger tourists. A better system of turnpikes and canals, mail delivery and Channel ferries, shortened the time and distance of a journey. Coaches had more comfortable innersprings and offered faster and more efficient service as timetables became more varied and inns regulated the maintenance of fresh horses. Moreover, Englishmen could count on a stable European civilization to encourage their excursions abroad. The greater accessibility to distant places would diminish the provincial differences between nations and foster a global consciousness in the lives and letters of contemporary citizens of the world. Thomas Macaulay may not have appreciated Johnson's love of touring but fully understood the impact of travel on social progress in eighteenth-century England: "Every improvement of the means of locomotion benefits mankind morally and intellectually as well as materially, and not only facilitates the interchange of the various productions of nature and art, but tends to remove national and provincial antipathies, and to bind together all the branches of the great human family."[16]

Johnson himself paid such a handsome tribute to travel. If Howell's guidebook made him aware of the Renaissance value of studying manners for moral and social betterment, Locke's philosophy clarified the intellectual and therapeutic benefits of travel. *An Essay concerning Human Understanding* had taught Johnson that man's basic drive is "a careful and constant pursuit of true and solid happiness" and that human psychology is, therefore, inherently dynamic.[17] Consequently, in his writings Johnson tended to conceive all intellectual activity in terms of travel by reference to Locke's doctrines. Thinking amounted to an act of empirical exploration for testing and comparing life's illusions and realities as the mind beat an increasingly ascending path to increasingly truer principles. The daily revelations of moral meaning proceeded from an active exposure to the data of existence and an inductive search for tentative generalizations about the human lot: "Some change in the form of life, gives from time to time a new epocha of existence. In a new place there is something new to be done, and a different system of thoughts rises in the mind."[18] Psychologically, men must be in constant motion, pursuing their worldly ambitions but readjusting their shortsighted goals, to attain that ultimate peace of mind from a religious perception of their final destiny. Earthly happiness is fundamentally a ceaseless process of traveling and seeking the new wonder and the new truth that lend excitement and purpose to living, "Every advance into knowledge opens new prospects, and produces new incitements to farther progress" (*Rambler* 103). Johnson had learned this principle from Locke: "Every step the mind takes in its progress toward knowledge makes some discovery, which is not only new, but the best too for the time at least."[19] The principal difference between the two thinkers is that the philosopher discusses an epistemological phenomenon and the moralist writes of its application to everyday behavior.

Whenever Johnson analyzes the mental satisfactions of touring or reading travel books, his explanation and phraseology are invariably Lockean in origin. Like travel literature, the activity of travel imparts a dual imaginative and intellectual pleasure. The tourist's imagination thrives on the romantic novelties of unfamiliar places while his rational curiosity searches out the universal truths of mankind. Besides affording pleasure, travel was an essential vehicle of instruction in the kind of factual knowledge promoted by the new science and Locke's teachings. Johnson stressed the empirical nature of the peripatetic learning process by alluding to Lucretius's key materialist tenet: "Ex nihilo nihil fit, says the moral as well as natural philosopher. By doing nothing and by knowing nothing no power of doing good can be obtained."[20] One had to study life at first hand to be useful to society. Howell's insistence upon eyewitness inquiry found reinforcement in Locke's teachings and the scientific movement of the eighteenth century. Although Johnson never read Bacon's works until the composition of the *Dictionary*, the assumptions of *The Great Instauration* permeated later philosophies to color Johnson's thinking about travel. Bacon had defined the work of the new science as a worldwide perambulation to collect factual data: "Those . . . who aspire not to guess and divine, but to discover and know . . . must go to the facts themselves for everything. Nor can the place of this labour and search and worldwide perambulation be supplied by any genius or meditation or argumentation."[21] This scientific program strongly appealed to Johnson, concerned as he always was with obtaining a clear-sighted knowledge of life free of fantasy and error.

The very idea of travel as a process of empirical validation, involving a psychological movement from untested conjectures to truth-telling realities, was a dominant intellectual pattern in Georgian literature and certainly Johnson's morality. He repeatedly emphasized the need to face the most minute facts of life directly to formulate accurate hypotheses about the true state of mankind. He had himself conducted "philosophical" journeys of scientific inquiry when examining the process of shipbuilding at Plymouth in 1762, weighing the evidence for the second sight in the Hebrides in 1773, investigating the bogus Rowley poems in Bristol in 1776, and refuting erroneous theories about Stonehenge near Salisbury in 1783. His description of this last expedition conveniently illustrates the empirical and inductive tendency of his learning process: "I told [William Bowles] that the view had enabled me to confute two opinions which have been advanced about it. One that the materials are not natural stones, but an artificial composition hardened by time. . . . The other opinion, advanced by Dr Charlton, is that [it] was erected by the Danes. Mr Bowles made me observe that the transverse stones were fixed on the perpendicular supporters, by a knob formed on the top of the upright stone, which entered into a hollow cut in the crossing stone. This is a proof, that the enormous Edifice was raised by a people who [had] not yet the knowledge of mortar, which cannot be supposed of the Danes. . . . This proves likewise the stones not to be factitious, for they that could mould such durable masses, could do much more than make mortar. . . . It is, in my opinion to be refered to the earliest habitation of the Island, as a Druidical monument of at least 2,000 years, probably the most ancient work of Man upon the Island."[22] Such was the remarkable care for detail necessary to ground tentative conclusions about phenomena. Johnson found congenial the eighteenth-century role of the scientist-traveler—a composite geographer, botanist, zoologist, anthropologist, and historian—provided it serve the great end of travel, the study of human life. In his case modern scientific principles regulated the mode of investigation, but Renaissance moral ideals governed the humanist focus of inquiry.

Since travel in the broadest sense was equated with intellectual growth, no wonder Johnson treated man in his morality as a perpetual traveler and relished touring himself. Whatever joy and knowledge that life afforded, sprang from a daily renovation of the mind and spirit by some novel fact and novel feeling acquired from the psyche's restless forays abroad. Traveling constituted both the means and end of temporal happiness and human fulfillment. *Rasselas* embodied this notion, and his theory of travel revolved around this psychological maxim. There was an immense therapeutic value to touring. Although *Rambler* 6 discounted the curative effects associated with a change of place, Johnson's sentiments changed in later life when failing health forced him to seek a remedy in motion: "That the *mind is its own place* is the boast of a fallen angel, that had learned to lie. External locality has great effects, at least upon all embodied Beings. I hope this little journey will afford me at least some suspense of melancholy."[23] The simplest jaunt through the countryside could provide the needed medicine for disburdening the mind of melancholy and exercising the diseased body into health.

The letters of his old age continually lament his unhealthy sedentary existence in London. He loved life dearly and projected eleventh-hour plans to convalesce in Italy in 1784 to ward off the looming specter of death. Robert Burton's warning in *The Anatomy of Melancholy*, "Be not solitary, be not idle," became for Johnson a prescribed course of action. Mrs. Thrale noted his pathetic attempts to experience the curative uplift of travel in his old age: "On this account, he wished to travel all over the world, for the very act of going forward was delightful to him."[24] Perhaps the closest analogue in fiction to his therapeutic delight in travel is Tristram Shandy's exuberant race with death in what Sterne considered the key section of his novel. The hero's vivacious grand tour in the seventh book of *Tristram Shandy* dramatizes the formless vitality and flowing process pervading the entire story: "—had I not better, Eugenius, fly for my life? . . . I will lead him a dance he little thinks of—for I will gallop, quoth I, without looking once behind me, to the banks of the Garonne; and if I hear him clattering at my heels— I'll scamper away to Mount Vesuvius, and from Joppa to the world's end, where, if he follows me, I pray God he may break his neck." This Shandean zest for movement to cure a stagnant mind and listless body expressed Johnson's own fondness for rambling in dispelling boredom and allaying his fears of mortality.

Appropriately, he liked to compare himself to the great classical exemplar of travel, Ulysses, when abroad: "We see *mores hominum multorum*. You that waste your lives over a book at home, must take life upon trust."[25] No doubt, travel had a personally epic significance for him in promoting his moral, intellectual, and emotional well-being. The writings of Howell and Locke offered him an ethical and psychological rationale that made any journey a possible conveyer of important private and public rewards. To all three authors, travel remained a prime symbol and vehicle of mental growth and social progress. For they saw life as an ordained cycle of exploration and discovery in a world imbued with a meaningful order of truths, only dimly perceived by man on earth but fully experienced in the hereafter. Johnson's receptivity to the newer scientific and epistemological trends of his century caused him to modify and enrich the doctrines expounded in *Instructions for Forreine Travell*. Nevertheless, a Renaissance vision of the invaluable moral education derived from an eyewitness study of mankind dominated his approach to touring. Indeed, the ultimate goal of travel, central to Johnson's moral essays and *Rasselas*, was that religious discovery of ourselves and our Creator inculcated by Howell: "All this is but vanity and superficial Knowledge, . . . unlesse by seeing . . . the Great World, one learne to know the Little, which is himselfe, unles one learne to governe and check the passions, our Domestique Enemies, that which nothing can conduce more to gentlenes of mind, to Elegancy of Manners, and Solid Wisdom. But principally, unlesse by surveying and admiring his works abroad one improve himself in the knowledge of his Creator, . . . in comparison whereof the best of sublunary blessings are but bables, and this indeed, this *Unum necessarium*, should be the center to which *Travell* should tend" (pp. 71–72). The worldwide survey of man's undisciplined desires and wandering aspirations in *The Vanity of Human Wishes* imparts virtually the same lessons.

All the energy expended in Johnson's later touring expressed such a drive for psychological and spiritual fulfillment fully examined in his previous moral writings. The moral tales of his middle age present numerous travelers who bear an uncanny autobiographical reference to their creator and his habits of travel. The typical Johnsonian protagonist is a disillusioned moral tourist who not only embodies several traditions of travel but also undergoes a harrowing experience reminiscent of the first and most crucial trip of Johnson's career. In 1737 Johnson left Lichfield with Garrick in hopes of securing a literary reputation in London. Arthur Murphy likened their unhappy venture to a real life *Paradise Lost* in the capital: "The two fellow-travellers had the world before them, and each was to choose his road to fortune and to fame."[26] Few details survive of what was to become a recurring journey plot in his fiction, except to confirm that Johnson's exposure to London resulted in poverty and failure and forced his return home without finding a job or a producer for *Irene*. The majority of his protagonists suffer this sad initiation into life as they reenact a veritable *Paradise Lost* from happy rural innocence into disillusioning urban experience that sends them home with all their ambitions defeated. Their misadventures relate to a historical reality of Johnson's life and industrial age when the lure of London seduced many provincials to the city. Arthur Young even feared for the depopulation of the countryside: "Young men and women in the country villages, fix their eyes on *London*, as the last stage of their hope; they enter into service in the country for little else but to raise money enough to go to *London*."[27]

Georgian literature dramatized the revolutionary shift from an agrarian to an industrial economy in countless stories portraying the migration of rustic heroes to urban centers of culture and corruption. Numerous English authors were provincials who came to London and eventually adopted metropolitan standards. These were the men most obsessed with transforming their travels into favorite literary vehicles. Goldsmith in *The Citizen of the World*, Fielding in *Joseph Andrews* and *Tom Jones*, Smollett in *Roderick Random* and *Pere-*

grine Pickle, and Johnson in *London* and *Rasselas* comprise a notable few of the many authors preoccupied with physical travel into and out of a city as an emblem of mental and moral discovery. Johnson exploited this travel theme in tales of provincial pupils and poets, who embark for the cruel metropolis and soon depart with failure at their heels. The abortive hopes of such city adventurers as Gelaleddin (*Idler* 75), Eumathes' pupil (*Ramblers* 132, 194, and 195), Polyphilus (*Rambler* 19), Liberalis (*Rambler* 163), and the hero of *Rasselas* all seem to spring from Johnson's troubled memory of his initial visit to London. Mrs. Thrale heard him confess to an autobiographical impulse behind the production of one of these tales: "he had his own outset into life in his eye when he wrote the eastern story of Gelaleddin."[28] As if exorcising the recollection, he kept telling the same sad story of disappointed expectations in his fiction. Certainly his famous love of London was actually a bittersweet affair, mingling the pain of early rejection and the pleasure of later acclaim in the bustling social life of the city.

Once established in London by 1738, he traveled little for the next two decades and channeled his restless energies into the sedentary business of a brilliant writing career. James Howell would have considered these years of learning and literature an ideal preparation for effective travel later on: "Thus the life of a Traveller is spent either in *Reading*, in *Meditation*, or in *Discours;* by the first he converseth with the *Dead*, by the second with *Himselfe*, and by the last with the *Living*" (p. 25). Johnson passed through all three stages of wide reading in his youth, moral meditation in the works of his middle age, and extensive touring in his old age to become one of the most distinguished travelers of his day. Even during his long sojourn in London, he portrayed his future wanderlust in the surrogate of fiction. For many of his tales look ahead to his later tendencies in touring.

Johnson's return to Lichfield after twenty years away realized the frustrating homecomings of Serotinus (*Rambler* 165) and Imlac (*Rasselas*, chap. 12). The two characters anticipated his own discovery of a changed society and indifferent friends after a similar period of absence: "Last winter I went down to my native home, where I found the streets . . . inhabited by a new race of people, to whom I was very little known. My play-fellows were grown old. . . . My only remaining friend has changed his principles."[29] Johnson's experience of hardship and misery in the world had similarly turned his thoughts homeward in later life when he sorely felt the ravages of time and the uncertainty of his future: "In age we feel again that love of our native place and our early friends, which in the bustle and amusements of middle age were overborn and suspended. . . . In our walk through life we have dropped our companions and are now to pick up such as chance may offer us, or to travel on alone."[30] Fortunately, his life's journey, like Imlac's in *Rasselas*, would be lightened by the friendship of a real life Rasselas in Boswell, who was preparing to execute his own grand tour in 1763. To reinforce the analogy, Johnson virtually repeated Imlac's warning about making a choice of life for Boswell's benefit on the Continent: "Let all such fancies, illusive and destructive, be banished henceforward from your thoughts for ever. Resolve, and keep your resolution; choose, and pursue your choice."[31] Other grand tourists received advice to pursue the principal study of *Rasselas* and compare expectations at home with realities abroad: "I know not any thing more pleasant or more instructive than to compare experience with expectation, or to register from time to time the difference between Idea and Reality."[32]

So often had Johnson's later life fulfilled the lessons of his fiction that biographers often referred to him by the names of Imlac, Rasselas, and other characters in his tales. Certainly Viator's interest in the snobbish conversation heard in stagecoaches (*Adventurer* 84) reflects his creator's favorite pastime and the class-conscious conditions of Georgian travel. As Mrs. Thrale reported, "I asked him why he doated on a coach so? and received for answer, 'That in the first place, the company was shut in with him *there*; and could not escape as out of a room: in the next place, he heard all that was said in a carriage, where it was my turn to be deaf.' "[33] Another character, Dick Shifter (*Idler* 71), prefigured Johnson's back and forth movements from city to country, between London and Lichfield, in search of novelty for a tedious life: "I was glad to go abroad, and, perhaps, glad to come home; . . . I was, I am afraid, weary of being home, and weary of being abroad. Is not this the state of life" repeatedly dramatized by his career and writings?[34] Johnson himself was the ultimate model for his traveling protagonists, all of whom express a resignation to the vanity of human wishes typical of his attitude on the road: "I suppose it is the condition of humanity to design what never will be done, and to hope what never will be obtained."[35] His characters possessed the most exacting moral authenticity possible by simultaneously originating in and predicting his intellectual and psychological responses to touring. They were ethical and empiricial travelers of life's disappointing realities envisioned by Howell and Locke and engendered from Johnson's personal experience.

The resemblances between characters and creator go beyond common moral attitudes and include even specific similarities in the methods of inquiry. Johnson's later sightseeing tours of Staffordshire and Derbyshire recall Vagulus's domestic survey of antiquities, scenery, and villas in rural England: "As we were unwilling to travel without improvement, we turned often from the direct road to please ourselves with the view of nature or of art; we examined every wild mountain and medicinal spring, criticised every edifice, contemplated every ruin, and compared every scene of action with the narratives of historians" (*Rambler* 142). Vagulus's activities might serve as a summary of most of Johnson's local tours. Boswell records a characteristic trip to the middle counties in 1777. During a visit to John Taylor's home at Ashbourne, Johnson studied all the curiosities of nature and art indiscriminately, from the manufacturing of porcelain and silk to the sublime beauties of Derbyshire scenery and the palatial estates at Ilam and Keddlestone. Little escaped the notice of this man of seemingly inexhaustible interests. He had definite ideas about architecture and preferred a functional design to a purely decorative style in villas. He took moderate pleasure in landscaping since "to embellish the form of nature is an innocent amusement, and some praise must be allowed by the most supercilious observer to him who does best what such multitudes are contending to do well."[36]

Johnson, as much as Vagulus, delighted in this fashionable form of domestic tourism that had familiarized Britain to eighteenth-century Englishmen as never before. Every county and hamlet had its topographer, and every natural wonder and rural community drew the middle-class tourist to view them and experience a greater national pride of place from knowing his homeland more intimately. Johnson lived in a very patriotic age when John Arbuthnot popularized Britain's national symbol in *The History of John Bull*; Defoe took stock of the national resources in his *Tour through the Whole Island of Great Britain*; John Wesley surveyed all the spiritual resources in his *Diary*; Arthur Young chronicled the agricultural resources in a series of *Farmer's Letters*; Thomas Pennant cataloged the natural resources in his zoological *Tours*; the political union of the realm attracted Scots and Irishmen to the capital in a cultural harmony with the English; the empire extended the island's power and language to the farthest reaches of the globe; and Johnson could proclaim for Europe and the world that the man who tired of London, tired of life itself. The last twenty-five years of the moralist's life testify to this patriotic spirit in the number of trips undertaken within the boundaries of his island. The range of his local tours would encompass most of England from Newcastle in the north, and Salisbury in the south to Plymouth in the east and Cambridge in the west. This John Bull of English literature grew to love his homeland better by knowing it better than most subjects could boast before or after.

After 1761 his visits to Lichfield and Oxford occurred almost annually. These cities were the sites of his birth and education dearest to his British heart next to London. The places visited on this yearly

pilgrimage comprised in his eyes a compact British civilization unsurpassed anywhere else in the world: "On Monday we hope to see
Birmingham, the seat of the mechanick arts, and know not whether
our next stage will be Oxford, the mansion of the liberal arts, or
London the residence of all the arts together."[37] To break this routine in his touring, there were more ambitious trips farther afield
covering practically the full extent of the island. By 1777 Boswell
could write that his friend had seen "all the cathedrals in England,
except that of Carlisle" in dozens of cities filled with nostalgic re-
minders of the glories of church and crown. While not strictly true,
Boswell's claim suggests Johnson's keen curiosity about studying
the heroic history of his island at first hand. Touring the bishoprics
had the quality of a patriotic and religious act, strengthening his
national pride and spiritual ties with a rich and passing Anglican
heritage. The emotional value of these sentimental excursions into
Britain's storied past proved a helpful restorative to the body and
mind of a man saddened by his old age and the cultural changes in
his milieu. Hence, near the end of his life, he relished his feat of extensive domestic travel: "You and I, Sir, have, I think, seen together
the extremes of what can be seen in Britain—the wild rough island
of Mull, and Blenheim Park."[38] Having completed the survey of his
beloved England, he was ready for more distant expeditions outside
the pale of his native land. The gratification of national prejudices
in travel had, in fact, preceded his more cosmopolitan rambles to
foreign places.

His local tours could never completely satisfy a lifelong ambition
to see very different forms of human life. His mind demanded more
of a journey than the emotional satisfactions of seeing familiar
faces and places around Lichfield and neighboring towns of the
realm: "Having seen nothing that I had not seen before, I have nothing to relate. Time has left that part of the island few antiquities;
and commerce has left the people no singularities."[39] There were intellectual and moral ends to be served traveling by to unfamiliar parts
of his island, the Continent, and the non-European world. Only

there did radically new scenes of humanity exist worthy of serious and comprehensive investigation. Accordingly, in the 1770s his restless quest for novelty, filling the psychological void of his inquisitive mind, inspired grandiose schemes of foreign travel only partially realized by his tours of Scotland, Wales, and France. The important episode of his Highland expedition in 1773 deserves a separate chapter of its own since his *Journey to the Western Islands of Scotland* represents the culmination of his varied interests in travel. An analysis of the travel book provides a convenient summary of his complex relationship to the subject reviewed near the end of this study. We might note in passing that the excursion was the happiest and most successful of his tours and displayed the same moral purpose of all his travels, namely, his desire to study "a new species of human existence" and perfect his knowledge of mankind.

A year later in 1774 he was off again on a less celebrated tour of Wales, which proved by comparison to the previous trip a great disappointment. Mrs. Thrale was responsible for their three-month sojourn in five of the six northern counties of Wales. She was a Cambrian by birth and went with her family to take possession of her ancestral estate of Bach-y-Graig and review the memories of her childhood. Two diaries of the tour by her and Johnson shed further light on his traveling habits. Without her personal ties to the area, he was curious to see "a new part of the island." But, unlike Scotland, Wales turned out to be "so little different from England, that it offers nothing to the speculation of the traveller."[40] The region abounded in exceptional scenery but lacked a sufficiently unique culture to merit the kind of intensive moral inquiry pursued in Scotland. There was now no Boswell to arrange introductions with the native gentry and treat the moralist to an intimate glimpse of unusual manners for his description and analysis. Instead, only a few Welshmen welcomed Johnson's conversation and exhibited the respect and kindness of his Scottish hosts. Despite Mrs. Thrale's assertion that "Mr. J's fame has penetrated thus far," he felt neglected by the boorish inhabitants.[41] His mind constantly compared Scotland and Wales and perceived a distinct falling off in the quality of Welsh scenery and hospitality. Moreover, worse health and poorer weather on this trip made him cranky and curtailed his opportunities of satisfactorily studying Welsh customs and history.

Consequently, while his diary indicates preparation for another travel book, the dearth of significant information about Wales put a stop to the project. There were already enough descriptions of Welsh landscapes on the market, and he preferred more substantial material on manners to justify publishing a travel book. Scenery alone was devoid of serious intellectual interest, and Welsh scenery was only a tamer version of Highland sublimity anyway. As he told Boswell, "instead of bleak and barren mountains, there were green and fertile ones."[42] Johnson's verdict finds support today from vacationing Englishmen lured to this beautiful region by brochures describing Wales as a little Scotland. Because little Scotland aroused as little enthusiasm in his mind, biographers have insisted that his poor eyesight and preoccupation with manners left him blind to the charms of nature. Mrs. Thrale for one heard him grumble that "a blade of grass is always a blade of grass, whether in one country or another; . . . men and women are my subjects of enquiry; let us see how these differ from those we have left behind."[43] Although her testimony seems convincing, the evidence of his Welsh diary shows that he could occasionally respond to scenery with great emotion.

No doubt, nearsightedness hampered a full appreciation of natural beauty by closing his field of vision to striking details in distant prospects. His perfunctory diary entry on Mount Snowdon, that magnificent peak which had terrified Defoe and Lyttelton and would enrapture Cradock and Wordsworth, suggests only indifference from his inability to see and climb easily enough to enjoy the majestic view: "On the side of Snowden are the remains of a large fort, to which we climbed with great labour. I was breathless and harassed. The lakes have no great breadth so that the boat is always near one bank or the other."[44] Myopia may have had as much influence upon his well-known penchant for abstract description as any rhetorical habit in his writing. Imlac's ideal poet "does not number the streaks of the tulip" in *Rasselas* possibly because he may not see them very well. Compared to Johnson's diary, Mrs. Thrale's journal contains contrary examples of sweeping vistas at Snowdon and elsewhere described in enthusiastic detail: "When the eye is tempted further a country of long extent and high cultivation detains it from the Welsh mountains, which lying at a great distance, terminate the prospect."[45] While Johnson's one good eye could not see so far and tended to focus on human life at close hand, he could take pleasure in natural scenery when nothing better offered. At the time, the principal pastime of Welsh tourists was viewing the wild scenery. If by no means a nature enthusiast himself, he came close to sharing the romantic feelings of fellow prospect-hunters before the sublime and beautiful landscapes of Wales.

The fame of Welsh scenery at first grew slowly in the eighteenth century. The region remained *terra incognita* as long as aesthetic tastes for the softer beauties of elegance and harmony generally held sway. Defoe was repelled by the rugged Cambrian "Alps" in 1726 and respected the preference of Renaissance topographers like Camden for scenes suggesting fertility and the regularity of a garden: "We have but little remarkable in the road from Conway to Hollywell, but crags and rocks all along the N. shore of Denbeigh, till we came to Denbeigh town. This is the county town . . . but that which was most surprising, after such a tiresome and fatiguing journey, over the unhospitable mountains of Merioneth, and Carnarvonshire, was, that descending now from the hills, we came into a most pleasant, fruitful, populous, and delicious vale, full of villages and towns, the fields shining with corn, just ready for reapers, the meadows green and flowery, . . . which made us think our selves in England, all on a sudden."[46] By the time of Lord Lyttelton's *An Account of a Journey into Wales* (1756), criticized by Johnson for "too much affectation of delight" in the area, there existed a more balanced appreciation of both sublime and beautiful prospects. However, Lyttelton still registered some of the older distaste for barren Welsh

mountains since they "strongly excite the idea of Burnet, of their
being the fragment of a demolished world."[47] Not all Georgian
tourists in the second half of the century enjoyed uncultivated
scenery, but travel books increasingly manifested a special fascination for romantic sights. A gradual shift of interest in the sublime,
apparent from the beginning of the century in Addison's *Spectator*
414, the picturesque nature poetry and art of Thomson, Pope, Pous-
sin, and Lorrain, and the melancholy graveyard poets, would make
Wales a popular tourist attraction.[48] When Johnson went there, a
crowd of sightseers was already thrilling to primitive scenes and
gothic ruins.

   The vogue of romantic tourism involved an enthusiasm for the
wilder aspects of nature and a resurgence of antiquarian research
in the traditions of the people. A new curiosity to explore primitive
Welsh geography and history resulted in the production of Gray's
The Bard (1757), Evan Evans's *Some Specimens of the Poetry of
the Ancient Welsh Bards* (1764), Joseph Cradock's *Letters from
Snowdon* (1770) and *An Account of ... North Wales* (1777), William Gilpin's *Observations on the River Wye, and Several Parts of
South Wales* (1782), numerous other picturesque descriptions, and,
greatest of all, Wordsworth's transcendent account of his Welsh
tour in *The Prelude*:

> In one of those excursions (may they ne'er
> Fade from remembrance!) through the Northern tracts
> Of Cambria ranging with a youthful friend,
> I left Bethgelert's huts at couching-time,
> And westward took my way, to see the sun
> Rise from the top of Snowdon.   (14.1–6)

Johnson visited Wales in the heyday of romantic tourism when nature worshipers, picturesque painters, and sentimental antiquarians
roved the craggy terrain in search of "reliques" of the bygone
culture. For all his hardheadedness, he was a highly emotional man,
sensitive to the sublimity of secluded cathedral towns, ruined castles,
and awesome mountains. Concerning the mountain range of Snow-

donia, he privately told friends that "he would not have the images he has gained since he left the vale erased for £110."[49] Instead of studying new manners that were lacking, he turned his attention to Welsh scenery and antiquities with nostalgic feeling and medieval associations.

In a qualified sense his trip was part of the current wave of romantic tourism in Wales. If in nothing else, this tour excelled the Highland expedition in the magnificent spectacle of well-preserved castles: "one of the castles in Wales could contain all of the castles he had seen in Scotland."[50] According to his diary, Carnarvon Castle "surpassed my ideas" of gothic magnificence while Beaumaris Castle carried medieval romance into the present: "This castle corresponds with all the representations of romancing narratives. Here is not wanting the private passage, the dark cavity, the deep dungeon or the lofty tower."[51] His romantic sightseeing had a time-tunnel effect upon his imagination in Wales as in Scotland. Touring the contemporary geography of a region laden with tradition became a nostalgic expedition through its ancient history in a peripatetic process of establishing an imaginative communion between the past and the present. Wordsworth would make this form of imaginative communion famous in *The Prelude* although Johnson was already seeking an emotional empathy with Britain's storied heritage in his romantic travels.

His response to Welsh landscapes was almost as romantic as his reaction to gothic ruins. The sublime so "agitated and distended" his mind that he preferred a stabilizing admixture of the beautiful to subdue the overpowering sensations evoked by primitive sights. His aesthetic creed was a compromise between older standards of elegance and new tastes for wild scenery. This desired synthesis of contrary qualities was in keeping with his artistic ideal in literary criticism, that of combining romance and reality in belles lettres so as to enliven truth and ground wonders in fact. For he sought a harmonious interaction of the imagination and reason, whether it be in the creation of fiction or in his response to nature, for a controlled appreciation of the marvelous phenomena that invigorate our mundane existence. His only discussion of the sublime and beautiful and the ideal merging of the two appears in his Welsh diary. In an entry of elaborate description, he compared Hawkstone and Ilam estates according to the aesthetic criteria found in Edmund Burke's *Philosophical Enquiry into the Origin of Our Ideas of the Sublime and Beautiful* (1756). Hawkstone Park possessed all the Burkeian elements of sublimity: "terrifick grandeur," religious "awefulness," artless irregularity, and the immensity of "inaccessible altitude" and horrifying profundity. The spectacle left Johnson feeling a "turbulent pleasure between fright and admiration" inferior to the unadulterated pleasure imparted by Ilam Park with its perfect blend of aesthetic qualities: "Ilam has grandeur tempered with softness," tranquilizing the painful emotions of fear and loneliness in a mind acutely aware of the fearful loneliness of the human condition.

Powerfully moved by wild scenery, Johnson looked for elements of elegance in landscapes, for some sign of man's reassuring control over nature. What distinguished him from other romantic tourists was his emotional reservations about primitive grandeur stemming from his rational faith in civilization as the proper environment for a truly human life. Man best served his needs by taming the wilderness into a garden wrought in his own image. Perhaps nature enthusiasts were sufficiently self-possessed to permit themselves release in a wild physical world. But an unsettled man like Johnson, personally struggling to achieve a rational stability in his mind and publicly proclaiming the virtue of self-discipline, favored a civilized order over a primitive formlessness in landscapes and in life. He might vacation in the country, but he lived and died in London: "Walking in a wood when it rained was, I think, the only rural image he pleased his fancy with; 'for (says he) after one has gathered the apples in an orchard one wishes them well baked and removed to a London eating-house for enjoyment.' "[52] Nature was most appealing when it suggested some usefulness to man and society. The sight of castles and natural curiosities as often gave rise to scientific investigation as to romantic sensations. Where Mrs. Thrale examined the folklore of the Nantwich well, her companion studied salt processing nearby. Anything in his diary that wins the expression of having "enlarged my views" usually pertains to technical and cultural information rather than natural scenery. Unfortunately, there was too little information of intellectual value to make the trip fully worthwhile: "But Wales has nothing that can much excite or gratify curiosity. The mode of life is entirely English."[53]

His tour of France with the Thrales in 1775 did offer the opportunity of viewing a new mode of life missing in Wales. However, his short sojourn abroad failed to produce much more satisfaction because of the disappointing manners that he saw. Curious as he was, he initially welcomed the chance to leave his beloved island for the first and only time in his life and visit his country's oldest rival at the age of sixty-six. The trip was a conventional three-month vacation tour of France following the route of a horde of English tourists visiting Paris by way of Calais and Amiens. No respectable tourist could forgo the experience of surveying the cultural capital of Europe and expect to be considered refined and cosmopolitan. Hence, many of the most distinguished travelers of the age, from Boswell to Wordsworth, flocked to the *grande ville* to see, describe, and usually criticize. James Howell had long ago reminded grand tourists that "The first Countrey that is most requisite for the *English* to know, is France" (p. 19). France was to be Johnson's last country to investigate even though he wanted to push on to Italy, the most popular tourist attraction of the century. To his sorrow, the French tour would afford him his only glimpse of the Continent, studied in the hurried and superficial manner typical of the debased grand tour of his day.

If not exactly a neophyte's introduction to the Continent, Johnson's journey exhibited the kind of hasty inquiry that made him critical of grand touring at an early age: "Time may be employed to more advantage from nineteen to twenty-four almost in any way than in travelling, . . . how much more would a young man improve were he to study during those years."[54] The degenerate state of much contemporary tourism helps to account for his view. What Thomas Coryate ascribed to the Renaissance grand tour—the accession of wisdom, political expertise, learning, and glory—could seldom be predicated of its eighteenth-century counterpart. In place of long educational sojourns abroad, the Georgian jaunt to the Continent tended to be a brief and amateurish survey of routine curiosities and places. The earlier ethical goals of Continental travel often yielded to the less serious pursuit of instant polish and reputation, a taste for foreign vices and fashions, and a dilettantish knowledge of art, antiquities, and natural curiosities. Boswell managed his grand tour in the current mode and yet perceptibly gained more sophistication, self-assurance, and insight into European civilization from an experience that considerably matured him. Although Johnson opposed sending immature youth abroad, he and his contemporaries probably exaggerated the evils of grand touring. In any case he had nothing to fear from his exposure to France because his ingrained English prejudices protected him from her charms. He might deplore the insularity of British tourists, but he was susceptible himself to the fashionable English contempt for French customs.

Nations in all ages have succumbed to the habit of stereotyping their neighbors, and England was notorious for the practice. The reader will recall the encouragement that Renaissance guidebooks gave to propagating the notion of distinct national traits. Howell's *Instructions for Forreine Travell* advertised in detail the standard categories of French gaiety, Italian licentiousness, Spanish formality, Dutch industriousness, Swiss hardiness, German stupidity, and English eccentricity. National traits, in turn, were linked to the specific physical environment and the secondary influences of astrology, moral flaws, and the devil upon a country's populace. Geography determined a Briton's reputed melancholy or a Swiss's supposed valor: *"Mountaignous people are the most pious; so are they observed to be the hardiest, as also the barrener a Countrey is, the more Masculine and Warlike the spirits of the Inhabitants are"* (p. 29).

In the Highlands Johnson similarly related comparable qualities in the inhabitants to their rugged habitat "for the manners of mountaineers are commonly savage, but they are rather produced by their situation than derived from their ancestors."[55] From a belief in environmental conditioning, French physiocrats developed radical doctrines of political economy based on the natural laws of national geography. Hector Saint John de Crèvecoeur justified the decentralized social system of America by appealing to its sprawling topography: "Men are like plants; the goodness and flavour of the fruit proceeds from the peculiar soil and exposition in which they grow."[56] Indeed, proponents of Alexander von Humboldt's physical geography in the nineteenth century would seek such an explanation to analyze the interplay of natural and human phenomena in the formation of the world's cultures.

Theoretically, Johnson denied that climate controlled individual behavior or totally accounted for national character. His opinion is clearly stated in *Adventurer* 131: "the manners of the world are not a regular system, planned by philosophers upon settled principles, in which every cause has a congruous effect, and one part has a just reference to another. Of the fashions prevalent in every country, a few have arisen, perhaps, from particular temperatures of the clime, a few more from the constitution of the government, but the greater part have grown up by chance, been started by caprice, been continued by affectation, or borrowed without any just motives of choice from other countries." However, in practice, Johnson certainly stereotyped the French people in a prejudicial manner. Englishmen were fond of observing how the happy climate and fertility of France made her subjects as effervescent and gay as the fine wines produced in the countryside. Taking their cue from Renaissance guidebooks, Gilbert Burnet and Joseph Addison turned their Continental travels into a tour de force attack on French and Italian types to publicize Protestant virtues: "*Switzerland* lies between *France* and *Italy*, that are both of them countries incomparably more rich . . . than it is; and yet *Italy* is almost quite dispeopl'd, . . .

and *France* . . . is reduc'd to a Poverty. . . . On the contrary, *Switzerland* is extream full of People, . . . Plenty, and Wealth. . . . So an easy Government, tho' join'd to an ill Soil, . . . keeps People in it; whereas a severe Government . . . drives its subjects even out of Best, and most desirable Seats."[57] Others would carry on the traditional English animosity toward the Catholic countries.

In the same vein Lady Mary Wortley Montagu preferred not to dispel her illusions about her country's old enemy: "I shall not perhaps stay here long enough to form a just idea of French manners and characters; tho' this, I believe, would require but little study, as there is no great depth in either. It appears on a superficial view to be a frivolous, restless, and agreeable people."[58] European stereotypes flourished in Georgian literature and travel. Prejudiced reporting of national traits provoked controversies among Giuseppe Baretti, Samuel Sharp, Tobias Smollett, and Philip Thicknesse over the validity of their Continental descriptions. Smollett became infamous for indicting French customs by reference to the stock generalizations about a people "remarkable for a natural levity, which hinders their youth from cultivating [their] capacity."[59] Philip Thicknesse, in turn, libeled Smollett's jaundiced *Travels through France and Italy* (1766) as mere "*Quarrels* through France and Italy for the cure of a pulmonic disorder." The very existence of travel controversies indicates a changed attitude toward national stereotypes.

At the time of Johnson's tour, enlightened travelers were already reacting against the traditional classifications of cultures. A more scientific approach to travel occasionally replaced the careless tourist techniques that had served only to intensify English prejudices in the past. From the time of the Renaissance, British tourists tended to concentrate on high stations in courts and universities abroad and were often as much interested in advancing their homeland's glory as in surveying foreign manners. The preoccupation with aristocratic sights obscured the complexities in cultures that might have led to a revision of stereotypes. But in Johnson's milieu there were a few true sociologists intent on gathering detailed facts from all levels of society for an accurate appraisal of Continental manners. Joseph Cradock's *Travels in France* (1783) defended the accumulation of minute details, and Arthur Young's *Travels in France and Italy* (1792) exemplified the process in a thorough reexamination of the countries: "To note such trifles may seem superfluous to many: but what is life when trifles are withdrawn? and they mark the temper of a nation better than objects of importance. In the moments of council, victory, flight, or death, mankind, I suppose, are nearly the same. Trifles discriminate better, and the number is infinite that gives me an opinion of the good temper of the French."[60] Young pointedly rejected the usual aristocratic focus of tourist inquiry to pursue an intensive study of common life and correct homebred myths about nations: "One circumstance I must remark . . . is the taciturnity of the French. I came to the kingdom expecting to have my ears constantly fatigued with the infinite volubility and spirits of the people, of whom so many persons have written, sitting, I suppose, by their English fire-sides" (p. 44). A growing habit of conscientious geographical research was helping to undermine cherished English prejudices.

In testimony to the emergent cosmopolitanism, Johnson and his fellow writers severely criticized the choleric reports of Continental travelers. Sterne remains the outstanding satirist of contemptuous British tourism in *A Sentimental Journey through France and Italy* (1768). His novel simultaneously exploits and undercuts the national stereotypes implicit in Yorick's English eccentricity and his French hosts' gay levity during a psychological fact-finding mission foreshadowing Young's own empirical journey: "I think I can see the precise and distinguishing marks of national character more in these nonsensical *minutiae*, than in the most important matters of state; where great men of all nations talk and stalk so much alike, that I would not give ninepence to chuse amongst them."[61] Sterne presents a scientific tourist of benevolent emotions who eventually avoids the conventional aristocratic sights and conducts an inductive search for love among nations in the meaningful minutiae of existence. The lesson learned is the falsity of national character types that becloud the fundamental oneness of the human family: "*Le POUR and le CONTRE se trouvent en chaque nation;* there is a balance . . . of good and bad every where; and nothing but the knowing it is so can emancipate one half of the world from the prepossessions which it holds against the other—that . . . travel . . . taught us mutual toleration; and mutual toleration . . . taught us mutual love" (pp. 62–63). Other English authors followed Sterne's lead in opposing the residual English insularity toward foreign cultures. Samuel Paterson's Shandean *Another Traveller!* (1767) had already ridiculed Continental stereotypes, and John Moore's *View of Society and Manners in France* (1779) would dramatically document a prejudiced Briton's gradual admiration for Gallic customs. When Wordsworth visited Paris, the French Revolution introduced a radical cultural transition that rendered the poet's preconceptions of French character meaningless:

> I scanned them all,
> Watched every gesture uncontrollable,
> Of anger, and vexation, and despite,
> All side by side, and struggling face to face,
> With gaiety and dissolute idleness.

Johnson can be forgiven his prejudices on the French tour since he had neither time nor opportunity to execute the detailed scientific inquiries that he demanded of other Continental travelers. Political conditions in France warranted at least his contemptuous remarks on her government. An oppressive church and crown enslaved the lower classes and obstructed the rise of a strong middle class to preserve social liberty and economic mobility in between. Young himself recognized good reasons in the climate of pre-Revolutionary France for Britons to lapse into biased generalizations about the national character: "There have been writers who look upon such observations as rising merely from the petulance of travellers, but it shows their extreme ignorance. Such circumstances are political

data" (p. 49). Observing the depressing social system, Johnson denounced the emptiness and insensitivity of the upper classes and the
"gross, incommodious" state of "common life" without economic
opportunities for social betterment. Public charity and the maintenance of the poor had always been a humanitarian concern of his
travels, and the spectacle of neglected beggars lessened his opinion
of France all the more.

Ripe for the revolution that would redress the abuses recorded
in his journals, this "gross, ill bred, untaught" people extended him
none of the hospitality and recognition that he was accustomed to
receiving at home. Hume and Sterne enjoyed notoriety in Paris,
and Boswell and Young conversed with eminent French thinkers
and scientists. But Johnson passed virtually unnoticed through
Paris and met relatively obscure figures. Except for Madame Du
Boccage and Julien-David Le Roy, he saw no significant writers and
no radical *philosophes* important to the coming Revolution. He
toured the brewery of the later revolutionary Antoine-Joseph San-
terre, but concentrated on the more conservative sights of monasteries, academies, and other hated symbols of the *ancien régime*. His
warmest friendships were with Benedictines, his most interesting entries dealt with the virtue of monastic life so offensive to the future
sansculotte, and his most noteworthy experience was viewing the
fated Louis and Antoinette at dinner instead of at the guillotine.
However, his round of inquiries was dictated more by the usual
course of sightseeing in France than by any settled purpose to bask
in the faded glories of monarchy. For what he saw of the waste and
frivolity in aristocratic circles and the hopeless poverty of the masses
outraged his sense of human decency and Christian charity. If the
Welsh tour brought him little instruction but some pleasure from
surveying impressive scenery, the French tour gave little pleasure
but much useful instruction about a corrupt social system: "What I
gained by being in France was, learning to be better satisfied with
my own country."[62]

Like his Welsh diary, his two extant French journals lack the fullness and appreciative tone of Mrs. Thrale's notebooks. His attention was usually fixed on urban curiosities revealing the French way of life in cathedrals, palaces, and whatever else contributed to his favorite study of manners. Technical research in natural history and manufacturing processes was subordinated to the examination of the national culture and state of learning in colleges, libraries, and monasteries. He partially fulfilled James Howell's injunction to investigate the country's aristocracy: "Hee must apply himselfe also to know the fashion and garb of the Court, observe the Person and Genius of the Prince, enquire of the greatest Noble-men, . . . and if there bee any famous man, to seek conversation with him" (p. 26). However, his unwillingness to speak French (he conversed in English and Latin) and the brevity of his trip interfered with an adequate and sympathetic survey of the complexities of the culture. As a consequence, his prejudices went unrevised, and his social conscience accentuated the national shortcomings. Having failed to curry much first-rate acquaintance with the French, he was forced to study the nation at second hand through her artifacts rather than her people: "The sight of palaces and other great buildings leaves no very distinct images, unless to those who talk of them and impress them."[63] Thus, despite Boswell's request for a *Journey of Paris*, Johnson refused to violate his own critical dictum against publishing travel books lacking valuable new material. In his case, France was "to a hasty traveller, not so fertile of novelty, nor affords so many opportunities of remark. I cannot pretend to tell the publick anything of a place better known to many of my readers than to myself."[64]

Readers wanted more than the repetitious information already supplied by hundreds of "modish travels" crowding the bookstalls of London. For that reason he had earlier dissuaded Boswell from publishing his Continental journals even though Boswell promised the standard tourist potpourri of "many incidents, anecdotes, jeux d'esprit, and remarks so as to make very pleasant reading," if not a substantial contribution to learning.[65] Johnson's own tour provided few deep insights into manners necessary to produce a travel book that could match his recent achievement in *A Journey to the Western Islands of Scotland*. To have published his rushed impressions would have made him a living parody of the hasty grand tourist satirized in *Idler* 97 for his confused memory of palaces and churches and his guessing at national manners by spending one night at an inn. In fact, a few journal entries come dangerously close to realizing such useless observations: "At night we came to Noyon an Episcopal City. The Cathedral is very beautiful. . . . Noyon is walled, and is said to be three miles around."[66] Superficial remarks like these could never lead to a travel book worthy of the Rambler's name or fame.

Whatever his dissatisfactions on his tours of France and Great Britain, he always valued a ramble for the moral, intellectual, and therapeutic benefits discussed in his writings and experienced in his life. He shared with characters in his fiction a tireless energy to explore the varied wonders and truths of human life in a process of moral discovery defined by Howell and Locke. To these authors he was indebted for his humanist and empirical habits of travel; from them he imbibed a lifelong desire to test notions against facts, illusions against realities, in a world replete with moral meaning. As Howell had insisted, "No, an ingenious and discerning Traveller will . . . strive to distinguish 'twixt good and evill, 'twixt that which is gracefull, and what's phantastique, 'twixt what is to be followed, and what's to be shunned, and bring home the best" (p. 68). The need to sift the grain from the chaff of human manners everywhere became a guiding moral imperative in Johnson's touring and in his philosophy of human nature: "As providence has made the human soul an active being, always impatient for novelty, and struggling for something yet unenjoyed with unwearied progression, the world seems to have been eminently adapted to this disposition of mind: it is formed to raise expectations by constant vicissitudes, and to obviate satiety by perpetual change" (*Rambler* 80). Ultimately,

Johnson's ever-widening excursions to Lichfield, then Inverness and Carnarvon, and finally across the sea to Paris dramatized the drives of the unsatisfied human spirit brilliantly analyzed in his moral essays.

Rowlandson's Johnson and Boswell *Walking Up the High Street.*
Courtesy of the Harvard College Library.

4

MORALITY AND THE
METAPHOR OF TRAVEL

Be thou, O Christ, in this our Navigation both Load-starre and
Sunne, for direction of our course and knowledge of our true
height and latitude.   Samuel Purchas, *Purchas his Pilgrimes*

ON ONE OF his frequent tours through Derbyshire, a contented
Samuel Johnson sat back in his coach and whimsically remarked that
if life had no moral or religious duties, "I would spend my life in
driving briskly in a post-chaise with a pretty woman."[1] His playful
daydream points to a deep-seated need in his personality for the
activity of travel to avoid indolence and the concomitant evil of
melancholy. Those troubled walks in his youth between Lichfield
and Birmingham and all his later tours of the British Isles manifested a natural human drive to liberate the mind from neurotic
introspection by the discovery of a corrective order of truths in the
objective world. Either to remain motionless or to travel distracting
bypaths away from the appointed journey of life resulted in mental
and moral stagnation conducive to the spiritual death of the soul.
Johnson's morality revolves around this dynamic concept of human
behavior dramatized in his writings by the metaphor of travel. He
portrayed man metaphorically as a universal pilgrim-Ulysses of
Quixotic travel on an endless quest for eternal happiness beyond the
narrow horizon of his earthly hopes and fears. His moral perspective on life was not far removed from James Howell's exhortation
to release the psyche's pent-up energies in travel: "the Genius of
all active and generous Spirits [is] . . . a desire of *Travell*, and not to
be bounded, and confined within the shoares and narrow circum-
ference of an *Island*, . . . whereas on the other side, meane and vulgar

spirits, whose *Soules* sore no higher than their Sense, love to hover ever about home, lying still as it were at dead anchor."[2] This guidebook directive could serve as a summary of the fundamental psychological principle in the Johnsonian ethic.

Previous chapters of this study have dealt with Johnson's lively interest in geography and travel that broadened his empirical knowledge of mankind. This chapter will concentrate on a principal rhetorical strategy that helped him to organize the disparate data of human experience into an integrated moral journey clarifying man's conduct and ultimate destiny in his moral writings. The realities of eighteenth-century travel influenced his dynamic philosophy of man since the journeys of his day captured for him the exuberant spirit of human nature. However, there was also a literary heritage of travel themes handed down from Homer, the Bible, and Cervantes that served to structure his firsthand observations of life. He may have surveyed mankind from China to Peru in geography, but he translated the drives and desires of the human family into a common metaphorical quest of an everyman Ulysses-pilgrim-Quixote in morality. His vivid imagination exploited these classic themes of travel to order the discordant actualities of a restless humanity in the artifact of style and fiction. Art and nature, literature and life, cooperated in the production of his perceptive moral commentary. His own account of composing essays underscores the dual impact of books and eyewitness investigation upon his mind: "A careless glance upon a favourite author, or transient survey of the varieties of life, is sufficient to supply the first hint or seminal idea, which enlarged by the gradual accretion of matter stored in the mind, is by the warmth of fancy easily expanded into flowers, and sometimes ripened into fruit" (*Rambler* 184). Such was the organic process of creation governing his writing habits and engendering his metaphor of travel in moral discussion.

If the style of great writers be expressive of their ideas, "the furthest elaboration of the one concept in the center," then Johnson's imagery, sentences, and paragraph structure should all mirror the

propulsive quality of his moral principles.[3] His style is invigorated
by active verbs, metaphors, and an expansive unfolding of ideas. His
prose and poetry characteristically reach downward to embrace the
particulars of experience and then proceed upward by accumulating
concrete images and allusions to summary generalizations and ordered verities in abstract diction and balanced phrasing. The propulsive tendency of his style is strikingly apparent in the scholar's
portrait of *The Vanity of Human Wishes*. There is a poetic thrust
to amass specific data, building upward through a catalog of abstractions about the sorry human condition to validate the couplet gen-
eralization that says it all: "Yet hope not life from grief or danger
free, / Nor think the doom of man revers'd for thee." His imagery
was especially geared to communicate the energy and thrust of the
searching human spirit. His dynamic morality evoked a favorite
cluster of active metaphors which predominate over all other types
in his works. Together they constitute a pervasive metaphor of travel
and fall into four categories: (1) the journey and pilgrimage of
life; (2) the race of life; (3) the voyage of life; and (4) the flight
through life. Expressing movement by land, sea, and air, all of them
relate to travel and the physics of motion and force. They combine
to form an overall metaphorical pattern in his morality illustrating
psychological growth and ethical discovery.

His *Dictionary* definitions of journey, pilgrimage, race, voyage,
and flight all converge around his primary meaning of motion as the
"act of changing place: opposed to rest." Analogously, his travel
metaphors were produced by energizing the root physical meaning
of such dead metaphors as "progress" and "intellectual advances"
to dramatize the actual process of forward movement. Thus, instead
of expressing his moral venture abstractly, the Rambler portrayed
his intention to so roam "the regions through which the intellect
has already made its progress, as may tempt it to return, and take a
second view of things hastily passed over, or negligently regarded"
(*Rambler* 3). Travel metaphors sprang from a physical concept of
human motion and gave rise to elaborate allegories and tales of the

human journey that adumbrate the moral quest in *Rasselas*. In other words they underwent a metamorphosis into higher literary forms and played a central part in the creation of Johnson's fiction. His fondness for travel metaphors helps to explain why he considered Pope's famous Alpine simile of the traveler's mental growth in *An Essay on Criticism* (ll. 225–232) the best in the language: "it assists the apprehension, and elevates the fancy."[4] His own nonsensory metaphors serve the same double rhetorical purpose of reinforcing moral meaning and enlivening didactic discussion. They elevate men in his morality to the imaginative plane of travelers, voyagers, racers, and fliers acting out their hopes and fears for the better edification of readers.

The metaphor of travel not only dramatized the Rambler's moral ideas but also expressed the imperial temper of his age when a nation's economic fortunes depended upon an expanding navigation and foreign trade. More than once in his Shakespeare criticism he had associated the playwright's many voyage metaphors with naval operations around the world. The same explanation holds true for his own. The growth of the Georgian Empire inspired an excellent symbol of human progress in *Rambler* 154: "This can only be effected by looking out upon the wastes of the intellectual world, and extending the power of learning over regions yet undisciplined and barbarous; or by surveying more exactly her antient dominions, and driving ignorance from the fortresses and retreats where she skulks undetected and undisturbed." In a well-traveled era Johnson instinctively turned to travel metaphors to describe all manifestations of enterprising conduct. Travelers were the very "sons [of] enterprize" (*Idler* 97), symbolizing "that ardent spirit of adventure, and that indefatigable patience" (*Life of Drake*) necessary for success in life. Travel and discovery comprised "the only project in which men of adventure and enterprise could exert their qualities" in normal times of peace when men extended their horizons of knowledge instead of narrowing them in parochial wars.[5] The wealth of geographical allusions in the essays further testifies to the impact of travel and discovery upon his writing. He illustrated domestic manners by citing foreign examples of Mohammedan law, Continental statecraft, Russian marriage, Chinese architecture, Indian scenery, South American culture, and North American colonization. His tales employed the distancing medium of exotic settings in Greenland, America, Africa, and the Orient to inculcate virtue more forcefully at home.

His rhetorical habits proclaim his inquisitive age. Voyages and travels easily shaded into effective metaphors describing the perennial human impulse to explore life actively and empirically and attain some distant good for mind and soul. In the seventeenth century Samuel Purchas devoted the first volume of *Purchas His Pilgrimes* to relating the "Allegoricall and Anagogicall sense" of his collection of travels to the entire spiritual history of man's pilgrimage on earth. Johnson did much the same with the voyaging and traveling of his day. He basically saw life in terms of the Christian *mythos* of pilgrimage and transformed didactic discussion into a continuing story of moral and spiritual discovery. He might have had Anson's starcrossed voyage in mind when he summarized the perils of the human voyage in *Rambler* 184: "We set out on a tempestuous sea, in quest of some port, where we expect to find rest, but where we are not sure of admission; we are not only in danger of sinking in the way, but of being misled by meteors mistaken for stars, of being driven from our course by the changes of the wind, and of losing it by unskilful steerage; yet it sometimes happens, that cross winds blow us to a safer coast, that meteors draw us aside from whirlpools, and that negligence or error contributes to our escape from mischiefs to which a direct course would have exposed us." In stressing the journey motif Johnson made use of perhaps the most universal metaphor in world literature, the archetypal image of the quester, to present a new interpretation of the mythic search for truth and selffulfillment.

The metaphor of travel proliferates everywhere in his work, from his earliest magazine reviews, throughout the moral essays of his middle age, to his final achievement in *The Lives of the English Poets*. Concomitant with his lifelong interest in travel, this recurring cluster of metaphors was a favorite rhetorical device for presenting all human endeavor in the process of vigorous motion. His literary criticism gives peripatetic roles to both the critic and authors criticized, fellow travelers alike in their quest for truth and beauty. Because the English author enjoyed the blessings of liberty and free inquiry, his mind was especially creative and active in beating "new tracks, where she is, indeed, sometimes lost in a labyrinth . . . yet, sometimes, makes useful discoveries, or finds out nearer paths to knowledge."[6] The same independent spirit characterized Johnson's labors in writing moral essays, the *Dictionary*, and his edition of Shakespeare. He chose an apt Horatian epigraph for the *Ramblers*, *Nullius addictus jurare in verba magistri / Quo me cunque rapit tempestas, deferor hospes*, to stress the exploratory nature of his morality by a Latin voyage metaphor. He probably knew that the Royal Society had already used this motto to express free inquiry in the sciences. In his early *Plan of a Dictionary* (1747) his rash ambition of civilizing a barbarous language yielded in his later *Preface to the English Dictionary* (1755) to a more conservative role of mere "pionier of literature" unable to fully tame a wilderness of words. Similarly, he is a brave Aeneas in his *Preface to Shakespeare* (1765) who knows the perils of settling new laws upon the ancient empire of dramatic criticism: "To dread the shore which he sees spread with wrecks, is natural to the sailor. I had before my eye, so many critical adventures ended in miscarriage, that caution was forced upon me."[7]

Johnson's biographers succumbed to his metaphorical habits and depicted his struggles in Grubstreet as an epic journey, race, and odyssey of life. Boswell equated *The Life of Johnson* with the *Odyssey* in his preface. Hawkins likened his friend's entrance into London to a hazardous voyage of discovery: "Bred to no profession, without relations, friends, or interest, Johnson was an adventurer in the wide world, and had his fortunes to make."[8] The facts of Johnson's painful journey to London in 1737 are reflected in much of his fiction

and gave his biographers ample warrant for employing travel metaphors. He never forgot this disappointing trip to London, an experience that left him afterward feeling like a storm-tossed sailor "in
the wild of life." The reader will recall that his initial failure to
realize his literary ambitions reappeared in his prose and poetry
thereafter. His fiction tended to repeat a pattern of disappointing
events pertaining to his career and the misfortunes of other London
adventurers. The pattern always appears as an unhappy journey,
beginning with an idealistic protagonist's exposure to a harsh metropolis, leading to his disillusionment with society, and often ending
with his departure for a rural seat. In the process, the protagonist
either falls victim to urban corruption or grows wise in the ways of
the world. This journey motif was a convention of Georgian literature that reflected the Horatian-Juvenalian myth of retirement. But
its presentation in his work has a peculiar emotional force.

Johnson's personal hardships converted a popular literary theme
into a powerful moral fable for his fiction. A pattern of exposure,
disappointment, and departure appears in his earliest performances,
passes into his *Life of Savage* and *The Vanity of Human Wishes*,
pervades his essay tales, and finds supreme expression in *Rasselas*.
Wherever it is found, the metaphor of travel almost always ac-
companies it to focus attention on the underlying thematic movement of his story. A voyage simile in an early poem, *The Young
Author*, introduces the typical journey motif present in all his later
tales of unfortunate authors and scholars in the metropolis:

> So the young author panting for a name,
> And fir'd with pleasing hope of endless fame,
> Intrusts his happiness to human kind,
> More false, more cruel than the seas and wind.
>   (Ll. 11–14)

London and *Irene* are political interpretations of the same disillusioning experience. Their respective protagonists, Thales and Deme-
trius, leave capital cities corrupted by the tyranny of Walpole and
the Turk (the two are synonymous) and escape to retired seats of

peace and virtue. In *London* that great aphorism which Johnson
added to his imitation of Juvenal's *Satire III,* "*Slow rises worth, by
poverty depress'd,*" has an autobiographical relevance to his own
career. The poem could also be used to summarize the misadventures
of his literary friend Richard Savage. In fact, the journey pattern of
London emerges again in the *Life of Savage* to structure the century's classic portrait of the Grubstreet odyssey to failure.

Johnson fortunately survived his struggles in Grubstreet to write
his moving biography of the luckless Savage in 1744. The work is
infinitely more tragic than his chill and lifeless tragedy *Irene* and
conveys a compelling sense of personal immediacy to the subject at
hand seldom matched in his other writings. Here can be found all
his later thematic concerns with the Quixotic journey of life, his
moralizing tendency, and the various metaphorical usages of travel
that distinguish his prose and poetry. A Johnsonian pattern of exposure, disappointment, and departure integrates the biography and
gives rise to travel metaphors emphasizing the tragicomic quest of
all men in a world always more tragic than comic to the biographer.
By alluding to literary figures looming large in all his tales, Johnson
portrays Savage as a Don Quixote of Grubstreet, driven by the
obstinate ambitions of a Ulysses but doomed to a pilgrim's life of
exile. He need only have remembered Savage's self-portrait in *The
Wanderer* for his own metaphorical perspective on this hapless
"knight-errant" in quest of free dinners and delusive dreams during
an abortive odyssey to find his family and rightful home. So Savage
had described his errant career in his finest poem:

> Forlorn, a friendless Orphan oft to roam,
> Craving some kind, some hospitable Home;
> Or, like *Ulysses,* a low Lazar stand,
> Beseeching Pity's Eye, and Bounty's Hand.

The biography elaborates upon this autobiographical theme to tragic
proportions. A heartless mother early cast Savage "upon the ocean
of life, only that he might be swallowed by its quicksands, or dashed

upon its rocks."[9] Thereafter, egotism and self-delusion kept this Ulysses adrift in a Quixotic search for recognition that left him treading "the same steps, on the same circle . . . to amuse himself with phantoms of happiness, which were dancing before him" and speeding him to his destruction.

The tragic course of his Quixotic odyssey followed the rising and falling movement of fortune's wheel. This traditional European concept of man's fated reversals helped Johnson to organize his biography and raise his subject's career to the dramatic plane of tragedy. Fortune's fatal rotations underlie Savage's rise from low obscurity to a peak "interval of prosperity" with noble patrons, followed by a precipitate fall into poverty, imprisonment, and death. Within the overall tragic framework, minor successes and failures occur in his life to retard or advance the inexorable momentum of fortune's wheel. His follies cooperated with the decrees of fortune to ensure his inevitable ruin. At the height of his prosperity midway in the narrative, he surrendered to the classic tragic sin of hubris, plunging him to his doom: "Examples need not be sought at any great distance to prove that superiority of fortune has a natural tendency to kindle pride, and that pride seldom fails to exert itself in contempt and insult" (8:138). After pride cometh the fall, and fortune has her revenge. The last half of the biography unfolds his "precipitation from plenty to indigence" concluding with the final act of the hero's fall from public favor and his edifying death in prison.

What Johnson accomplished in his *Life of Savage* was the imposition of a tragic, tripartite order of events upon the poet's wayward career. By allusions and metaphors he had raised a common man to the heroic stature of a Ulysses worthy of a central role in high tragedy, if debased by his lowlier comic role as the Don Quixote of minor English poets. The *Life of Savage* was, after all, implementing his critical demand for familiar biography of ordinary heroes and average people who surpass great historical figures in the moral instruction that their lives afford readers (*Rambler* 60; *Idler*

102). Since few men pursued lives of high tragedy, the tragicomic
dimension of familiar biography had more relevance to actual experience and more educative value for the general public. The
magnificent prelude to the biography suggests this point of view;
it not only elevates an ordinary hero to a tragic dignity but impli-
cates us all in the tragedy of everyday life: "It has been observed,
in all ages, that . . . those whom the splendour of their rank, or the extent of their capacity have placed upon the summits of human life,
have not often given any just occasion to envy in those who look up
to them from a lower station; whether it be that apparent superiority
incites great designs . . . liable to fatal miscarriages, or that the general
lot of mankind is misery, and the misfortunes of those whose eminence drew upon them an universal attention have been more carefully recorded, because they were more generally observed, and
have in reality been only more conspicuous than those of others, not
more frequent, or more severe" (8:96). Johnson's tragicomic treatment of a minor poet artistically reversed the Shakespearean achievement of approximating the remote and familiarizing the wonderful
by a more democratic process of exalting the familiar and ennobling
the common.

Five years later *The Vanity of Human Wishes* (1749) enshrined
this tragicomic perspective on the misguided human journey in the
massive dignity of generalized poetic statement. The poem sweeps
through the lives of the great and small with an aphoristic finality.
Its portraits comprehend the various tragedies of the human condition and are essentially jewellike distillations of the *Life of Savage*
in theme and style. Once again the lesson communicated is the vanity
of undisciplined desires, subjecting all men to Savage's fate on the
tragic wheel of fortune. In place of Savage, the reader must undergo
a process of exposure, disappointment, and departure for spiritual
rewards promised at the end. For Johnson invites his audience to
survey a tragicomic mankind and participate in the Quixotic quest
for a nonexistent heaven on earth. Man's shortsighted hopes and fears
create a psychological "maze of fate" that further perplexes the

inherently chaotic and unhappy state of life, "Where wav'ring man, [is] betray'd by vent'rous pride, / To tread the dreary paths without a guide." This opening travel metaphor reappears throughout the poem in the subsequent vignette of the robbed wealthy traveler, the portraits of rising and falling historical figures, and the final prayer of mankind "panting for a happier seat" in paradise. The earthly journey becomes a race for fame propelling the searching and supplicating wanderer on to the road of Christian pilgrimage.[10]

"Delusive fortune" dominates the metaphorical patterns in *The Vanity of Human Wishes*. Rising and falling images convey the fate of a doomed humanity betrayed by natural drives to strive but without reason enough to aim for truly fulfilling goals. Hopeful multitudes reverence "growing names" and "growing wealth" but scorn the "sinking" statesman and the distorted portrait of fallen eminence. Fortune obeys their irrational cry to rise and heeds their self-defeating desires: "They mount, they shine, evaporate, and fall." Her fatal rotations structure the incisive portraits that follow. The wheel of fortune collaborates with the tragic hubris of humanity to dictate a rising and falling movement in the lives of the scholar, Cardinal Wolsey, Charles XII, Xerxes, and Charles Albert of Bavaria. Of the entire group the Wolsey portrait exhibits the most perfect structural symmetry ordained by the tragic concept. A sad victim of hubris, the cardinal unwisely piles Pelion on Ossa in the form of cumulative regal honors plunging him to his downfall. Exactly midway in the verse paragraph, he raises himself to the treacherous Olympian heights of power. Thereafter, falling images replace rising metaphors when the monarch frowns and the cardinal's enormous edifice of honors piece by piece comes down. The pathetic wheellike revolutions of human fortunes in all the portraits contribute to a powerfully organized argument for *The Vanity of Human Wishes*.

While imitating Juvenal's *Satire X*, Johnson introduced a unique metaphorical stress on the journey of life and the wheel of fortune in his poem. The very attitude toward fortune differs between the two

writers. Juvenal stoically rejects fortune as an irrational illusion of
the mind. But Johnson deifies her sometimes as an overruling fate
for ill beyond human control and sometimes as an extension of misguided human desires lacking the direction of reason to clarify
worthwhile Christian goals. As his title suggests, the melancholy
religious tone of his review is less Juvenalian than biblical in origin
and captures the spirit of his favorite scriptural text, Ecclesiastes:
"The wisest of men terminated all his experiments in search of happiness, by the mournful confession that 'all is vanity' " (*Adventurer*
120). Unlike Juvenal or the laughing Democritus mentioned in the
poem, the compassionate Johnsonian spectator finds human folly
too sad to satirize or laugh at. The scholar's race for fame might
realize all the evils outlined in Robert Burton's admired treatise,
The Anatomy of Melancholy: "But our Patrons of Learning are so
far nowadays from respecting the *Muses*, and giving that Honour
to scholars, or reward, . . . that, after all the pains taken in the
Universities, cost and charge, expences, irksome hours, labourious
tasks, wearisome days, dangers, hazards, . . . they shall in the end
be rejected, contemned, exposed to want, poverty, and beggary."[11]
Yet, Johnson's personal experience of those evils blunted any possibilities for satire in his scholar's portrait. He felt the miseries that
his poem exposes. Roman cynicism gave way to a warm sympathy
for human suffering; Stoic *apatheia* yielded to a humane acceptance
of man's irrepressible desires for temporal and eternal fulfillment.

   The Vanity of Human Wishes changed a cutting survey of pagan
vices into a charitable Christian quest through life's dissatisfactions.
The poem beautifully incorporated the metaphorical movement
most basic to his writings, the disillusioning pilgrimage of the clear-
sighted traveler beating a perilous path to eternity: "As it is the
business of a traveller to view the way before him, whatever dangers
may threaten, or difficulties obstruct him, and however void may
be the prospect of elegance or pleasure; it is our duty, in the pilgrimage of life, to proceed with our eyes open, and to see our state; not
as hope or fancy may delineate it, but as it has been in reality ap-

pointed by Divine providence." [12] So summarized, this travel metaphor permeated his work to illustrate the epistemological paradox
of subjective and objective realities in need of correlation through
reason and prayer for the good of mind and soul. Whether it be
the traveler, racer, or voyager of Johnson's morality, whether it be
Savage exploring London or Wolsey rotating on fortune's wheel,
all their earthly journeys have but one safe and satisfying destination.
Unfortunately, when human pride keeps subjective and objective
realities separate, too many pilgrims mistake their will-o'-the-wisp
desires for true landmarks and lose forever the road to paradise.

Johnson wrote his moral essays in the 1750s for the charitable
purpose of directing his fellow pilgrims in the proper course of
virtuous conduct to obtain that final spiritual goal. Before beginning
the *Rambler*, he prayed that his undertaking would promote God's
glory and "the Salvation both of myself and others." [13] Morality was
intended to serve the higher ends of religion. No group of writings
more often employed the metaphor of travel to depict the human
pilgrimage than his *Rambler* (1750–1752) and *Idler* (1758–1760).
The cluster of journey, racing, voyage, and flight metaphors constitutes the major image pattern of both essay series and unifies their
seemingly disconnected moral discussions. The *Rambler* is especially rife with active metaphors. From the outset, the Rambler
quietly establishes his literary role as an adventurer in morality,
sharing the same propulsive psychological energy examined in his
fellow humanity thereafter. *Rambler* 1 portrays the essayist torn
between a cautious desire to sail with the *Aura popularis* and a bold
ambition to embark on an unconventional voyage of moral discovery. The decision is made in *Rambler* 2 to follow the latter course
and avoid the clichés of former moralists "more inclined to pursue
a track so smooth and so flowery, than attentively to consider
whether it leads to truth." *Rambler* 3 commences the exploration of
new ethical frontiers and the embellishment of time-tested paths to
wisdom. He dons the heroic mantle of Ulysses, Aeneas, and other
epic travelers to withstand the Argus and Cerberus of criticism and

oversee the manners of many men on their various moral odysseys in life.

As the essays unfold, the Rambler's dynamic personality finds further definition by other telling facets of characterization. Sometimes he postures as a laughing Democritus (*Rambler* 179) and the omniscient surveyor (*Rambler* 50) in *The Vanity of Human Wishes*. Always he appears as "the grave and humourless philosopher" to set himself apart from previous essayists, particularly Joseph Addison. His series may conform to the conventional essay format of interspersing didactic discussion with entertaining jeux d'esprit, tales, correspondence, and literary criticism. But he is at pains to distinguish himself from the lighter and more eccentric Spectator, the most popular essayist of the century. Instead of the Spectator's more explicit self-portrayal, the uncompromising Rambler characterizes himself by contrasting negatives: he will not discuss his life history (*Rambler* 23) nor Addison's topical morality and feminine matters (*Rambler* 107) nor veer from the masculine dignity of truth (*Rambler* 207). On the contrary, he will live up to his name in a philosophical ramble to discover new ways of looking at life and recover forgotten moral truths. Fearlessly he rejects old chestnuts like Neoplatonic notions of innate ideas, Stoic doctrines of *apatheia* and the golden mean, and classical dismissals of rash conduct. *Carpe diem* morality is readjusted to fit a dynamic Christian ethic that asks every man to pluck the day and keep the journey of life in motion. Moderation is less a virtue than a bold initiative to activate the psyche's quest from false hope, through tentative hope, to eternal hope. The Rambler endorses a new science in morality. Bacon's call for a naturalistic psychology finds a response in these experimental essays expounding a moral physics of human behavior. Locke's empirical epistemology evolves into a dynamic philosophy of moral growth requiring men to exercise properly, rather than to repress totally, their inner drives and desires.

As befits his title, the Rambler praised all enterprising activity. Even temerity was preferable to "timorous prudence" in conduct.

Cautious enterprise, mingling a conservative respect for past precedent and a liberal openness to new discovery, expressed an ethical
ideal that characterized Johnson's outlook as a man, a moralist, and
a writer in general. The Rambler emphasizes his essential oneness
with mankind by applying the same travel metaphors defining his
enterprising personality to all other moral adventurers in the essays.
Rambler 2 plays a crucial part in the series by initiating the travel
concept that governs his entire moral discussion. According to this
essay all men are naturally active beings and born moral travelers
progressing from hope to hope, never resting long in static intervals
of pleasure, and ever renewing the Quixotic quest for happiness in
the elusive horizon: "This quality of looking forward into futurity
seems the unavoidable condition of a being, whose motions are
gradual, and whose life is progressive: as his powers are limited, he
must use means for the attainment of his ends, and intend first what
he performs last: as, by continual advances from his first stage of
existence, he is perpetually varying the horizon of his prospects, he
must always discover new motives of action, new excitements of
fear, and allurements of desire." In the essay the Rambler subsequently unleashes the latent energy of such dead metaphors above
as *motions*, *progress*, and *action* and introduces travel metaphors of
enterprising conduct: "The natural flights of the human mind are
not from pleasure to pleasure, but from hope to hope."

Rambler 2 is important not only for enunciating the underlying
ethic of his essays but also for revealing the integrated development
of ideas and metaphors in his moral discussion. The key moral assumptions in this essay and throughout the series are reducible to a
physical concept of matter in motion. If Bacon had requested a
theory of psychology based on naturalistic tenets, then Johnson
partially obliged by propounding a moral physics of human behavior. The very language of the *Ramblers* often has a primitive
mechanical connotation and expresses the attainment of virtue as
"steps to a certain point" equivalent to the course of activated matter. A root concept of physical energy in *Rambler* 2 sets off a chain

reaction of moral analysis, travel metaphors, and closing illustrations
of man's active nature. A mechanical principle of force and motion
becomes translated into moral discussion of human movements and
motives, then related metaphors of the mind in motion, and finally
the drama of Don Quixote and the Quixotic Rambler on the move
in a futile search for fame. The rhetorical evolution of ideas in
Rambler 2 might be likened to Newton's procedure of elaborating
a complex theory of the universe from a simple formula of gravity in
the *Principia*. Although Johnson never allowed morality the mathematical precision of physics, the act of writing his essay came close to
being a Newtonian exercise in producing a comprehensive explanation of psychology from a single physical theorem. The *Ramblers*
exploit the physical analogy fully and display an organic growth of
meaning through successive didactic, metaphorical, and narrative
interpretations of basic moral principles.

There is a thematic interrelatedness within and between the essays
in the series that underscores their essential unity individually and
as a group. The *Ramblers* are not a haphazard collection of detach-
able essays on unrelated subjects, but a unified moral statement pool-
ing all the Johnsonian wine and vinegar of a lifelong study of man.
Ramblers 5 and 6, for example, continue the psychological analysis
of *Rambler* 2. Having established the active nature of man, the
Rambler now turns to the psychological dilemma springing from it;
namely, the mind's need for constant motion and yet its impossible
desire for rest in this life: "day and night, labour and rest, hurry and
retirement, endear each other; such are the changes that keep the
mind in action; we desire, we pursue, we obtain, we are satiated; we
desire something else, and begin a new persuit" (*Rambler* 6). Change
is of the essence of existence; rest is, therefore, antithetical to the
demands of living and mortally dangerous to the health of the psyche. Any attempt to abstract oneself from the vital flux of human
affairs and rest in limited worldly goals is a fatal psychological trap
productive of an unhealthy stasis in the mind and soul leading to
madness and melancholy introspection. The involuted psyche must

push outward, spurred on by the Don Quixote imagination and reined in by reason, because it was created to love the chase even if fated to lose the prize. As useless as a single inert particle of matter, the psyche must obey the mental physics of motion, escape the "equipoise of an empty mind" by reacting against fear and moving forward with hope, and cohere with other selves in society in the common search for happiness (*Rambler* 5). Unfortunately, life cannot grant man ultimate happiness, and the great moral question remains: "Where then shall hope and fear their objects find?"

At regular intervals in the essays thereafter, the answer to that question gradually emerges to irradiate life's clouded maze of fate. The resolution of the Quixotic dilemma of striving but desiring rest is found in the great human aspiration for the peace of paradise. If the mind would only direct its energies through worldly pursuits and fly to the sole hope that cannot deceive, then "Beyond this termination of our material existence we are therefore, obliged to extend our hopes" (*Rambler* 203). Without faith in an afterlife of permanent rest, "the progress of life could only have been the natural descent of negligent despair from crime to crime" on a regressive evolutionary scale (*Rambler* 110). Only religion can truly civilize humanity and raise the beast to the beatitude of manhood and godhead. Like *The Vanity of Human Wishes*, the Rambler converts the troubled earthly journey into a purposeful spiritual pilgrimage. Moral essay becomes a sermon. Not surprisingly, Johnson's sermons examine the Christian pilgrimage more fully and less tentatively than his experimental essays. But they still assume the same physical principles of psychological growth. Christian revelation established the truth of a heaven with the religious consequence "that we are here, not in our total, nor in our ultimate existence, but in a state of exercise and probation."[14] According to the Johnsonian physics of the mind, moral improvement and spiritual progress were proportionate to the energy expended in propelling a man on the path to paradise. Conversely, sin implied either the arrest or misdirection of the soul's potential force for doing good. Woe to

the idle and wayward pilgrim! Idleness ever remained the worst of
vices conducive to mental stasis, moral lassitude, and spiritual coma
in terrible sequence. His recurring metaphor of travel served a per-
formative function of exorcising the vice in the very process of expressing the contrary virtue of activity throughout the moral essays.

The consistent metaphorical equation of mankind with travelers
gave rise to a representative tragicomic hero of the *Rambler* essays,
a Quixotic pilgrim on a continuing odyssey to recover his spiritual
home and moral happiness. As the wise Sancho Panza of the expedition, the Rambler conducts his Quixotic readers and ramblers
of the series on an instructive course of exposure, disappointment,
and departure on a summary scale. We join the people in the essays
on the typical moral quest of his writings: to see life as it is; realize
its tendency to disappoint our expectations; and detach ourselves
from its vanities for a perception of substantial spiritual goals. Journey and pilgrimage metaphors reinforce this lesson. They are so
predominant in the *Ramblers* that an allegorical pilgrimage envelops
the series to emphasize the driving force uniting all men psychologically in a moral physics of heaven-directed motion. The constant
barrage of quest images forces the reader to recognize an unfolding
story of moral travel in the work. If told in the expansive fashion
of an essay format, this tale contains essentially the same narrative
elements synthesized in his *Vision of Theodore*, *The Vanity of
Human Wishes*, and *Rasselas*. Johnson's obsession with the journey
motif suggests that he habitually conceived life as an allegorical
pilgrimage before any act of writing took place. Such a preconcep-
tion suited his Christian temperament and would have provided him
with a useful intellectual framework for harmonizing the observed
complexities of life in the creation of his essays and fiction. Certainly
his writings abundantly testify that this religious assumption lay at
the heart of his moral meaning and literary manner.

The Rambler gives peculiar stress to the journey metaphor. Religion requires Christian soldiers to march unswervingly to holiness
(*Rambler* 7), and morality facilitates their march by ingraining the

habit of cautious enterprise on the road (*Rambler* 25). Similarly, worldly success depends upon activating our inner energies; therefore, even presumption excels sluggish despondency and mediocre moderation in performing great achievements on the "roads of life" (*Rambler* 43). Any accomplishment requires the channeling of all mental energies in one definite direction and ceases when the mind rests in idleness or moves haphazardly from its proper path: "In the journey of life some are left behind, because they are naturally feeble and slow; some because they miss the way, and many because they leave it by choice, and instead of pressing onward with a steady pace, delight themselves with momentary deviations, turn aside to pluck every flower, and repose in every shade" (*Rambler* 89). This elaborate travel metaphor epitomizes Johnson's narrative perspective on the hazardous course of human endeavor and virtually condenses the journey plots of his more ambitious allegories and tales. *Rambler* 134 resumes the attack against idleness by expressly evoking the laws of physics and developing its discussion from that starting point. The essayist describes indolence as a *vis inertiae*, then as a "constant desire of avoiding labour," and finally as a metaphorical "pause in the choice of his road," all in a naturally evolving order of presentation.

Always the advocate of moral activity, the Rambler favored the hopeful vitality of youth (*Rambler* 69) over the despondent lethargy of old age (*Rambler* 50). He commended intellectual discoveries opening up new frontiers of learning (*Rambler* 121) and recommended resolution in avoiding those delusive pleasures that obstruct the road to progress (*Rambler* 196). Perseverance brought moral travelers closer to the destination of their desires: "The traveller that resolutely follows a rough and winding path, will sooner reach the end of his journey, than he that is always changing his direction, and wastes the hours of daylight in looking for smoother ground, and shorter passages" (*Rambler* 63). However, because of the inescapable instability of life, neither resolution nor caution can save the human journey, race, and voyage from frustration and misfortune: "Some there are who appear to walk the road of life with more circumspection, and make no step till they think themselves secure from the hazard of a precipice; when neither pleasure nor profit can tempt them from the beaten path; who refuse to climb lest they should fall, or to run lest they should stumble, and move slowly forward without any compliance to those passions by which the heady and vehement are seduced and betrayed. Yet even the timorous prudence of this judicious class is far from exempting them from the dominion of chance, a subtle and insidious power, who will intrude upon privacy and embarrass caution" (*Rambler* 184). Gathering together the four types of travel metaphors, *Rambler* 184 closes with a complex voyage image of the psychological tempests and immoral whirlpools that detour the human pilgrimage from the promised port of paradise.

The cluster of travel metaphors coordinates the various interests and subjects of the essays into a meaningful journey of human aspiration. Race, flight, and voyage images assist in the work of establishing this journey motif in the *Ramblers*. His *Dictionary* definitions of race as a "Progress," "process," and "Contest in running" connote the dynamism of his many racing metaphors. These active images present the tragic rising and falling movement of the search for fame in *Ramblers* 17, 19, 127, 146, and 164. "Every man pants for the highest eminence" (*Rambler* 193), but "When those who started with us in the race of life, leave us so far behind" that we cannot catch up (*Rambler* 172), envy arises from the frustration of the psyche's innate drive to aspire. The soul races to assert and fulfill itself and "formed for eternal life, naturally springs forward" to enjoy the worldly satisfactions at hand in partial appeasement of its infinite aspirations (*Rambler* 49). While the soul races, the mind usually flies in the *Ramblers*. The mental faculties either happily soar from hope to hope (*Rambler* 2) or unhappily lie grounded in torpor and despondency (*Rambler* 5). Curiosity and imagination metaphorically take wing in the essays, actually sprout allegorical wings in *Rambler* 67, and have their narrative embodiment in the aviator's flying chariot in *Rasselas*. If thoughts fly, they also flow into a marriage of true minds (*Rambler* 167) and into a stream of life and time (*Ramblers* 29, 42, 61, 124, and 165). Worldly success and mental well-being are measured by the varying rapidity of the current's psychological flow since "the stream of life, if it is not ruffled by obstructions, will go putrid by stagnation."

When the stream of life expands into an ocean of human endeavor, voyage metaphors surface in the *Ramblers* with enough frequency to rival the recurrence of journey metaphors in the series. They most directly mirror the vogue of eighteenth-century travel and discovery. One voyage metaphor, for example, corresponds to Johnson's survey of man's ever-widening forays on the sea in his *Introduction to the World Displayed*. According to this work, "Navigation was now brought nearer to perfection. The Portuguese claim the honour of many inventions by which the sailor is assisted, and which enable him to leave sight of land, and commit himself to the boundless ocean."[15] Under his pen the history of primitive navigation inspired a fine nautical image of man's gradual surrender to evil: "A man ventures upon wickedness, as upon waters with which he is unacquainted. He looks upon them with horror and shudders at the thought of quitting the shore, and committing his life to the inconstancy of the weather; but by degrees the scene grows familiar, his aversion abates, and is succeeded by curiosity. He launches out with fear and caution, always anxious and apprehensive, lest his vessel should be dashed against a rock, sucked in by a quicksand, or hurried by the currents beyond the sight of shore. . . . In time he loses all sense of danger, ventures out with full security, and roves without inclination to return, till he is driven into the boundless ocean, tossed about by the tempests, and at last swallowed by the waves."[16] Exciting voyage narratives like his *Life of Drake* might have suggested his reference to piracy in foreign ports to illustrate human fraud in *Rambler* 79. Anson's *Voyage Round the World* probably underlies his metaphorical crosswinds of fortune (*Rambler* 184), stormy seas of wickedness (*Rambler* 174), and challenging routes for "discovering and conquering new regions of the intellectual world" (*Rambler* 137).

The expanding British Empire offered the Rambler an apt symbol of the manifold dangers and sole destination of the human voyage in his essays. Sailors searching for fame and fortune had best embark on their exploration with the essayist's even keel of cautious enterprise (*Rambler* 25) and requisite abilities (*Rambler* 20). They must subsequently safeguard their cruise from the envy of less able seamen (*Rambler* 172) and the treachery of wicked pirates "without anchor, and without compass" (*Rambler* 95). Finally, they must steer a resolute and hopeful course with the prospect of temporal and eternal happiness always in the horizon to protect them from despondency: "A man thus cut off from the prospect of that port to which his address and fortitude had been employed to steer him, often abandons himself to chance and to the wind, and glides careless and idle down the current of life, without resolution to make another effort, till he is swallowed up by the gulph of mortality" (*Rambler* 127). However frustrating human experience may be, any despairing lapse into inactivity was anathema to the enterprising Rambler. To lie becalmed on the ocean of life betrayed those innate drives infused in man by a "Master who will regard his endeavours, and not his success" in the voyage for truth and self-fulfillment.

Scattered allusions to the *Odyssey* and the *Aeneid* elevate the Quixotic pilgrimage in the *Ramblers* to the heroic plane of an epic odyssey to regain a symbolic Ithaca of happiness. Calypso's isle represents all enervating paradises of pleasure arresting the appointed voyage of life (*Rambler* 102). Spendthrifts risk both the Sirens and Cyclops of financial shipwreck (*Rambler* 53). Crazed virtuosos collecting useless curiosities are mere Lotus-eaters of learning refusing to explore valuable human knowledge (*Rambler* 83). Marriage suitors must bypass the lures of Scylla and Charybdis and many a female harpy in their search for genuine love (*Rambler* 115). Unknown poets tread an easy path to the hell of London poverty (*Rambler* 26) and face the infernal torments of Tantalus at the

hands of stingy patrons (*Rambler* 163). As the Rambler had begun
his series with voyage metaphors, so he concludes his moral odyssey
with a determination to sustain his intellectual energy for the return
home: "To faint or loiter, when only the last efforts are required,
is to steer the ship through tempests, and abandon it to the winds
in sight of land" (*Rambler* 207). Land is sighted in the last essay,
where the Rambler reviews his previous moral explorations and
dedicates his venture to God, the supreme Judge of everyman's
Quixotic pilgrimage on earth: "Celestial pow'rs! that piety regard, /
From you my labours wait their last reward."

So lofty a dedication was withheld from the considerably lighter
Idlers six years later. If the title of the *Ramblers* connotes the active
ethic set forth in the series, then the title of the *Idlers* indicates a reduced vigor and seriousness in the presentation of religious precepts
and moral principles. The Idler relaxes the Rambler's accustomed
gravity and cultivates the casual and languorous pose of the topical
Spectator. His idleness is the chief concern of a series that reflects
the vice in its shorter essays, less philosophical outlook, and fewer
travel metaphors. He presides over a world of idlers reading newspapers out of boredom (*Idler* 7), sleeping by day and restless by
night (*Idler* 17), and surrounded by a rogue's gallery of lazy fools.
There are humorous portraits of Sober, Ned Drugget, Dick Linger,
Dick Minim, Dick Snug, and Mr. Ginger, all of whom manifest
their creator's besetting sin. The laws of physics serve to define
idleness as a human "*vis inertiae*, the quality of resisting all external
impulse" (*Idler* 9). To underscore the negation of physical force in
the series, his travel metaphors are less propulsive, his characters are
less active, and the moral discussion is less energetic than in the
Ramblers.

When they appear, travel metaphors now dramatize the failure
of motion in an indolent humanity. The Idler himself treads a conventional "track of life" (*Idler* 1) trodden by previous moralists
(*Idler* 3) because of his refusal to "go far in quest" of new ideas
(*Idler* 24). Instead, he waits for the help of correspondents to set

his listless literary voyage in motion: "He that embarks in the voyage
of life, will always wish to advance rather by the impulse of the
wind, than the strokes of the oar; and many founder in the passage,
while they lie waiting for the gale that is to waft them to their wish"
(*Idler* 2). Travel metaphors lose their momentum to portray the
mental inertia of fellow idlers, prone to "quit the beaten track" of
disciplined study and persevering effort (*Idler* 36) for a lazy "passage of life" (*Idler* 24). Rather than stress a successful "progress of
life" (*Idler* 94), the Idler emphasizes the difficulties of the human
journey. He bemoans the irksome labor of activating one's moral
travels and notes the probable failure of most human enterprises.
However, the Rambler and Idler do finally agree about the absolute
human need to avoid idleness and keep life constantly active. For
his moral and religious well-being, man must "advance himself to a
higher and happier state of existence by unremitted vigilance of
caution, and activity of virtue" (*Idler* 43). Both series possess a
thematic unity in a common moral vision and metaphor of spiritual
travel, generated by a psychological physics of men in motion on a
ceaseless quest for happiness in the world.

Johnson's essays reveal a deliberate attempt to formulate something of a new science in morality. He admitted to having "familiarized the terms of philosophy by applying them to popular ideas"
in his final *Rambler* 208 and had brilliantly propounded a Newtonian
physics of the mind. He was not the first thinker to experiment
with a scientific ethic. Rationalists like Richard Cumberland, Samuel
Clarke, and Francis Hutcheson had less successfully searched for a
system of moral philosophy as clear-cut as a mathematical theorem
or a physical law. Yet, Johnson is certainly the most enduring moralist to relate conduct to physics without exaggerating the analogy
between an exact science and variable human behavior: "Life is not
the object of science: we see a little, very little; and what is beyond
we only can conjecture" (*Adventurer* 107). Ethics resisted tidy
formulas but did warrant the use of physical principles to clarify
man's restless nature. Hence, conduct breaks down into a simple

physics of motion-producing metaphors and tales of travel to illustrate the dynamics of his moral philosophy. *Rambler* 127 exemplifies the rhetorical elaboration of a physical concept in the development of its moral discussion: "The advance of the human mind towards any object of laudable persuit, may be compared to the progress of a body driven by a blow. It moves for a time with great velocity and vigour, but the force of the first impulse is perpetually decreasing, and though it should encounter no obstacle capable of quelling it by a sudden stop, the resistance of the medium through which it passes, and the latent inequalities of the smoothest surface will in a short time by continued retardation wholly overpower it. Some hindrances will be found in every road of life." A law of physics becomes a symbolic moral journey.

The gradual unfolding of meaning in this essay pervades the series. Moral vicissitudes in the journey, race, flight, and voyage of life merge into one grand psychological movement of one great physical motion propelling all mankind on a Quixotic *Pilgrim's Progress*. So forceful was this dynamic vision that the metaphor of travel itself exhibited a dynamic metamorphosis into other literary forms. His rhetorical technique paralleled his philosophy; style reflected meaning. We have seen how a root concept of physics engendered travel metaphors of spiritual and moral aspiration. But there were further stages in the artistic process of portraying man's perennial quest for happiness. For his numerous quest images, in turn, evolved into the allegorical journeys recounted in *The Vision of Theodore* as well as in *Ramblers* 65, 67, and 102. Finally, these allegories represented prior experimentation with the Quixotic journey theme treated summarily in *Rasselas*. An eighteenth-century editor of Spenser, John Hughes, had defined allegory as a "kind of continued Simile or an Assemblage of Similitudes drawn out at full length."[17] His definition expresses the Rambler's own rhetorical habit of drawing out dead physical metaphors at full length to create images, allegories, and tales of moral pilgrimage.

Sometimes the metamorphosis of travel metaphor into allegory occurs within a single essay. *Rambler* 102 is a case in point. The essay evolves from an initial statement of the "incessant fluctuation" of human wishes, through a nautical metaphor of shifting desires into a full-blown allegory of the haphazard human voyage. Its Ovidian epigraph and opening Senecan quotation introduce voyage images for the Rambler's elaboration thereafter. The simple allegory that resulted is reminiscent of Addison's "Vision of Mirza" (*Spectator* 159) and especially Spenser's *Faerie Queene* (2.12). But Johnson's ultimate source was the *Odyssey*. The Quixotic pilgrim of the *Ramblers* now emerges as an everyman Ulysses sailing past personified abstractions of Calypso, Scylla, Charybdis, and Circe: "In the midst of the current of life was the 'Gulph of Intemperance,' a dreadful whirlpool, interspersed with rocks, . . . on which Ease spread couches of repose, and . . . where Pleasure warbled the song of invitation. Within sight of these rocks all who sailed on the ocean of life must necessarily pass. Reason, indeed, was always at hand to steer the passengers through a narrow outlet by which they might escape." The reduction of the *Odyssey* to moral allegory was in keeping with the ethical interpretations of the epic by Spenser and other Renaissance poets and commentators.[18] Unlike Homer and Spenser, however, Johnson made a traditionally optimistic story conform to his somber view of human frailty and self-defeating mortality. His pessimistic outlook colors his transformation of voyage metaphors into odyssey allegory in *Rambler* 102 and looks ahead to his narrative adaptation of the *Odyssey* archetype in *Rasselas*.

Another allegory important to the archetypal overtones in *Rasselas* is his *Vision of Theodore* (1748). This work was his first published piece of prose fiction and his earliest treatment of the pilgrimage motif, hurriedly composed for inclusion in Robert Dodsley's *Preceptor*. Georgian and Victorian readers concurred with Johnson in considering the fable one of his best efforts in fiction. If not so popular today, the story deserves attention as an allegorical forerunner of *Rasselas* in miniature, skillfully compressing his moral creed. On the one hand, Theodore's pilgrimage expands simple journey metaphors like the following to allegorical proportions: "We are in danger from whatever can get in possession of our thoughts; all that can excite in us either pain or pleasure has a tendency to obstruct the way that leads to happiness, and either to turn us aside or retard our progress" (*Rambler* 7). On the other hand, Theodore's view of the Mountain of Existence past Education and Reason to Religion adumbrates Rasselas's ascent of the happy valley for his moral education and rational choice of eternity. There are classical antecedents behind *The Vision of Theodore* in *The Choice of Hercules* by Prodicus and *The Tablet* of Cebes.[19] However, its nearest predecessor in religious meaning and allegorical geography is none other than his favorite allegory, *The Pilgrim's Progress*. Both allegories present a dream vision of Christian pilgrimage with a mountain-climbing movement toward a spiritual destination. Theodore and Christian similarly find themselves burdened under overhanging hills, similarly observe proud pilgrims tempted into gulfs of despair, and similarly succumb to indolence and sleep on their respective mountains.[20] Johnson inculcated Bunyan's warning against idleness in his allegory but changed a Calvinistic Hill Difficulty into a morally abstract Mountain of Life for the better instruction of his eighteenth-century readers.

Bunyan's influence is also apparent in two later allegories. *Rambler* 67 discusses the necessity of hope in "urging us forward" and then allegorizes the metaphorical flights of hope up the Streight of Difficulty, so named after Bunyan's Hill Difficulty.[21] The metamorphosis of travel metaphors into journey allegory occurs again in *Rambler* 65. Obidah's trek across the plains of Indostan assumes a symbolic significance as he wanders by flowery groves and a pleasant river to escape the heat before losing his way in a stormy wilderness. A hermit afterward interprets Obidah's experience as a wayward journey of life through immoral bypaths of sensuality into storms of despair. The whole story merits comparison with a well-known episode in *The Pilgrim's Progress*, Christian's sinful walk through By-path Meadow into spiritual storms of Despair: "Now their way lay just upon the bank of the River . . . on either side, were *green Trees* that bore all manner of Fruit; and the leaves of the Trees . . . they eat to prevent . . . Diseases that are incident to those that heat their blood by Travels. . . . And now it began to rain, and thunder in a very dreadful manner, and the water rose amain. Then *Hopeful* groaned in himself, saying, *Oh that I had kept on my way! . . .* Then for their encouragement, they heard the voice of one, saying, *Let thine heart be towards the High-way, even the way that thou wentest, turn again.*"[22] Obidah's journey runs a parallel narrative and thematic course to teach the same lesson of perseverance in the pursuit of virtue. The evidence suggests that whenever Johnson wrote a story of moral pilgrimage, be it *The Vision of Theodore* or *Rasselas*, *The Pilgrim's Progress* remained a preferred model of the journey archetype in his fiction.

His mind seems to have instinctively pictured the course of all human conduct as an allegorical pilgrimage and then worked from this concept to produce fiction portraying a coherent interpretation of man's restless nature. Of all his writings, his abstract allegories come closest to capturing the basic design of his moral thought responsible for the journey structure in so much of his prose and poetry. Allegorical literature especially appealed to him precisely because it communicated an ordered pattern of ideas directly without lapsing into the distracting details of a complex story. The fable was less important than the lessons conveyed, and, according to his critical priorities, "The most artful fiction must give way to truth."[23] The aim of allegory was to teach rather than to titillate, and he implemented that aim with his moralizing tendency toward allegory, personified abstractions, and didactic stories. John Hughes had specified four qualities of good allegory in his *Essay on Allegorical Poetry* (1715): elegance free of mixed metaphors, clarity, consistency, and dramatic liveliness.[24] Johnson's allegories excelled in the first three qualities but lacked liveliness due to their stark simplicity and avoidance of pictorial detail. He shied away from the vivid symbolic concreteness of Spenser and Bunyan and cre-

ated thoroughly abstract moral parables with bloodless personifications and generalized settings to hammer the message home. Although recurring Spenserian symbols of enervating bowers of bliss
and happy valleys do appear in his works, his ideal was always a
complete clarity of meaning. In fact, in his literary criticism he
demanded that even personified abstractions should be restricted to
their precise denotative sense alone: "Discord may raise a mutiny
but Discord cannot conduct a march, nor beseige a town."[25] His
fondness for allegory and his allegorical way of looking at life were
integral to the moral seriousness and abstract style of a man who
preferred instruction to amusement in literature.

The metaphor of travel underwent a further metamorphosis beyond allegorical pilgrimages and odysseys into moral tales of Quixotic journeys in his writings. Whether the destination be Cairo in
Rasselas or London in the moral essays, these disillusioning urban
journeys represent the final transformation of the protean travel
metaphor into story. They portray the same process of psychological
growth recounted in Johnson's metaphors and allegories. Moreover,
their adventures correspond to a favorite plot pattern, symbolic of
the human life cycle, in world literature. Johnson's protagonists repeatedly pass from youthful innocence to mature experience in a
world that chastens their mortal hopes and instills a spiritual wisdom
about their ultimate goals. Their journeys implicitly circumscribe
all the stages of human development. The very stories that Johnson
most admired—*Don Quixote*, *The Pilgrim's Progress*, and *Robinson
Crusoe*—embody this archetypal growth process in the form of an
antiromantic quest, a Christian pilgrimage, and a geographical odyssey respectively.[26] His own prose fiction exploited all three versions
of the journey plot; the characteristic hero in his moral fables is a
pilgrim-Ulysses of Quixotic travel. While his allegories stressed the
pilgrimage and odyssey motifs, his moral tales emphasized the
Quixotic pattern of frustrated idealism.

Don Quixote offered Johnson an ironic interpretation of the human journey, balancing a fool-hero's illusions against a knave-society

for a dual satire on both.[27] His description of Quixote is relevant to his characterization of romanticizing protagonists in fiction: "Cervantes shews a man who, having . . . subjected his understanding to his imagination, and familiarised his mind by pertinacious meditation to trains of incredible events and scenes of impossible existence, goes out in the pride of knighthood to redress wrongs and defend virgins, to rescue captive princesses, and tumble usurpers from their thrones."[28] Imprisoned in his happy valley of illusions, Rasselas lets his Quixotic imagination revel in the same romantic feats: "One day, as he was sitting on a bank, he feigned to himself an orphan virgin robbed of her little portion by a treacherous lover, and crying after him for restitution and redress. So strongly was the image impressed upon his mind, that he started up in the maid's defence, and run forward . . . with all the eagerness of real persuit."[29] Johnson's Quixotes all participate in a journey of exposure, disappointment, and departure from inhospitable cities that crush their naive dreams and provincial hopes of happiness. Quixotic antiromance originates in the thematic juxtaposition of their high ideals against corrective urban realities, with Johnson's satire directed against both in varying proportions. His pessimistic portrayal of the Cervantic quest seldom allows his unfortunate heroes the benefit of a cunning Sancho to save them from inevitable defeat on the road.

Travel metaphors often epitomized the journey plots of these tales: "To youth, therefore, it should be carefully inculcated, that to enter the road of life without caution or reserve, in expectation of general fidelity and justice, is to launch on the wide ocean without the instruments of steerage, and to hope, that every wind will be prosperous, and that every coast will afford a harbour" (*Rambler* 175). Johnson had only to amplify such a metaphor to narrative length to create the Quixotic London journeys of Polyphilus, Liberalis, Zosima, Betty Broom, and Eumathes' spoiled pupil. A few essays demonstrate the metamorphosis of travel metaphor into tale. In *Ramblers* 26 and 27, Eubulus's metaphorical dreams of exploring the "new world" of London become a reality of Quixotic travel through the inhospitable capital. A nautical metaphor sums up the rake's progress to ruin in Misella's tale: "I have heard of barbarians, who, when tempests drive ships upon the coast, decoy them to the rocks that they may plunder their lading, . . . yet how light is this guilt to the crime of him, who . . . cuts away the anchor of piety, and when he has drawn aside credulity from the paths of virtue, hides the light of heaven which would direct her to return" (*Rambler* 171). Johnson metaphorically elevated the rake's progress of Misargyrus (*Adventurers* 34, 41, and 62) to a Vergilian descent into the hell of London vice in the manner of Fielding's prose epic, *Amelia* (1751). Misargyrus's epic misadventures similarly open in medias res in Newgate prison, where this crestfallen Aeneas reviews his "progress of vice" and "persuit of pleasure" leading by "no unbeaten track" to his present predicament.

However dangerous or disappointing, these Quixotic journeys were meant to be imitated by readers. London might have been the hell that Johnson, Fielding, and Defoe all describe, but all men were obliged to see it for themselves: "To know the world is necessary, since we were born for the help of one another; and to know it early is convenient, if it be only that we may learn early to despise it" (*Idler* 80). The psychological propellants of Quixotic travel were curiosity and imagination. Curiosity was an intellectual drive for novelty in life and cooperated with the imagination in arousing romantic hopes that sent man in quest of their fulfillment. Johnson's protagonists personify these mental attributes and let their Quixotic imaginations set their journeys in motion. He considered the imagination a peculiarly restless faculty with an "innate inclination to hazard and adventure" in the "boundless ocean of possibility."[30] The faculty was a necessary force behind any creative activity and, because "it grasps greedily at wonders," generated fiction at one remove from the direct experience of reality. However, when unchecked by reason, the imagination produced wild romance twice removed from reality and fatal to the mind. Such an aberration afflicts his protagonists and violated his intellectual priorities.

An understood hierarchy of values governed his ironic treatment of the Quixotic journey. Whenever Johnson judged anything, he kept in mind the Aristotelian distinction between natural and artificial goals, between what is necessary and what is unnecessary to the truly human ends of life. Accordingly, religion ranked highest on his value scale, whereas even morality "entirely abstracted from religion, can have nothing meritorious in it."[31] Morality, in turn, had precedence over all other branches of learning, including science and history, because the "first requisite is the religious and moral knowledge of right and wrong."[32] Within morality there was a hierarchy of virtues: charity and active goodness excelled frugality and "timorous prudence" by removing the worst obstacles, poverty and indolence, in the way of spiritual progress. After morality, a clear-sighted knowledge of reality was essential to personal and social betterment. Empirical priorities dictated his outlook on the imagination and its by-product, fiction. As far as man's greatest wants were concerned, Johnson could subordinate his own livelihood of literature and deny "the necessity of our having poetry at all, it being merely a luxury, an instrument of pleasure, it can have no value, unless when exquisite in its kind."[33] Since the "only excellence of falsehood is its resemblance to truth," the best fiction communicated actual experience that might lead readers to recognize higher moral and religious truths.[34] Empirically inclined as he was, Johnson preferred factual literature like biography and autobiography to realistic fiction like the novel and, worst of all, purely fanciful writings like romances without any redeeming moral realism (*Rambler* 4). Imagination and fiction were important to man but not as necessary as reason and reality in moral and religious development.

These intellectual priorities are pertinent to the thematic progression of his moral tales. His pejorative *Dictionary* definition of romance as "A lie; a fiction" clearly equates the genre with the kind of psychological falsification of reality that speeds his Quixotic protagonists to disaster in the city. Whether as a literary form or a psychological malady, romance resulted from an imagination out of

control usually in a youthful mind when the faculty especially pre-
dominated. His young heroes are romanticizing victims of their wild
imaginations, projecting illusory dreams about life's possibilities until
the hard facts of urban experience prove them all lies. Their loss of
youthful innocence in the metropolis may be sad but is morally
necessary to their intellectual and spiritual growth. Johnson's hierarchy of values required this difficult maturation. The imagination
sweetened existence with its delightful fictions but tended to obstruct a rational grasp of life's limitations that promoted the ultimate
human needs of moral and religious improvement. Whatever the
cost to an idealizing mind, the falsehood of romance had to yield
always to the sanative stability of truth.

Romance strongly appealed to Johnson in its literary form. He
thoroughly enjoyed the *Morte d' Arthur, Guy of Warwick, Don
Bellianis*, and *Amadis de Gaul*. Having learned to read from *The
Seven Champions*, he recommended that children study the genre
to " 'stretch and stimulate their little minds.' "[35] However, he at-
tributed his unsettled mind to his fondness for reading romances
and denounced them as "thus incorrect, thus absurd, thus dangerous" to morals for contradicting his empirical standards of truth.[36]
Perhaps his criticism was partly a defensive reaction against his own
dangerous delight in the genre. As he wrote of Shakespeare's romantic tendencies, "Such is the power of the marvellous even over
those who despise it, that every man finds his mind more strongly
seized by the tragedies of Shakespeare than of any other writer."[37]
In his literary criticism at least, he was able to formulate a viable
solution for his paradoxical response to romance. Romance could
combine with reality to enliven, without falsifying, truth in Shakespeare's greatest plays, Pope's *Rape of the Lock*, and travel literature.
In fact, all the best literary productions displayed this ideal synthesis
of contrary qualities. Unfortunately, his artistic ideal was seldom
workable in life or in his tales. The enlivening romance of the imagination drives his Quixotic protagonists into a world of corrective
reality, but they gain reason only by sacrificing their romantic imagi-

nation. Theirs is an impossible quest to unite opposite mental qualities. Nekayah makes this discovery in *Rasselas:* " 'No man can taste
the fruits of autumn while he is delighting his scent with the flowers
of spring: no man can, at the same time, fill his cup from the source
and from the mouth of the Nile.' "[38] The lesson that his protagonists
come to learn is that romance and reality necessarily clash in life and
that only in an afterlife at the end of the human journey are the two
truly one and eternal.

Trapped by the essential antiromance of life, all Johnson's travelers renew Quixote's delusive quest for happiness to remind us of the
Quixotic nature of our own tragicomic lives: "When the knight of
La Mancha gravely recounts to his companion the adventures by
which he is to signalize himself in such a manner that he shall be sum-
moned to the support of empires, solicited to accept the heiress of
the crown which he has preserved, have honours and riches to scatter
about him, ... very few readers, amidst their mirth or pity, can deny
that they have admitted visions of the same kind; though they have
not, perhaps, expected events equally strange, or by means equally
inadequate. When we pity him, we reflect on our own disappointments; and when we laugh, our hearts inform us that he is not more
ridiculous than ourselves, except that he tells what we have only
thought" (*Rambler* 2). With his tales of Quixotic travel the metamorphosis of metaphor through allegory into story had reached a climactic and sophisticated stage of literary development. The metaphor of travel bound his moral writings in a dramatic saga of moral
pilgrimage undertaken by a Christian everyman possessing the fortitude of Ulysses and the fantasies of Quixote. This hero would reappear in *Rasselas*, where the archetypal human quest would be played
out for the last and greatest time in his fiction. Of all his prose and
poetry, this oriental romance is the most representative document of
Johnson's complex response to travel in imaginative literature. Travel
myths and travel books interacted in his imagination to power forth
his finest parable of the journey of life.

5

MYTHIC AND HISTORIC TRAVEL IN THE CREATION OF *RASSELAS*

> If between these two countries there are some countries which Homer leaves out, one might pardon him for the professed geographer himself omits many details. And we might pardon the poet even if he has inserted many things of a mythical nature in his historical and didactic narrative.   Strabo, *Geography*

JOHNSON'S PERVASIVE VISION of a dynamic and disillusioning journey of life culminated in *Rasselas*, his most distinguished grand tour through life's elusive satisfactions. When in 1759 he hurriedly wrote the work "in the evenings of one week," he drew upon a lifetime of reading and experience that tied his oriental romance to the great traditions of Western literature.[1] His tale is a classic formed from other classics of travel and travel literature. His princely hero emerges as a true pilgrim-Ulysses of Quixotic travel on a romantic quest for happiness grounded in the historical realities of oriental exploration. His story magnificently mirrors his profound knowledge of geography and his concern for maintaining historical authenticity in the portrayal of characters and setting. To study its development from the resources within his mind and writings can deepen our understanding of his achievement. Johnson himself was always curious about the process of creating fiction: "Among the inquiries, to which ardour of criticism has naturally given occasion, ... none is ... more worthy of rational curiosity, than a retrospection of the progress of this mighty genius in the construction of his work, a view of the fabrick gradually rising, perhaps from small beginnings, till its foundation rests in the centre, and its turrets sparkle in the skies."[2] So he wrote of *Paradise Lost*. No doubt, he would have approved the use of the same procedure for analyzing *Rasselas*.

One of the major questions about *Rasselas* is whether Johnson really wrote it within a week's time to pay for his mother's funeral. No one doubted his ability to compose such a masterful work so quickly until recently. The evidence of numerous sources used in its setting has given rise to the theory that he prepared drafts of his oriental romance long before its actual composition.[3] This view contradicts not only traditional opinion but also our knowledge of his casual writing habits and phenomenal powers of mind that enabled him to compose fiction rapidly without mechanical aids. There was a heritage of literary models both within and outside of his writings that would have helped him to produce his tale with speed and spontaneity. His own explanation of the creation of prose fiction implies no lengthy premeditation on the author's part: "Even the relator of feigned adventures, when once the principal characters are established, and the great events regularly connected, finds incidents and episodes crouding upon his mind; every change opens new views and the latter part of the story grows without labour out of the former" (*Rambler* 184). On the contrary, Johnson considered the writing process a naturally evolving elaboration of narrative details dictated by a controlling thematic purpose and a general plot structure. In the case of *Rasselas*, he could depend upon a ready-made narrative and thematic blueprint from previous works to assist him in rapidly developing the incidents and episodes of his story.

His earlier writings clearly experiment with its journey plot in the form of metaphors, allegories, and tales portraying the restless search for human fulfillment. The Seged tale (*Rambler* 204 and 205) has long been recognized as a forerunner of *Rasselas* with its Abyssinian setting and happy valley situation proving the impossibility of happiness. Characters elsewhere in his fiction like Nouradin, Morad, Euphelia, and Generosa's unsociable astronomer adumbrate Imlac's father, the Egyptian hermit, Nekayah, and the mad astronomer respectively. A few moral essays even deal with the theme that suggested its original title, "The Choice of Life." Polyphilus's abortive journey to London to make his choice of life (*Rambler* 19) foreshadows Rasselas's trip to Cairo. Moreover, in *Adventurer* 107 Posiddipus asks "Through which of the paths of life is it eligible to pass" and answers pessimistically that neither public and private life, native and foreign life, celibacy and marriage, nor youth and age can lead to happiness. Rasselas would survey all these contrasting options and come to the same unhappy conclusion. Perhaps the closest antecedents in overall design were Johnson's allegories of the voyage and pilgrimage of life (*Rambler* 102; *The Vision of Theodore*), which are essentially abridged variations on stories found in the *Odyssey* and *The Pilgrim's Progress* respectively. As such, they constitute a key link between *Rasselas* and two great literary paradigms of travel. For his oriental romance embodies a fable of moral pilgrimage reminiscent of the quest motif treated by Homer and Bunyan and made unheroic by Cervantes.

Johnson acknowledged the existence of certain recurrent stories in literature adapted by authors to the flourishing genres of their times: "Yet, whatever hope may persuade, or reason evince, experience can boast of very few additions to ancient fable. . . . accordingly we find, that besides the universal and acknowledged practice of copying the ancients, there has prevailed in every age a particular species of fiction" (*Rambler* 121). In his own case, a legacy of travel themes in Homer, the Bible, and Cervantes passed into the popular eighteenth-century genre of oriental romance. *Rasselas* presents a mythic journey of life found in works as different as the *Odyssey*, *The Pilgrim's Progress*, and *Don Quixote*. All these stories contain perhaps literature's most basic plot: an innocent hero's quest for some ideal good by way of trials with evil and descent into underworlds of despair for his growth in wisdom and final passage to new worlds of happiness.[4] Behind the narrative trappings, Rasselas's moral travels conform to this perennial quest pattern. He traverses life's gradual journey from happy valley innocence to maturity in Cairo (where he, like Ulysses, *Mores hominum multorum vidit*) and descends into the depressing world of the dead (the pyramids and catacombs) to perceive ultimate truths about death and an afterlife by the Nile. He is an archetypal traveler, following in the footsteps of Quixote, Ulysses, and the Christian pilgrim on a sweeping moral survey of mankind: "Wandering from clime to clime, observant stray'd / Their manners noted, and their states survey'd" (Pope's *Odyssey*, 1.5–6).

No poet, according to Johnson, exerted more influence upon later writers than Homer: "nation after nation, and century after century, has been able to do little more than to transpose his incidents, new name his characters, and paraphrase his sentiments."[5] The moralist naturally preferred the *Odyssey* over other epics because of its unusual domestic and ethical dimension and frequently adapted its adventures for the purpose of allegory and moral illustration in the *Ramblers*. He was well aware of the Renaissance allegorical tradition that made the poem the great classical prototype of the humanistic grand tour. Roger Ascham, for example, warned young tourists of the need for reason and grace in their earthly pilgrimage by pointing to the moral significance of all the *Odyssey* episodes: "For he shall not always, in his absence out of England, light upon a gentle Alcinous and walk in his fair gardens full of all harmless pleasures; but he shall sometimes fall either into the hands of some cruel Cyclops or into the lap of some wanton and dallying Dame Calypso, and so suffer the dangers of many a deadly den, not so full of perils to distroy the body as full of vain pleasures to poison the mind."[6] Rasselas's own moral grand tour relates to this tradition. His resilient curiosity about mankind, his circular return home, and the tale within a tale framework of his story, all bear comparison with the *Odyssey* archetype. Renaissance ethical interpretations of the epic could apply to his unhappy odyssey from a Calypso of happy valley pleasures through the Siren songs of false philosophers and the Scylla and Charybdis of high and low stations into the hell of moral incertitude at the end. Certainly Imlac showed great wisdom when he appropriately summarized the pitfalls of the human journey by an odyssey metaphor anticipating Rasselas's travels in chapter 12 of *Rasselas*.

While the *Odyssey* provides a useful critical perspective on the archetypal overtones of *Rasselas*, there is evidence to suggest that Johnson imitated *The Pilgrim's Progress* in his story. His admiration for this allegory is well known. His allegorical journeys in *The Vision of Theodore* and both *Ramblers* 65 and 67 had already assimilated episodes of Christian's quest. Such a pilgrimage archetype has a bearing on the narrative development of *Rasselas*.[7] From the standpoint of the Puritan allegory, the oriental romance redefined Bunyan's emotional valleys and spiritual plains, giant Satanic compulsions and wise heavenly helpers in moral terms. Rasselas leaves the City of Destruction behind in the enervating happy valley, passes through a Slough of Despond when he first fails to escape, and climbs up through an Abyssinian Hill Difficulty to enter the Vanity Fair of Cairo. Put off by the city's vanities, he then visits another Hill Lucre at the pyramids and learns of Pekuah's captivity in an Arab's Doubting Castle under the psychological bondage of a giant Despair. Back in Cairo he encounters presumptuous Ignorance anew in the person of the mad astronomer, foolishly convinced himself of a divine election ordaining his supernatural powers over the universe. Left only with the final choice of eternity at the end, he can only hope in a Celestial City before returning to a state of unrealized happiness. The overall parallel between the two journeys extends to specific similarities in language and narrative treatment in individual episodes. The analogous progression of the stories serves to underscore Johnson's debt to Christian tradition and his penchant for adapting old religious truths to new moral uses in the creation of his fiction. However secularized for contemporary readers, Rasselas's moral odyssey has the heightened spiritual significance of a Christian pilgrimage.

His mythic journey revolves around a theme inherited from the classics. The choice of life was a major *topos* of Plato's *Republic*,

Aristotle's *Ethics*, *The Choice of Hercules* by Prodicus, and Cicero's *De Officiis*. The Socratic imperative to ponder life's diversity and perceive the ideal good beyond worldly illusions is especially pertinent to *Rasselas:* "it should be our main concern that each of us, neglecting all other studies, should seek after . . . the knowledge to distinguish the life that is good, . . . choose the best that the conditions allow, and . . . know . . . what are the effects of high and low birth and private station and office . . . with his eyes fixed on the nature of his soul."[8] As if acting out this Platonic maxim, Rasselas rejects his native instruction to seek the best choices of life in high and low stations, public and private careers, before concluding his inquiries with a discussion of the soul. His education fulfills the philosopher-prince ideal of the *Republic*. Plato supposedly visited secretive Egyptian astronomers with certain pupils to further their instruction. Imlac has a similar interview in the mad astronomer episode while supervising the transformation of a hopeful prince into a disillusioned philosopher. The Platonic regimen of music and bodily exercise for a prince's early development corresponds to Rasselas's upbringing in the happy valley. Then came the Platonic study of society (Cairo), geometry (the pyramids), and astronomy (the mad astronomer) in preparation for public office (Rasselas's political destiny) and final philosophical retirement (Imlac's retreat from life). *Rasselas* may incorporate this educational scheme but is an anti-*Republic* in its denial of utopia and ideal choices of life.

   The tale consistently negates philosophical optimism and rejects the ultimately happy course of the odyssey and pilgrimage archetypes in its narrative. Johnson had in mind a third archetype that prevents his hero from realizing the successful outcome of Ulysses' voyage home and Christian's progress to paradise. The antiromance of *Don Quixote* pervades his journey through a world devoid of great classical heroes and promised spiritual rewards. Rasselas is, after all, a hapless Quixote, whose idealism about life clashes with the hard realities of Cairo. Plato must bow to Locke in an empirical search for corrective facts bursting the idle dreams of visionary speculation. Like Quixote's illusion-producing romances, Rasselas's empty Platonic hopes of utopia must give way to the more substantial phenomena of urban unhappiness, modern doubt, and moral uncertainty. Even Cervantes's genial acceptance of the human comedy has darkened considerably in Johnson's treatment of a potentially tragic quest activated by the comic expectations of the prince's Quixotic imagination. The romance of the happy valley gives way to the antiromance of Cairo, where Imlac (Johnson's wiser Sancho Panza) asserts the prerogatives of reason over the imagination and leads his disappointed companion home. The irony of Rasselas's impossible search for perfect happiness is that the Quixotic quest itself, his ceaseless progression from hope to hope, is the greatest possible happiness afforded by this imperfect world. Life is a state of flux, and its moral pilgrims must dance to its changing rhythms and keep the mind in constant and disciplined motion for the pursuit of that one great eternal hope in objective reality. The act of travel is both the means and end of temporal happiness for Rasselas and for all mankind.

The impact of the *Don Quixote* archetype upon the others in the story radically altered the normal format of oriental romance. The success of the earliest collections of Eastern tales, Antoine Galland's *Arabian Nights* (1704–1717) and Pétis de la Croix's *Turkish Tales* (1707), started a lively eighteenth-century market for numerous imitations and translations. Worried about paying for his mother's funeral, Johnson capitalized on their popularity by writing an oriental romance without compromising his antiromantic outlook on life. All the conventions of the genre—a questing prince in disguise, a forlorn princess, erotic intrigues, wise hermits, damsels in distress, and happy endings—are purposely deflated to present an original study of everyman's Quixotic journey.[9]

Since its first appearance, *Rasselas* has most often invited comparison with Voltaire's *Candide* (1759). The general resemblance between the two works caused even Johnson to confess that readers might accuse either author of plagiarizing the other when in fact this was not the case. Both tales use a journey plot influenced by travel books and present an innocent hero and older guide on a panoramic survey of the negatives of existence that allow no savory choices of life and illustrate the folly of optimism. But there the real similarities end. The differences are more revealing. Voltaire worked in the picaresque mode of a low-born protagonist engaged in satiric social survey to attack a single thesis (philosophical optimism) and recover a specific love interest (Cunégonde). *Candide* is often irreligious and obscene and unmercifully ironical and fatalistic about the misery of mankind. Voltaire's characters arrive only at a static state of cynicism, where tending a garden substitutes for hoping, thinking, and living. Johnson, by contrast, mutes the potential satire in his tale and at least allows his indecisive characters a true freedom of choice, an ultimate hopefulness despite pervasive disappointment, keeping them dynamically alive and intellectually alert in their endless earthly journey. He is a compassionate moral philosopher, who created a royal grand tour of life's summary limitations and handled his subject with reverence and grand generality. His different moral outlook and sources dictated his unique treatment. The influence of the journey archetypes alone helped to suffuse *Rasselas* with a combination of classical seriousness, Christian piety, and humane acceptance of Quixotic aspirations missing in Voltaire's mocking exposé.

The impression which Johnson's aphoristic tale so often gives the reader, that here is the history of human experience distilled, is true in part by nature of the fund of learning absorbed in the narrative. What he had accomplished in the *Dictionary* four years before is relevant to the synthesis of multiple sources in *Rasselas*. Ever a moral teacher, the lexicographer had intended to illustrate word usage by instructive quotations from literary authorities: "I therefore extracted from philosophers principles of science; from historians remarkable facts; from chymists complete processes; from divines striking exhortations; and from poets beautiful descriptions."[10] This moral design became a rhetorical habit when writing his tale. *Rasselas* assimilated and communicates back to readers a legacy of great ideas from his wide reading. Its plot recalls journey patterns made famous by Homer, Bunyan, and Cervantes and treats a Platonic topic ironically. Its thematic organization corresponds to the development of Ecclesiastes as elaborated in Simon Patrick's *Paraphrase upon . . . Ecclesiastes*.[11] Characters like the mad astronomer mirror Johnson's life and his biographies of Thomas Browne and other eccentric scholars. Almost every chapter paraphrased some work admired by Johnson and either modified borrowed passages for a related moral purpose or slyly burlesqued them for violating the Johnsonian ethic. There are echoes of Sidney's *Defense of Poesy* (chapter 10), John Wilkins's *Mathematical Magick* (chapter 6), Samuel Clarke's *Demonstration of the Being and Attributes of God* (chapters 22 and 48), Locke's *Essay concerning Human Understanding* (chapter 44), William Law's *Serious Call to a Devout and Holy Life* (chapter 6), Thomas Browne's writings (chapters 40 and 41), Bacon's essays on marriage (chapter 29), Stoic doctrines (chapter 18), and commentaries on the Book of Job (chapters 27 and 28). All in all, the readers of *Rasselas* are invited to feast on a rich intellectual repast of Western wisdom served up in the rhetorical container of oriental romance.

Johnson's vivid imagination operated on all his sources to fashion a new creation from the learning of the past. The tale is a finished mosaic of interlocking literary influences transformed by his personal moral outlook and sensitivity to current cultural tendencies into an original work of art. His adaptation of sources reveals a mind caught between different world views and intent upon synthesizing diverse intellectual values. The story attempts to enunciate a coherent interpretation of human behavior from often contradictory philosophical traditions. His moral discussion accommodates the wisdom of Plato and Locke, Bunyan and Homer, the Bible and the new science, and Renaissance humanism and Georgian skepticism. The rhetorical generality and transcendent serenity of his somber survey reflect the harmonious moral vision wrung from the intellectual tensions within the author and his age. Those confusions and frustrations frequently disturbing his mind found release and resolution in the marmoreal stability and wholeness of his art. The moral artistry of this fundamentally Christian tale supplied what his own life often denied him. His solutions for the perplexing moral problems of mankind are paradoxically expressed by negative discoveries: no philosophical position can perfectly explain or alleviate the human plight. *Rasselas* attacks some ideologies and life-styles as nonsensical and even harmful to true human fulfillment. Other choices of life only partially realize and illuminate man's purpose for being. But unless the reader grasps the larger humanist vision that life at best offers only limited satisfactions, he will miss the implicit religious conclusion of the tale. Mankind experiences partial happiness and predominant misery to chasten, not suppress, his earthly desires in preparation for making his final choice of eternity.

Rasselas is obviously not a religious sermon but a searching rational analysis of the human condition that avoids overt religious answers to moral problems. The intrusive spiritual message concluding *The Vanity of Human Wishes* barely surfaces at the end of the tale. However, the author of *Rasselas* is clearly a devoted Christian at heart, who reaffirmed the bleak truths of Ecclesiastes in a moralized *Pilgrim's Progress* through a secular moral universe. At the time of his mother's death, Johnson prayed for the strength to fulfill his spiritual obligations as a man and as a writer: "Make me to remember her good precepts, and good example, and to reform my life according to thy holy word, that I may lose no more opportunities of good; I am sorrowful, O Lord, let not my sorrow be without fruit."[12] Reverence for the holy word did bear fruit in the creation of a story that essentially reduces the human search for happiness to a biblical quest for an elusive paradise on earth. Johnson muted the religious implications in *Rasselas* to concentrate on the ethical dilemmas of man in the here and now. His concern with practical morality dictated a largely secular focus on the conduct of the natural man guided by reason and not by revelation. Hence, he was prevented from openly offering religious solutions and directly appealing to the optimistic doctrines of Scriptures. There is no victorious home-coming on this moral odyssey, nor do his Quixotic pilgrims attain a divine haven of rest. There is only a final chapter, "The conclusion, in which nothing is concluded," that leaves his archetypal travelers without a destination. Johnson may have depended heavily on pro-cess of imitation to produce his work, but he converted traditional sources into a new moral parable of the modern everyman.

The subject of imitation, the importance of investigating sources and distinguishing between outright plagiarism and legitimate bor-rowing, intrigued Johnson. Usually he was at pains to clear authors of the charge of plagiarism because he believed that most writers copied a few stock stories in literature and revised them according to the needs and conventions of their times. As Imlac remarked, "Whatever be the reason, it is commonly observed that the early writers are in possession of nature, and their followers of art: that the first excel in strength and invention, and the latter in elegance and refinement" (chap. 10). Johnson himself was obviously a great practitioner of elegant imitation. He probably acquired the skill from grammar school exercises in the classics and perfected that skill during his later writing career by paraphrasing works in maga-zine reviews and moral essays with an editor's eye for improving an author's style and arguments.

His biographers were amazed by his ability to remember volumes of biblical and classical passages for use in fiction whenever the pressures of publication required him to write. His imagination brought special insight to bear upon his store of learning and pro-duced modifications in remembered texts to suit his moral intention. His imitative technique of creation was integral to his aims as a moralist and critic in the *Ramblers*, the *Dictionary*, and the *Lives of the English Poets*. For in all his greatest writings, he was similarly concerned with assessing and transmitting the time-tested wisdom of the past to illuminate man's present state and promote his future welfare. Although he failed in his school at Edial early in life, he spent the rest of his career successfully teaching the public old truths in new literary forms. Writing was a sacred ministry of the printed word, authorized by the Bible and an approved literary tradition, for the edification of his congregation of readers.[13]

A detailed analysis of the creation of *Rasselas* would entail an endless safari of source-hunting. A more useful approach, consistent with our study of Johnson's varied interests in travel, is to isolate the crucial influence of geography upon his creative process. When writing the tale, he not only achieved a new interpretation of revered travel archetypes but also enriched them with the color and conventions of travel literature. He used his expert knowledge of geography to portray the people, places, and events of his oriental romance and give his moral fable a firm foundation in fact. As a consequence, a mythic journey of life possessed a historical validity in the truths of oriental travel that added authenticity to its moral lessons. Rasselas follows a course of ethical inquiry in the tracks of real explorers as well as literary wanderers celebrated by Homer, Bunyan, and Cervantes.

Johnson's critical demand for truth in literature best explains his dependence upon travel literature to produce stories that never stray far from the realities recorded of man and his globe. Since "The only excellence of falsehood is . . . its resemblance to truth," what better way could fiction represent the actual state of life than to imitate historical examples? As early as *Irene* (1749), he had consulted Richard Knolles's *Generall Historie of the Turkes*, George Sandys's *Relation of a Journey*, and Barthelemy Herbelot's *Bibliothèque Orientale* to document his plot and characterization. Oriental history would continue to validate his Indian and Persian tales in the moral essays. His knowledge of *The Six Voyages of Monsieur Tavernier* (1678) facilitated the creation of his Morad tale in *Rambler* 190. Moreover, his research in Herbelot's treatise provided him with concise portraits of Obidah, Nouradin, Gelaleddin, Ortogrul, and Omar in his other oriental essays. Of all his Eastern fiction, the Seged tale in *Ramblers* 204 and 205 most closely approximates *Rasselas* and evolved from a similar combination of travel book sources. Apparently the data of geography and history constituted a necessary stimulus for this fact-minded man to create fiction having an exacting moral authenticity. He severely criticized other authors whenever they violated historical and geographical truth in their prose and poetry. What he required of others, he implemented himself.

The relationship between *Rasselas* and travel literature is complex and intimate. Not only did its generalized setting originate in the topographical details of travel reports, but its plot also paralleled the format of geographical literature. Like other Georgian writers, Johnson was keenly aware of the narrative possibilities of travel books for imitation in fiction. When he listed the contents of voyages and travels, he could have been describing the materials and concerns of a large body of contemporary prose fiction: "The different Appearances of Nature, and the various Customs of Men, the Gradual Discovery of the World, and the Accidents and Hardships of a naval Life, all concur to fill the Mind with Expectation and with Wonder; and as Science, when it can be connected with Events is always more easily learned, and more certainly remembered, the History of a Voyage may be considered the most useful Treatise on Geography."[14] We need only substitute the subject of morality for the science of geography to make this description serve as an adequate synopsis of the peripatetic education presented and imparted to readers in the history of Rasselas's voyage of discovery.

The overall sequence of Rasselas's adventures—his preparations for travel, his tour of Cairo manners and Egyptian ruins, mishaps with Arabs, and interviews with sages—could be found in most of the oriental travel books read by Johnson. Furthermore, Rasselas and Imlac are ideal Johnsonian travelers who put their creator's theory of travel into practice during their moral survey. Their mode of inquiry reflects Renaissance and eighteenth-century trends of tourism since they stress the ethical study of human life and observe Lockean standards of empirical research: "Whatever be the consequence of my experiment, I am resolved to judge with my own eyes of the various conditions of men, and then to make deliberately my *choice of life*" (chapter 12). In this key statement of purpose, Rasselas accepts the role of a scientific humanist in travel and will carry out the tourist principles promoted by Johnson and defined by James Howell. Howell's influential *Instructions for Forreine Travell* had, in fact, enunciated the philosophical rationale for Rasselas's journey and predicted the meaning and movement of his unsatisfying review of foreign sights.

While the archetypal journey patterns of *Rasselas* shed light on its thematic development, there is a more apparent tradition of travel underlying the procedures and subjects of investigation. Renaissance commentators had viewed the grand tour as a necessary moral and political education for princes in need of worldly wisdom to prepare them for ruling. James Howell had strongly endorsed this educational ideal and proposed that royal tourists undertake a circular journey around Asia and Africa before permanently returning home. His reasons for recommending this oriental itinerary were, as Imlac repeats in chapter 30 of *Rasselas*, to examine the revolutions of learning originating in the East and spreading to the West. He advised princes to make a comparative study of manners abroad, visit courts and scholars, and finally learn the moral uniformity of man and the ultimate vanity of life. Prior consultation with merchants provided princes with helpful geographical information to "distinguish 'twixt good and evill, . . . and what's phantastique" in their moral travels. Above all, their exposure to the world was meant to teach them life's universal limitations and leave them contented "to live and dye an *Islander* without treading any more *Continents*."[15] So conceived, the Renaissance grand tour of Howell's guidebook is precisely the kind of traveling performed by Rasselas.

All of Howell's principles find expression in *Rasselas*. The prince of Abyssinia executes a royal grand tour around the East before unhappily returning home with no more plans to resume his travels. The circularity of his tour is symbolic of the tale's thematic inconclusiveness and corresponds to the geographical pattern that Howell mapped out for Renaissance princes. Rasselas receives a political and moral education abroad and learns the uniform misery of man and the vanity of human hopes among rulers and scholars. The merchant-philosopher, Imlac, prepares him for these lessons, and a comparative study of cultures confirms the pervasive frustrations of life. Rasselas acts like a grand tourist; he measures monuments, surveys cities and ruins, theorizes on foreign customs, and bemoans his hardships abroad. He concentrates on the ethical subject of manners until the narrative shifts in travel book fashion to antiquarian research and an account of Arab treachery. The very itinerary of *Rasselas* coincides with an actual trade route from Abyssinia to Cairo by way of the Red Sea along the African coastline. Howell's *Instructions for Forreine Travell* had dictated the moral approach and thematic direction of Rasselas's travels and proclaimed the underlying religious premise of the tale. For, according to the guidebook, every tourist must ultimately consider his journey a symbolic pilgrimage exposing the vanity of all worldly pursuits: "Nor are the observations of the Eye any thing profitable, unless the Mind draw something from the Externe object to enrich the Soule withall , . . . that by the perlustration of such famous Cities, Castles, Amphitheaters, and Palaces; . . . he come to discerne, the best of all earthly things to be frayle and transitory. That this world at the best is but a huge Inne, and we but wayfaring men, but Pilgrimes, and a company of rambling passengers. That we enter first into this World by Travaile, and so passe along with Cries, by weeping cross: So that it was no improper Character the Wisest of Kings gave of this life to be nought else but a continuall Travell" (pp. 69–70).

Rasselas does indeed inculcate the same theme in the course of a Quixotic pilgrimage imbued with the spirit of Ecclesiastes. Its journey embodies the rules of grand touring and transforms the realities of oriental travel into an oriental romance of moral exploration. Just the wealth of geographical information that went into the creation of the tale indicates Johnson's wide familiarity with travel literature. Years of casual reading in accounts of Abyssinia and Egypt supplied all the necessary geographical data for the scenery of the story. By the time that he translated *Lobo's Voyage to Abyssinia* in 1735, he had already consulted Job Ludolf's *New History of Ethiopia* and Michael Geddes's *Church History of Ethiopia*. He would create the Abyssinian setting of *Rasselas* from these and other descriptions by the Jesuit missionaries, Francisco Alvarez and Balthazar Tellez; the pseudohistorians, Luis de Urreta and Giacomo Baratti; the French physician, Charles Poncet; and probably additional African travelers. Numerous classical and modern geographies of Egypt by Herodotus, Strabo, Diodorus Siculus, Pliny, George Sandys, John Greaves, Aaron Hill, Richard Pococke, and Alexander Russell made contributions to the Egyptian locale of the tale. Thanks to the valuable research of recent critics, we now know that a complex synthesis of travel reports produced the geography of *Rasselas*.[16] To compare Johnson's key sources with the end product can enhance our knowledge of his creative process, his large literary debt to travel books, and the totality of his achievement.

Travel books significantly influenced his literary design. They corroborated and often suggested the universal moral lessons of the tale. Johnson paid close attention to the information and attitudes of oriental travelers. Although he felt free to modify his sources for new moral purposes, his uncompromising drive for truth in fiction seldom allowed him to unduly contradict historical or geographical evidence in his fable. Just as Rasselas cannot escape the limitations of his world, so also his creator could not evade the restrictions of his sources. Johnson's imagination might engender an original moral interpretation, but the dictates of his reason required a fairly steady compliance with the data of his reading. His conscientious concern for accuracy contrasts sharply with the creative process of a writer like Coleridge, whose exuberant imagination completely transcended the bounds of geographical evidence to conceive that preternatural *Rime of the Ancient Mariner*.[17] The differences in literary procedure between the two authors underscore their distinctly opposite treatment of subject matter. Where Coleridge converted mundane fact into captivating fantasy, Johnson reduced exotic fantasy to familiar facts about human nature. The moralist's respect for the evidence of his sources was consistent with his intention to present a true moral analysis of life. The empirical tendency of his creating mind was responsible for the empirical ethic of his creation, and history authenticated the mythic travels of *Rasselas*.

His heavy reliance on travel literature helps to explain the antiromantic thrust of his tale. *Rasselas* continually juxtaposes romance and reality in the development of themes, in the psychology of characters, and in the presentation of setting. Such a juxtaposition was implicitly present in his sources. Travel books read like romance but communicated frequently sobering realities to readers. They combined contrary aesthetic qualities and fulfilled an ideal of Johnson's literary criticism that was closely related to the proper mental balance of reason and imagination advocated in his morality. Their blend of fact and fantasy was the literary equivalent of the psychological harmony that Rasselas gradually acquires as the realities of life correct his fanciful notions. His imagination is the mental stimulus of his initially romantic explorations, but his reason eventually disciplines his extravagant hopes through the antiromantic discoveries of the tour. Johnson's sources foreshadowed this psychological dichotomy and authorized his disillusioning treatment of foreign manners and scenes. The romance of travel books permeates the tale, but the true facts of disappointing journeys through the East document the unhappy outcome of Rasselas's inquiries.

Not surprisingly, the pessimistic movement of *Rasselas* has a specific historical counterpart in travel literature. Rasselas's Quixotic journey reflects the disillusioning course, the early hopes and final disappointments, of Jesuit missionary efforts in Abyssinia during the sixteenth and seventeenth centuries. Successive religious expeditions reported in Johnson's sources had begun in happy valley hopes of converting a nation of Coptic Christians to a Roman Catholic choice of life. However, the Jesuits experienced a growing frustration in their activities that culminated in their permanent expulsion in 1634. The unhappy record of abortive religious labors could have reinforced the pattern of moral reversals in *Rasselas* since its protagonists and episodes directly relate to the history of Jesuit misfortunes in Abyssinia. His own translation of *Lobo's Voyage to Abyssinia* succinctly chronicles the sad unfolding of historical events pertinent to the Quixotic progression of the tale. Here was a Jesuit description of an exciting and disappointing journey, which, stripped of religious references and distracting geographical details, would surface again in *Rasselas*.

Johnson's preface to *Lobo's Voyage* enunciates several notions dramatized in the story. First, there is a Lockean insistence on eyewitness investigation to correct "the romantic absurdities or incredible fictions" of false geographical reports. Such an empirical mode of inquiry enables Rasselas to readjust his romantic outlook on life when the cumulative facts of his African travels demonstrate the impossibility of perfect happiness. The preface next affirms the moral uniformity of men and the geographical compensations of nations; human beings and their habitats exhibit basically the same mixture of good and evil. A central thesis of the tale is that universal moral and psychological truths exist in any environment of the East and West. Finally, the preface acknowledges the translator's willingness to modify and curtail the original text so as to publish "every thing either useful or entertaining." This literary aim would govern the assimilation of Lobo's journey in *Rasselas*. Johnson's revisions in his translation resulted in a travel book that stands midway between an originally complex account of religious adventures and his later tale of moral travel. His many deletions of Catholic references and geographical observations served to minimize the doctrinaire religious tone of Lobo's narrative and simplify the historical journey for the better instruction of his Protestant readers. He even reduced Lobo's three voyages to a single expedition that more closely corresponds to Rasselas's unified tour. The changes foreshadowed the radical transformation of Lobo's emphatically religious travels through the Orient into a completely moralized oriental romance.

Despite the vast differences in outlook, the general similarities in the journeys of Lobo and Rasselas are unmistakable. A comparable disillusioning series of events appears in the two works. Lobo and Rasselas pass from naive expectations at departure, through observation and discussion of a foreign people that increasingly disheartens them, to the final frustration of their high aspirations before returning home. They both set out in disguise in the company of an older traveler with vain hopes of finding happiness abroad in the form of a successful Christian ministry for the priest and an ideal choice of life for the prince. The word *hope* recurs throughout both narratives with increasingly ironic overtones as disappointments accumulate on the road. Often the actual details of *Lobo's Voyage* reappear in *Rasselas*, particularly at three points in the story: (1) the happy valley episode and Lobo's arrival at the exotic mountain valleys of Abyssinia; (2) the escape to Cairo for a study of political corruption and Lobo's flight to a port city notorious for political abuses; and (3) the Arab abduction of Pekuah and the Turkish captivity of Lobo. The verbal and narrative parallels in these analogous adventures attest that Johnson's travel book helped to map out the geographical course of his travel plot. He purposely adapted the historical journey to suit the moral demands of his fable. Spiritual trials become relatively tranquil moral inquiries. Personal suffering in a hostile geographical environment is replaced by detached observation in a generally hospitable moral setting. Finally, the romance of dangerous exploration fades before the antiromance of peaceful ethical discovery. Nevertheless, the act of reading and then translating *Lobo's Voyage* made an indelible impression upon Johnson's memory for quick recall twenty-five years later during the writing of *Rasselas*.

The travel book is a colorful chronicle of geographical discovery and religious persecution. Father Lobo arrived at a happy valley of unconverted souls among Abyssinian mountains filled with many natural delights and "subtle monkeys" found in Rasselas's paradise. However, in both cases, the idyllic pleasures of this African won- derland soon prove deceptive. Growing anti-Catholic sentiment ultimately forced the Jesuit to flee Abyssinia on a hazardous night journey that approximates Rasselas's escape from the happy valley. During his flight, Lobo witnessed mining operations by a supersti- tious prince and enjoyed the humble hospitality of shepherds, who eased the burdens of his dangerous passage to the Red Sea ports of Mazua and Suaquem. *Rasselas* recounts much the same itinerary in far less perilous terms: there are happy valley excavations by a super- stitious prince who later dines with hospitable shepherds and eventu- ally reaches the Red Sea coast during his escape to Cairo. Both Lobo and Rasselas express surprise at the indifference of the crowds in their respective cities and observe corrupt power politics unseating petty rulers by higher Turkish authorities. Subsequent events in the two journeys are broadly parallel although *Rasselas* characteristically minimizes the hazards of the historical expedition. The uneventful Pekuah episode is essentially a tame version of Lobo's terrifying captivity by a Turkish chieftan in the final phase of *Lobo's Voyage*. The prisoners in both works must travel to an island fortress, where their venal captors wrongly suppose them worth a huge ransom and are torn between a desire to retain or release them. Messengers eventually negotiate the price of ransom, and the captivities end with the tearful embraces of the principals at the moment of deliverance.

The differences between the two abductions are as significant as their similarities. The high romance of Lobo's hair-breadth escape from a cruel Turkish ruler is transformed into a lackluster story of a halcyon imprisonment by a kindly Arab chieftan, who grows to love, rather than hate, his helpless victim. The Pekuah episode initially captures the excitement of the actual experience but soon winds down into a mundane adventure revealing the boredom of harem life. The pervasive antiromance of *Rasselas* originated in part from Johnson's deflation of historical dangers to create and com-

municate practical moral lessons of greater relevance to our normally
uneventful lives. Instead of the chaos of specific evils narrated in
the travel book, the tale portrays a world so statically ordered and
generalized in its options that boredom is its major danger and unavoidable consequence. Its static presentation of human affairs coun-
ters its dynamic theme of actively searching for happiness and works
against Rasselas's hope for an exciting and fulfilling career in the
world. He remains a restless Quixote who rejects the inevitably
tedious and unhappy choices of life in the stationary moral episodes
of the tale. Like *Rasselas*, *Lobo's Voyage* ends abruptly and sadly.
The priest returns home without any more reason to hope in the
restoration of Roman Catholicism in Abyssinia than Rasselas has to
hope in the possibility of a conclusive choice of life upon his return.
Both journeys exhibit a futile pattern of irrepressible hopes and successive disappointments that lead to an indeterminate destination and
teach the lesson of life's tragic frustrations and reversals.[18] Johnson's
early biographers had noted the similarity of setting in *Lobo's Voyage* and *Rasselas*. But the relationship between the two works is far
greater than they recognized. Rasselas's archetypal grand tour of
humanity had a definite historical basis in the African travels of
Jesuit missionaries.

A key document anticipating the creative interplay of Abyssinian
travel books in *Rasselas* is the Seged tale of *Ramblers* 204 and 205.
Seged's abortive search for happiness inculcates the precepts of Ecclesiastes in an Abyssinian setting indebted to sources later affecting
the oriental romance. These *Rambler* essays show that by 1752 Johnson had supplemented his early reading in the works of Lobo, Job
Ludolf, and Michael Geddes with further research in geographical
descriptions by Balthazar Tellez, Francisco Alvarez, and Charles
Poncet. Johnson followed all these sources carefully in working out
the series of episodes and even the oriental style of address in the
story.[19] He modeled Seged on the biblical Solomon of 1 Kings and
Ecclesiastes but placed his protagonist in an African setting for a
good reason. History dictated the connection between Solomon and

Ethiopian monarchs. Since Abyssinian emperors even today claim Solomon and Sheba (or Belkis) for ancestors, no wonder Emperor Seged inherits the biblical experiences of his Jewish forebear and has a daughter named Balkis in the essays. Furthermore, there is a specific historical prototype for Seged's characterization in Sultan Segued of Abyssinia (fl. 1607–1632), whose unhappy reign had fully exemplified the vanity of human wishes.

Sultan Segued entered Abyssinian history during an unfortunate period of religious civil wars and foreign invasions. With the help of his brother, Ras Sela Christos (Johnson's Rasselas), Segued unseated the legitimate emperor and converted to Roman Catholicism for the promise of Portuguese military aid. When he tried to impose the new religion upon his Coptic subjects, warring factions arose and destroyed the peace of his kingdom. The Portuguese Jesuits were eventually banished, and the emperor himself was overthrown. His eleventh-hour concessions to the recalcitrant Coptic forces failed to restore civil order, and Segued died a broken man worn out by the cares of ruling. The events of his troubled reign underlie the action of *Ramblers* 204 and 205. Job Ludolf's *New History of Ethiopia* records all the reasons for Seged's retirement to an island palace and consequent unhappiness in the tale: *"However [Segued] was unhappy during his Reign, by reason of his continual Wars, and the frequent Rebellion of his subjects, whome he sent to compel by force to submit to what he thought convenient to enjoyn them.* . . . But at length Peter Pays built the King a Palace after the *European* manner. . . . He chose to build this House in a most commodious and delightful place . . . almost surrounded by the *Tzanic* Lake. . . . The King therefore . . . retir'd into *Dembea*, before the War was at an end. Which he did with so much hast . . . that as it diminish'd his own fame, so it gave courage to the Rebels."[20] Segued's misrule inspired Seged's misguided retreat to Lake Dambea, his futile edict commanding obedience to his will, and his final discovery of rebellion in his midst. The tale demonstrates Johnson's careful attention to sources in creating his pessimistic fiction. The creative interaction between

Abyssinian history and moral themes in the Seged essays would be all the more profoundly pervasive in the plot of *Rasselas* seven years later.

Rasselas fully exploited the historical link between Solomon of Ecclesiastes and Abyssinian monarchy. The basic assumptions of Ecclesiastes are dramatized in the story. Rasselas re-creates Solomon's disillusioning biblical survey of sensual pleasure, domestic pursuits, tyrants and fools, before concluding his study in the universal cemetery of death.[21] To reinforce the biblical analogy, he could claim a royal descent from Solomon by virtue of his relationship to Ras Sela Christos, prince of Abyssinia. This historical prince was actually the brother of Emperor Segued and the third of four royal sons rather than "the fourth son of the mighty emperour" in Johnson's pedigree. Nevertheless, he bequeathed to Rasselas the few character traits presented in the story: a regal pride of authority, an imprudent zeal for impossible principles, a rashness in action, and a preoccupation with politics. We might wonder why Johnson's protagonists and other characters in his fiction lack psychological complexity and completeness. Johnson was a brilliant student of human nature and a proponent of detailed psychological analysis in biographies. His portrayal of Rasselas was indebted to a comprehensive biography of Sela Christos in his sources. But he chose to generalize his characterization to emphasize the universal and archetypal significance of the moral adventures. Particularity would have interfered with the summary moral design of the tale.

The histories of Geddes, Ludolf, Lobo, and Tellez supplied Johnson with a full portrait of Sela Christos. This African prince was a hotheaded defender of Emperor Segued and the Roman Catholic faith. He secured the throne for Segued by his astute military leadership and subsequently won the post of *Ras* (commander in chief) and viceroy of an imperial province. His sincere loyalty to the Jesuit cause embroiled the state in disastrous religious wars and resulted in his dismissal from office and death around 1650 under Segued's anti-Catholic successor. The Protestant historians, Ludolf and Geddes, paint a very unfavorable picture of this Catholic martyr. Johnson, by contrast, showed more religious tolerance by making his hero a truly catholic everyman on a moral pilgrimage that transcends any theological bounds. His plot parallels the journey of a Jesuit missionary, and his protagonist embodies the personality of a Catholic prince who protected the Jesuit mission at the cost of his life. Despite the Protestant bias evident in his translation of *Lobo's Voyage*, Johnson apparently came to sympathize with the misfortunes of Catholicism in Abyssinia. *Rasselas* moralized the sad religious history and transmitted an authentic study of human disappointments applicable to all mankind.

The career of Sela Christos explains Rasselas's characterization and political desires. The seeds of Rasselas's political destiny were implanted in the happy valley and needed only the nurture of time and experience to fully flower in maturity. His impatience with native instructors (chap. 3), his intention to reform the empire (chap. 8), and his fondness for debate all reflect the iconoclastic temperament of the reform-minded warrior in history. Sela Christos had similarly rejected his native traditions to propagate new religious ideals of public happiness in just such a little kingdom that Rasselas dreams of ruling (chap. 49). According to Balthazar Tellez, "In the Yr. 1612, the Emperour going to *Gojam*, made his brother Rae Cella Christos Viceroy of that Kingdom, which was almost the same as making him King, because he enjoy'd all the Revenues of that Country, and was obey'd like the Emperour himself. The new Viceroy was affable, and generous, and a great favourer of the Fathers, . . . and therefore lov'd to hear the disputes between the Fathers, and the Native learned men."[22] Moreover, rumors that Sela Christos plotted against his brother for control of the empire account for Rasselas's startling wish to murder the royal family and found a political utopia (chap. 44). Certainly all the allusions in *Rasselas* to savage invasions and public calamities pertain to civil turmoils and conspiracies surrounding Sela Christos's life. History provided the tragic background for the tale and grimly fulfilled Rasselas's youthful ambitions. His happy valley hopes were consistent with historical facts.

One of the most subtle ironies in *Rasselas* is the hero's unknowing exposure to his political destiny in Egypt. There he encounters several characters who presage the misfortunes that await him back in Abyssinia. The prosperous Egyptian (chap. 20), the exiled hermit (chap. 21), and the banished bassa (chap. 24) together reconstruct the successive stages of his future downfall. The prosperous Egyptian arouses the jealousy of neighboring princes; the hermit fell victim to intrigues during his military career; and the Cairo bassa suffers disgrace from court factions and the Turkish emperor. Johnson's gloomy review of political treachery coincides with the course of Sela Christos's ruin. The growing prosperity and military successes of Sela Christos had similarly stirred up enemies eager to plot his destruction. History records that Sela Christos lost his estate and military command but, like the hermit of *Rasselas*, eventually returned from exile. However, court intrigues aroused the emperor's suspicions once again and precipitated Sela Christos's overthrow and death under Segued's anti-Catholic successor. The spectacle of the calumniated bassa of *Rasselas*, carried in chains before Turkish authorities, mirrors the true outcome of Rasselas's political ambitions in history. Surely Imlac's conviction that life is to be more endured than enjoyed proves too terribly true when not only a man's past and present but even his future seem doomed to unhappiness. If the grand tour were intended to be a political education for Renaissance princes, then Rasselas's expedition served this purpose very well. By studying the corruptions of Egyptian statecraft, the prince of *Rasselas* was effectively preparing for his ill-starred role in Abyssinian politics.

In the tale Imlac guides Rasselas on this prophetic grand tour and has equally close ties with Abyssinian figures in Johnson's sources. Imlac's name belonged to an ancient emperor, Icon Imlac, responsible for the cruel policy of imprisoning princes on Mount Amhara to prevent civil wars over the imperial succession.[23] In *Rasselas* Imlac ironically becomes the captive and severest critic of the mountain prison instituted by his historical namesake. Furthermore, the travel books consulted by Johnson mentioned several traveling philosophers, whose wisdom and wanderlust prefigure Imlac's characterization.[24] Ludolf's *New History of Ethiopia* chronicles the career of Gregory the Abyssinian, who bears an especially close resemblance to Imlac. In fact, the biography of Gregory in this treatise reads like a concise summary of Imlac's life history in *Rasselas* (chaps. 8 to 12). According to Ludolf, Gregory was a fifty-year-old philosopher who had sailed to India in his youth for greater knowledge than his backward homeland afforded. During his travels, he recommended himself to rulers and scholars as a "Person of great gravity and high credit," fully experienced in the world's misfortunes from East to West.[25] Gregory appears in Ludolf's work as a native authority on Abyssinia and engages in a series of dialogues on the state of foreign nations that foreshadow Imlac's conversations with Rasselas. Occasionally the geographical subjects discussed by Gregory reappear in Imlac's discourses. The numerous similarities between the two figures suggest that Johnson used Ludolf's philosopher as a model for his own.

Johnson's dependence upon Abyssinian history in characterizing his protagonists has important ramifications for the meaning of the tale. Just the evidence of Rasselas's connection with Sela Christos can settle a much debated question concerning the prince's destination at the close of *Rasselas*. History proves that he cannot end where he began. He returns to Abyssinia but not to the happy valley, and Sela Christos's career commences where Rasselas's story concludes. Rasselas's circular journey of life up and down the Nile becomes a parabolic curve demarcating his passage from youth to maturity in preparation for his political destiny. Fiction recounts the private education of a prince on a grand tour, and history unfolds the unhappy public responsibilities of his manhood. The culminating irony of many ironies in the tale is that Rasselas's last wish for a political choice of life would for once be granted him in the annals of Abyssinian civil war. The conclusion of *Rasselas* had to be inconclusive, and his archetypal journey of life was necessarily left unfinished because an essential part of the earthly pilgrimage lay before this statesman and Catholic martyr-to-be. Johnson scrupulously maintained his empirical priorities in his fable: fiction yielded to fact and let history write the last chapter of *Rasselas*.

History was not alone in supplying a denouement to Rasselas's story. Ellis Cornelia Knight later published a sentimental continuation of *Rasselas* in *Dinarbas* (1790), a minor novel completely unlike the original in its happy tone, optimistic moral, and undisciplined style. The authoress apparently had some knowledge of Abyssinian history but intended to refute Johnson's pessimistic thesis by presenting a rosy romance of Rasselas's subsequent career as a victorious warrior, emperor, and husband. There is nothing of the disillusioned spirit of Ecclesiastes in this inferior imitation, only an unconvincing argument for life's predominant happiness that Johnson heartily disavowed. Johnson's very different moral outlook shows a care for authenticity in creating fiction and representing the human condition. Where *Dinarbas* violates the sad facts of Abyssinian politics, *Rasselas* allows no compromise with either the data of sources or the realities of human experience. Johnson had himself planned a second part of *Rasselas* to illustrate the attainment of happiness but found life too miserable to carry off the project.[26] To have composed a continuation would have required taking liberties with history and his own moral convictions about mankind. He could not betray his exacting critical standards of truth in literature. As it was, his memory of Sela Christos's reversals and Father Lobo's frustrating voyage cast an appropriately dark shadow over the pages of *Rasselas*.

His care for authenticity in plot and characterization extended to the presentation of setting in the tale. He digested volumes of information from travel books to locate his vision of the vanity of things in a verifiable moral environment. By distancing his story in the exotic but true realms of geographical romance, he could more objectively bring home to readers the lessons of life's universal disappointments. Like the emerging British Empire, *Rasselas* offered the symbolic truth that the sun never set on mankind's tireless pursuit of happiness. If anchored in the realities of travel books, his generalized setting is an imaginary moral backdrop for communicating perennial human problems existing everywhere around the globe. The story proclaims the cosmopolitan viewpoint of Ecclesiastes within a remote oriental locale: "I have seen all the works that are done under the sun; and, behold, all *is* vanity and vexation of spirit." Fortunately, the shifting scenery of *Rasselas* is sufficiently detailed to indicate the specific sources in Johnson's mind. Travel books inspired the geography of the tale and influenced the moral course of Rasselas's explorations from Abyssinia to Egypt along the banks of the Nile. Johnson followed the lead of oriental travelers to create a wholly unique topography that forcefully illustrated his moral themes. He amalgamated true and false descriptions of Mount Amhara in his portrayal of an unsatisfying happy valley. He combined ancient and modern accounts of Egypt to expose the country's deflated wonders. And he conflated geographical controversies about the Nile to produce the major symbol of human vanity in *Rasselas*.

Johnson's sources show a preoccupation with the Nile that probably suggested the central geographical symbol of the tale. Rasselas's tour along the Nile raises the principal geographical phenomenon of northeast Africa to a new moral significance. The river symbolizes man's fluctuating desires and transient hopes and unites the two geographical realms of *Rasselas* in a common bond of unhappiness. Rasselas explores the route of the Nile in the footsteps of Portuguese travelers intent on solving the ancient mystery of the river's source. Father Lobo, for example, claimed the honor of discovering the source in the mountains of Abyssinia and charted the river's passage into Egypt: "As the empire of the Abyssins terminates at these desarts, and as I have followed the course of the Nile no farther, I here leave it to range over barbarous kingdoms, and convey wealth and plenty into Egypt, which owes to the annual inundations of this river its envied fertility."[27] *Rasselas* retraces the course of the Nile from its source in the happy valley through its northward passage by the hermitage and Arab fortress in upper Egypt to its outlet at Cairo. However, Johnson treats the river's geography ironically by reversing the normal route of Portuguese travelers in the itinerary of the tale. His story begins in the African *terra incognita* that had so fascinated historical explorers of the Nile but thoroughly bores Rasselas in the happy valley. Conversely, the better-known territory of Egypt turns out to be the actual no-man's-land of moral doubt at the conclusion of Rasselas's journey. The travelers in *Rasselas* are only too familiar with the mundane delights of their remote Abyssinian playground. Boredom as well as curiosity drive them into the civilized world to chart the sad course of human disappointments in the philosophical wilderness of Cairo at the end of the Nile.

The sobering moral exploration of the Nile paradoxically commences at its head in the happy valley of Mount Amhara. The happy valley is the most famous description in Johnson's writings and was created by a complex imaginative synthesis of sources. The episode refutes the myth of earthly paradises in a manner reminiscent of Solomon's attack on the vanity of pleasure gardens in Ecclesiastes, chapter 2. Contradictory travel reports of Mount Amhara guided Johnson in his antiromantic conception of the happy valley. The pseudohistorians, Luis de Urreta and Giacomo Baratti, had falsely represented Mount Amhara as a tropical paradise founded by Solomon's immediate Abyssinian ancestors.[28] Hence, there was a tenuous historical tradition authorizing Johnson's description of an African wonderland blest with the plenum of pleasures enumerated by Solomon in Ecclesiastes. However, the ironic portrayal in *Rasselas* deftly counterbalances the romantic fabrications of false geographers with true accounts of a forbidding Mount Amhara by reliable geographers like Job Ludolf. Far from being a paradise, the mountain actually contained a miserable prison for Abyssinian princes: "The custome is, that all the male children of the Kings, except the Heires, . . . they send them presently to a very great Rocke, which stands in the Province of Amara, and there they passe all their life, and never come out from thence, except the King which reigneth departeth this life without Heires, for they bring from the Rocke him that is neerest, to come and raigne."[29] Johnson purposely conflated contrary observations of Mount Amhara to produce an unhappy happy valley that confirmed the genuine hardships of royal confinement and aptly dramatized his theme. Travel books are partly responsible for his antiromantic treatment of an illusory paradise that conceals a true royal prison.

The whole episode assimilated a wide variety of geographical findings that substantiate Johnson's imaginary creation. Francisco Alvarez's *Prester John of the Indies* recorded the hidden entrances, iron gates, guards, and valley situation of Mount Amhara. While traversing the mountains of Abyssinia, Alvarez had encountered the heavy winter rains and royal guards that Rasselas impatiently endures inside his retreat. This Jesuit's pointed denial that rabbits existed in the country was ignored by Johnson since rabbit burrows become the escape route for his characters in the episode. Another missionary source, Balthazar Tellez's *Travels of the Jesuits in Ethiopia*, verified the mysterious happy valley palace. Tellez had witnessed the construction of a durable stone palace standing on a pleasant lake and containing a private room for Emperor Segued's personal use. Johnson located this structure in his paradise and added further architectural details, including winding passages and a fabulous cement arch, taken from accounts of the ancient Labyrinth by Herodotus and Pliny. The complexity of Johnson's creative process is apparent everywhere in his presentation. Seldom is any single source responsible for his conception of people, places, or events. His mind absorbed innumerable geographical facts and fables and selected whatever would best serve his moral intention at the moment. The happy valley episode pits true against false travel reports, antiromance against romance, to teach the vanity of earthly utopias. Geography confirms moral meaning, and the happy valley of fiction is the genuinely unhappy Mount Amhara of history.

Johnson continued to harmonize skillfully the diverse and sometimes discordant data of travel literature in the Egyptian setting of
Rasselas. George Sandys's *Relation of a Journey* and Richard Pococke's *Description of the East* probably had the greatest impact on
the remaining scenery of the tale. But there were also other sources
that deeply influenced his treatment of the Egyptian episodes. Several ancient and modern geographies merged in his imagination and
suggested an appropriate moral environment to exemplify his themes.
They not only documented his geographical landscape but also inspired many ideas discussed at length in the story. His antiromantic
portrayal of Egypt frequently juxtaposes descriptions of the early
glories and later ruins of the country. A major topic in the rest of
Rasselas concerns life's transience and decay in history. The theme
was inherent in his sources. He had only to contrast past and present
reports of Egyptian society and learning for an authentic record of
the destructive changes that shape human affairs. The pyramids and
catacombs of travel books became telling symbols of the world's
mutability in fiction.

Rasselas reaches the outlet of the Nile at Cairo and there repeats
the disillusioning discoveries of Johnson's previous London adventurers in the essay tales. Cairo is another London set in an Egyptian
locale and contains a microcosm of human diversity actually ascribed
by travelers to "This incorporate World of Grand Cairo."[30] Both
Sandys and Pococke fully described the oriental center of trade,
luxury, learning, and power politics presented in *Rasselas*. They had
similarly witnessed the city's mixed population, thriving commerce,
social assemblies, colleges of philosophy, and the rampant sensuality
of the inhabitants: "Hither the sacred thirst of gaine, and feare of
poverty, allureth the adventurous merchant from far removed nations. . . . Than Cairo, no Citie can be more populous, nor better
interserved with all sorts of provision."[31] The Nile made Cairo a
bustling thoroughfare of a worldwide humanity and drew Rasselas
to this ideal location for a summary review of the choices of life.
Here he renews Solomon's biblical survey of frivolity, loneliness,

foolish speech, political instability, domestic discord, and life's arbitrary calamities. The pronouncements of Ecclesiastes are reaffirmed in a geographically true Vanity Fair of oriental follies and intrigues.

Rasselas periodically leaves Cairo to follow the course of the Nile to its lower cataracts in southern Egypt. In a wilderness that had given rise to Western monasticism under Saint Anthony the hermit, the prince appropriately investigates religious retirement at a hermitage and a monastery of Saint Anthony. Richard Pococke confirmed Johnson's account of the monastery and had observed the flagrant political abuses that distresses Rasselas back in Cairo. The court intrigues that overthrow the bassa and sultan of *Rasselas* were typical of the devious Turkish policies recorded in Pococke's narrative: "There is this difference between the tumults here and those at Constantinople, that the latter are commonly begun by some resolute fellows among the janizaries, whereas the mob is generally raised by some great man who envies one that is rival to him."[32] *Rasselas* exposes the common unhappiness of an active and retired life at the hermit's retreat and the bassa's palace. Once again travel books helped to validate Rasselas's disappointments with Egyptian choices of life that lead to a moral dilemma almost arresting the journey of the prince and princess midway in the story.

At this point *Rasselas* enters a new narrative phase of antiquarian research among the pyramids of Gizeh. Johnson combined the different viewpoints of ancient and modern geographers to create another antiromantic episode that begins in heightened expectations of seeing historical marvels and ends in disappointment and despair. Imlac entices his reluctant companions to examine the pyramids by reiterating glowing classical accounts of Egypt's early intellectual and architectural achievements. Herodotus, Strabo, and Diodorus Siculus had all praised Egyptians for originating and perfecting the arts and sciences that civilized the West. Imlac's discussion in chapter 30 echoes their comments, but the ensuing exploration of the pyramids results in disillusionment and difficulties reported by modern travelers on the scene. The works of Sandys and Pococke largely inspired not only Johnson's description of the great pyramid but also the melancholy tone and unhappy outcome of the episode. The following passage is only a sample of Sandys's meditations on the ruins of time and the folly of the pharoahs that probably suggested Imlac's psychological critique in chapter 32 of *Rasselas:* "By these ... inventions exhausted they their treasure, and employed the people; for feare lest such infinite wealth should corrupt their successors, & dangerous idlenesse beget in the Subject a desire of innovation. Besides, they considering the frailty of man, that in an instant buds, blowes, and withereth; did endevour by such sumptuous and magnificent structures, in spite of death to give unto their fames eternity. But vainely." [33] In addition to Sandys's account, John Greaves's *Pyramidographia* (1646) provided documentation for Imlac's architectural analysis of the pyramids in chapter 31. All of Johnson's modern sources expressed a nostalgia for ancient ruins and a fear of Arab marauders that come to sadden his moral travelers. Pekuah realizes the perils of actual antiquarian research in her abduction by Arabs, and Rasselas ponders the somber meaning of fallen Egyptian grandeur. The disappointed expectations and deflated wonders of the episode mirror the shift in geographical sources away from classical eulogies of Egyptian monuments to modern elegies over the present decay and dangers of the Arab-infested region.

The curiosity of Johnson's travelers has potentially tragic consequences. Numerous archaeologists had complained of lawless Arabs at Gizeh, where Pekuah's misadventures take place. Pococke almost lost a servant to Arabs at the pyramids and appealed in vain to a lax Egyptian government for the recovery of his stolen property. His narrative documents experiences resembling the Pekuah episode and also inspired her Arab captor's island fortress and celestial observatory under the tropic of Cancer on the Nile: "On the height over Assouan are the ruins of antient Syene, which is exactly under the *tropic of Cancer*. The present fortress ... has water on three sides of it. . . . About the middle, . . . I found the building which might possibly be the observatory . . . for making astronomical observations. . . . The island is there twenty or thirty feet above the water, and there being a prospect about a mile south to the granite hills, where the Nile having made a turn, the view is . . . very extraordinary."[34] Such picturesque scenery in *Rasselas* fails to alleviate Pekuah's boring captivity. She fears a lovelorn Arab abductor who possesses all the racial traits associated with desert nomads by George Sandys: a predilection for thievery and skillful horsemanship, a fondness for collecting harems of submissive wives and extending hospitality to strangers, and a pride in their ancestry and absolute dominion over the desert.[35] Johnson's chieftan boasts of such a cultural inheritance and, true to the venal character of his race, releases Pekuah when money proves a greater incentive than love. She eventually returns with her friends along the Nile to Cairo in preparation for a fascinating encounter with two bizarre philosophers of the Nile.

The truths of travel books continued to shape the adventures of fiction in Johnson's final episodes. The mad astronomer and old man of *Rasselas* have an obvious autobiographical relevance to their creator's own melancholy life of learning. They also reflect the intellectual eccentricities chronicled in Johnson's biographies of deranged scholars like Thomas Browne and Zachariah Williams. His *Life of Browne*, for example, presented a case history of irrational scholarship that anticipates the mad astronomer's career. Imlac, in fact, practically repeats the following criticism of Browne's undisciplined imagination in chapter 44 of *Rasselas:* "The wonders probably were transacted in his own mind; self-love, co-operating with an imagination vigorous and fertile as that of Browne, will find or make objects of astonishment in every man's life; and, perhaps, there is no human being, however hid in the crowd from the observation of his fellow mortals, who . . . will not conclude his life in some sort a miracle, and imagine himself distinguished from all the rest of his species by many discriminations of nature or of fortune."[36] The characterization of the mad astronomer and the old man points to a biographical influence, but their speculations regarding the Nile originated in travel books. An old geographical controversy about the cause of the Nile's inundations by the sun, rain, or wind explains the mad astronomer's wild desire to control all three forces and regulate the Nile. His dangerous prevalence of imagination resembles the "Presumptuous Imagination" ascribed to arrogant theorists of the Nile's overflow in *Lobo's Voyage*.[37] Such boasted authority over the Nile represents the climactic attempt of many futile efforts in the tale to impose stability on the protean moral universe intersected by this symbolic river of worldly flux.

The concluding visit to the catacombs in *Rasselas* is Johnson's *memento mori* emphasizing the ultimate instability of man's mortal hopes and fears. The episode properly terminates the symbolic drama of human growth in the story. Rasselas passes from youthful innocence in the happy valley to maturity in Cairo and confronts the spectacle of old age and death before returning home. His archetypal journey circumscribes the human life cycle but allows him only a faint hope in the final choice of eternity at the end. Physically and morally, he is left stranded on the banks of the Nile. His travels constitute a moralized pilgrimage without a religious conclusion, a Quixotic grand tour without a romantic ending, and a modern odyssey of perpetual exile from any earthly haven of rest. He explores the wisdom of the West and the geography of the East and rediscovers the disillusioning lessons expounded in Ecclesiastes and authenticated in travel literature. All in all, the thematic movement of his tale evolved from classics of literary and historical travel that led to a new classic interpretation of the haphazard human quest for meaning and order in the world.

The intricate creation of *Rasselas* may not explain its greatness as fiction but does illuminate the awesome intellectual and imaginative powers that produced the story. His tale remains a remarkable feat of a literary genius who could incorporate a vast heritage of learning in a deceptively simple fable of human aspirations. Boswell isolated exactly those qualities of mind needed to condense a wealth of knowledge and experience in *Rasselas* during its rapid composition: "But his superiority over other learned men consisted chiefly in what may be called the art of thinking, the art of using his mind; a certain continual power of seizing the useful substance of all that he knew, and exhibiting it in a clear and forcible manner; so that knowledge, which we often see to be no better than lumber in men of dull understanding, was, in him, true, evident, and actual wisdom."[38] Having used his mind so brilliantly in *Rasselas*, Johnson climaxed his writing of prose fiction and solidified his reputation as the most celebrated moralist in English literature. With the exception of *The Fountains*, he never again published any fiction. The imaginary travels of *Rasselas* would be succeeded by an actual journey to Scotland for the same purpose of penetrating the mysteries of human life and historical change. The moral patterns of his tale would carry over into his only travel book.

The Aegyptian Pyramides & Colossus, from George Sandys' *Relation of a Journey begun An Dom: 1610* (1615), a travel book important to the Egyptian setting of *Rasselas*. Courtesy of the Harvard College Library.

6

PHILOSOPHIC ART AND
TRAVEL IN THE
HIGHLANDS

> Our geographers seem to be almost as much at a loss in the
> description of this north part of Scotland, as the Romans were
> to conquer it; and they are oblig'd to fill it up with hills and
> mountains, as they do the inner parts of Africa, with lyons and
> elephants, for want of knowing what else to place there. Yet
> this country is not of such difficult access as, to be pass'd unde-
> scrib'd, as if it were impenetrable.   Daniel Defoe, *A Tour
> through the Whole Island of Great Britain*

RASSELAS was a splendid prelude to Johnson's later career of restless
travel and distinctly foreshadowed the thematic concerns of his
Journey to the Western Islands of Scotland (1775). Only four years
after the tale appeared, he expressed a desire to undertake his own
moral tour of foreign manners in the remote isles of the Hebrides.
During the 1760s financial security and friendship with Boswell
created new opportunities for converting the journeys of fiction into
actual excursions in his life. With Boswell's encouragement through
a decade of planning, Johnson's youthful dream of visiting the region
of Martin Martin's *Description of the Western Islands of Scotland*
finally materialized in 1773. The elegant travel book that resulted
had combined the moral artistry displayed in *Rasselas* and the conventions of travel literature found in previous accounts of Scotland.
His study was a skillful blend of philosophic art and travel and
represents the culmination of his literary and intellectual adventures
with geography in his writings. In its pages the metaphor of travel
had come round full circle, from a dramatic expression of human

growth in his morality to a realized process of moral discovery on the road. The Highlands became a testing ground for examining those assumptions about man and principles of touring so memorably presented in *Rasselas*. Guided by scientific techniques of exploration, Johnson would now rely on direct observation to validate the lessons of his moral literature. As Boswell reported in Scotland, "He was pleased to say, 'You and I do not talk from books.' "[1]

In the complementary *Tour to the Hebrides* Boswell described Johnson as a Hercules, John Bull, and Socrates of Highland travel. The heroic conception aptly summarizes the nature of Johnson's Highland expedition. For the trip involved the Herculean labor of touring a primitive area at the age of sixty-four and led to a bullish defense of England's superiority over Scotland, which he studied with the shrewd moral insight of a Socrates. The Highlands today preserve memorials of his itinerary through a region now considerably tamed by economic and agricultural development. Modern tourists have the advantage of better roads and efficient transportation but can still appreciate Johnson's hardy curiosity and melancholy impression of the desolate Hebrides. There yet exists much of the barrenness and decay that made eighteenth-century travelers feel like daring explorers of a remote British *terra incognita*. Boswell so represented his Highland tour: "Martin's Account of those islands had impressed us with a notion that we might there contemplate a system of life almost totally different from what we had been accustomed to see; and to find simplicity and wildness, and all the circumstances of remote time or place, so near to our native great island, was an object within the reach of reasonable curiosity."[2] Johnson agreed with Boswell's estimate of their heroic project. The relative obscurity of the Hebrides in 1773 justified the moralist's notion of being a pioneer traveler: "I have now the pleasure of going where nobody goes, and of seeing what nobody sees."[3]

Johnson's tour was very much a part of the exciting geographical exploration taking place in 1773. Johnson was surveying Scotland when Cook crossed the Antarctic Circle for the first time, Constantine Phipps sailed for the North Pole, and James Bruce returned from Abyssinia. Joseph Banks had previously completed the first scientific study of Iceland by an Englishman, and Robert Chambers would soon embark on a distinguished career as a judge in India. The Highland expedition was worthy of a place in the annals of contemporary geographical discovery. Boswell, in fact, likened their trip to a voyage of discovery, and Johnson encouraged the analogy by his wealth of geographical allusions in the *Journey*. The Highlanders are treated as if they were Eskimos, Siberian nomads, American Indians, and Pacific savages. Johnson, of course, recognized the disparity between his local tour and distant voyages and expressed embarrassment when friends aggrandized his accomplishment: "I am really ashamed of the congratulations which we receive. We are addressed as if we had made a voyage to Nova Zembla, and suffered five persecutions in Japan."[4] But he could pride himself on enduring many of the perils of remote exploration while gathering information about a society almost "equally unknown with that of Borneo or Sumatra." He set out armed with two pistols for use against highwaymen, risked shipwreck at Coll and unhealthy lodgings at Glenelg, experienced bad health and wretched weather, and grew homesick from long separation. Yet, whatever his discomforts and dangers, he showed the fortitude of more renowned travelers in his journey through "scenes of adventures, stratagems, surprises and escapes."

His tour was symbolic of the geographical revolution in his century and the moral concerns of his writings. The *Journey* reflects a historical tradition of Highland travel and exploits themes and procedures made famous in *Rasselas*. The motives that drew Rasselas out of the happy valley, to test notions against facts, also propelled his creator out of his parochial London habitat into an unknown world to the north: "Having passed my time almost wholly in cities, I may have been surprised by modes of life and appearances of nature that are familiar to men of wider survey and more varied conversation."[5] Moreover, the *Journey* has a unified moral theme already enunciated in *Rasselas*, namely, a traveler's disillusionment with foreign manners as his fancied preconceptions clash with sad realities abroad in a growing threnody of disappointments. The thematic unity of his account has occasioned considerable debate concerning its precise status as travel literature: Is his report more a polished work of art related to his moral writings or a genuine travel book of unpremeditated geographical description?[6] The question really has only one adequate answer. The *Journey* is a two-fold triumph of art and travel, displaying the moral patterns of his travel tales and the usual format of contemporary travel books. When writing his account, he had recourse to favorite literary strategies in his fiction and implemented the prevailing scientific standards of inquiry in travel literature. The trip permitted him to practice his philosophy of travel and confirmed his moral vision of the vanity of human wishes by firsthand observation of the Highlands.

Obvious differences in genre and content have tended to obscure important similarities in the thematic development and tone of his oriental romance and travel book. Like *Rasselas*, the *Journey* invites comparison with great literary archetypes of travel that help to define the nature of his tour. Johnson played out the role of a pilgrim-Ulysses of Quixotic travel in Scotland. He directly alludes to the *Odyssey* adventures to emphasize the primitive conditions of a region requiring a truly heroic curiosity to travel there: "At Dunvegan I had tasted lotus, and was in danger of forgetting that I was ever to depart, till Mr. Boswell sagely reproached me with my sluggishness and softness" (p. 71). His tour was also a pilgrimage through the religious ruins of a formerly pious nation that had degenerated to a Bunyanesque City of Destruction at Iona and elsewhere in the isles: "The island, which was once the metropolis of learning and piety, has now no school for education, nor temple for worship, only two inhabitants that can speak English, and not one that can write or read" (p. 152). Most of all, he was doomed to be a real life Quixote of frustrated expectations when his romantic ideas of the Highland heritage collided with the facts of cultural upheaval: "Such is the

effect of the late regulations, that a longer journey than to the Highlands must be taken by him whose curiosity pants for savage virtues
and barbarous grandeur" (p. 58).

The very circumstances of the trip paralleled the human relation-
ships and geographical movement of *Rasselas* in reverse. In the *Journey* an aging Rasselas, as biographers often called Johnson, departed
from his bustling Cairo of London accompanied by another well-
traveled Imlac in Boswell, "a companion whose acuteness would
help my inquiry" in the unhappy valleys of pastoral Scotland. Like
Rasselas, he regarded himself as "one who has seen but little" of
the world and was eager to escape a parochial life, "in which little
has been done and little has been enjoyed," by foreign travel. However, his expedition was another case of long choosing and beginning
late. Years of poverty and sickness prevented him from realizing his
high hopes of finding happiness from a survey of unfamiliar manners.
He had planned to visit Scotland in 1772, but poor health forced him
to stay home. Boswell began to worry about Johnson's repeated
postponements of the trip and suspected him of stalling. Johnson,
however, was sincerely eager to embark on a tour that had been in
his mind since childhood. He fully shared Rasselas's curiosity about
human diversity and intended to examine a romantic realm of "anti-
quated life" in a country almost as mysterious to most fellow Englishmen as it was to himself. Unfortunately, when the trip took place
a year later, his hopes of seeing a pastoral Arcadia ended with the
discovery of pervasive social change and unhappiness in the Hebrides. His travel book would record his surprise and gradual dis-
enchantment with the total transformation of the old Highland
traditions: "The clans retain little now of their original character,
their ferocity of temper is softened, their military ardour is ex-
tinguished, their dignity of independence is depressed, their contempt of government subdued, and their reverence for their chiefs
abated" (p. 57). The progressive disappointments in *Rasselas* had
indeed found new expression in the *Journey*.

Both works are moving accounts of frustrated expectations and human misery discovered by eyewitness examination of a wholly new environment. Readers of the *Journey* once again follow the dashing of human hopes in the observer and the society before him and ponder the uncertain choices of life facing the Highlanders in the midst of a cultural revolution. His tour reaffirmed Imlac's pessimistic vision of a suffering humanity in the historically true spectacle of a defeated nation. Rasselas's recognition of a tragic mutability in human affairs was to be fully authenticated by the rapid alterations destroying Highland clans, ancient ceremonies, and a valuable heritage of learning. Nekayah's illusory dream of a pastoral idyll in *Rasselas* (chap. 19) was a myth of poets and philosophers to be exploded again by the empirical test of Highland travel. In Scotland Johnson was intent on familiarizing himself with the economic state of the masses and soon perceived the folly of idealizing the backward social system. The noble savages of Scotland turned out to be a miserable and ignorant race of human beings, not at all conforming to the romantic conceptions of primitivists at home. His own expectations of finding a happy primitive world faded before the realities of cultural decay and produced a series of disappointments duly recorded at regular intervals in his narrative. As a consequence, his travel book presents an increasingly disillusioning journey previously portrayed in *Rasselas*.

Hope and disappointment constituted a basic psychological pattern of the *Journey*, *Rasselas*, and all kinds of travel in his experience. Long before his touring began, *Idler* 58 had pointed out how a traveler's "journey of pleasure in his mind, with which he flatters his expectation" becomes a journey of disillusionment in the event: "It is seldom that we find either men or places such as we expect them." His letters and diaries of excursions to Lichfield, Wales, and France show that he meant the pattern to be a prime study of travel. Before his tour he even predicted his disappointed expectations of seeing radically new manners abroad from a conviction of mankind's moral uniformity: "I am afraid travel itself will end likewise in disappointment. One town, one country is very like another. Civilized nations

have the same customs, and barbarous nations have the same nature.
There are indeed minute discriminations both of places and of manners, which perhaps are not unworthy of curiosity, but which a
traveller seldom stays long enough to investigate and compare. The
dull utterly neglect them, the acute see a little, and supply the rest
by fancy and conjecture."[7] However, the Highland tour was the
only one of his many trips to afford him enough time and opportunity to uncover the minute discriminations of national character
worthy of publication in a travel book. If predisposed to being disappointed, he did enjoy the trip and gained positive intellectual
benefits from a disillusioning process of discovery anticipated in his
travel tales. By comparing ideas with realities, expectation with outcome, Johnson, Rasselas, or any traveler learned important and invariably sobering lessons about the world.

An ironic psychological juxtaposition of romance and reality,
imagination and reason, characterized the general tendency of mental and moral growth in *Rasselas* and the *Journey*. Fact comes to
regulate fancy, and successive disappointments gradually correct
false hopes. In Scotland the major disappointment of missing a vanished feudal society was attended with minor frustrations reinforcing his dissatisfaction with the impoverished state of the region. The
report of a comfortable inn "raised our expectation" but never gave
"much satisfaction on arrival." Curiosities encountered on the trip
caused a similar shift of emotions: "We had been disappointed already by one cave, and were not much elevated by the expectation
of another" (p. 145). He would afterward ask Boswell "if our jaunt
had answered expectation," knowing himself that the intellectual
rewards and emotional pleasures of the tour far outweighed its discomforts and disappointments.

The pattern of hope and disappointment in the *Journey* is an integral part of the inductive learning process enveloping the narrative. *Rasselas* anticipated this inductive procedure. The lessons of
the tale build to a convincing moral argument for universal unhappiness as the story progresses from description to discussion, from

discussion to tentative conclusions, and, by an accumulation of tested truths, to summary generalizations about a frustrating world. An analogous development of ideas distinguishes the logic of his disillusioned survey. The travel book passes from simple description and first impressions to moral reflections within chapters and onward to summary discourses on the region based on the previous data of the tour. Early in the work, his somber account of Saint Andrews initiates a succession of observations on dead or dying cultural values that demonstrate the futility of human hopes in the Highlands: "The city of St. Andrews, when it had lost its archiepiscopal preeminence, gradually decayed: One of its streets is now lost; and in those that remain, there is the silence and solitude of inactive indigence and gloomy depopulation" (p. 6). Thereafter, dormant cities and depopulated islands on his itinerary confirmed the sad meaning of Saint Andrews, that the ravages of war, greed, and poverty had forever buried an old way of life. Calvinist reformers and their commercial-minded descendants, irresponsible lairds and a vindictive English government had promoted cultural innovations that caused Johnson personal sorrow and disappointment. The disturbing conclusions emerging from his inquiries were not, after all, far removed from the increasingly disheartening discoveries of *Rasselas*.

What strengthens the ties between the *Journey* and *Rasselas* are common assumptions about the methods and ends of travel originating in James Howell's *Instructions for Forreine Travell*. This guidebook had recommended a comparative study of cultures to promote individual and social development and encourage a greater love of homeland. Johnson adopted this procedure and patriotic attitude on a tour that was a personal moral education productive of economic proposals for the general public good. He constantly evaluated the Highland culture by the norm of English civilization and, after the completion of the trip at Mull, had sufficient information to affirm his country's superiority over Scotland. The *Journey*, in fact, enunciates the fundamental rationale for all eighteenth-century travel by a Lockean interpretation of Howell's principle of comparative inquiry: "It is true that of far the greater part of things, we must content ourselves with such knowledge as description may exhibit, or analogy supply; but it is true likewise that these ideas are always incomplete, and that at least till we have compared them with realities, we do not know them to be just. As we see more, we become possessed of more certainties, and consequently gain more principles of reasoning, and found a wider basis of analogy" (p. 40). To ensure the success of this great educational function, Johnson carefully researched Scottish history before the trip and afterward preserved his impressions in a notebook. Howell had regarded such practices as essential tools in acquiring knowledge abroad. Above all, the *Instructions for Forreine Travell* stressed a study of foreign manners to clarify the ultimate vanity of human actions and accomplishments around the globe. Johnson took this lesson to heart because his travel book isolates Highland manners for special analysis and inculcates much the same theme.

Both *Rasselas* and the *Journey* exemplify the rules of Renaissance travel in settings far removed from the normal Continental destination of grand tourists. Nevertheless, Johnson favored the moral preoccupations of seventeenth-century tourism and retained the traditional humanist focus on mankind in his works. His tale and travel book share a distinct ethical concern for elucidating the past and present state of man and society. In Scotland he generally neglected the conventional travel book topics of natural history and antiquities to concentrate on the manners and history of the people. Contemporary readers of the *Journey* were quick to recognize its unusual moral emphasis because they were accustomed to finding miscellaneous observations on all the arts and sciences in travel reports. Johnson surprised the public with a uniquely integrated study. His early biographers rightly considered his predominant interest in cultural matters the greatest strength of his description. Perhaps the shrewdest appraisal at the time was Ralph Griffiths's review in the *Scots Magazine*. Griffiths's insight into the relationship that exists between Johnson's travel book and moral writings might well be remembered by modern critics of the *Journey:* "the learned English Rambler seems rather to confine his views to the naked truth,—to moralize on the occurrences of his journey, and to illustrate the characters and situation of the people whom he visited, by the sagacity of remark, and the profundity of reflection."[8] The statement sums up the intellectual procedure and moral perspective giving form and meaning not only to the *Journey* but also to *Rasselas*.

At the heart of Johnson's achievement in travel literature was precisely his ability to enrich his survey with a profundity of moral reflection typical of the *Ramblers* and *Rasselas*. More than any other excellence of the work, the Rambler's skill at moral analysis set his description apart from the common run of travel books in artistic quality and intellectual value. He was a moralist on his Scottish rambles and devoted his great mind to a philosophical examination of the inhabitants. As reluctant as Rasselas to explore ruins, he too preferred to investigate human life and deepen his understanding of human nature and social systems. At Saint Andrews and elsewhere, the sight of a "gloomy mansion" and other relics of cultural decay interested him less than the present condition of life: "The distance of a calamity from the present time seems to preclude the mind from contact or sympathy" (p. 9). But the unavoidable spectacle of ancient ruins gradually became for him, as it had for Rasselas, an indispensable part of his instruction in man's changing intellectual history and the degeneration of learning. Ruins made important contributions to his overriding thematic concern with a ruined people, caught between a Renaissance heritage and a brave new world of modern progress instigated by Whig reforms. This was the subject that passionately engaged Johnson's mind in moral reflection on the trip. His travel book chronicles a cumulative *memento mori* of a culture's demise and a people's degradation with much of the artistic and moral force of *Rasselas*. No doubt, the moral patterns and mode of inquiry in Rasselas's grand tour reappeared in the *Journey* to produce a unified exposé of human hopes and fears without equal in Georgian travel literature.

In the case of the *Journey*, however, Johnson fixed upon his central theme, not from any philosophical preconceptions about human misery, but from the evidence of the desolate environment before him. The travel book is obviously not a moral tale but an authentic report of an eye-opening excursion that allowed him to test his moral convictions and theory of travel in Scotland. Its elegant execution bears comparison with his previous moral writings, but its geographical information was the subject matter of travel literature. Johnson was, in fact, remarkably self-conscious about the conventions of travel books and the rules of geographical research in his description. As he studied the Highlanders, he also analyzed the proper methods of travel promoted in his essays and practiced in his age. His work not only records the substance of his discoveries but also discusses the mode of his explorations in the area. This pervasive interest in the correct procedures of investigation was unusual for Georgian narratives but reflected the analytical mind of a moralist conducting his first major experiment in travel. Perhaps its closest parallel in eighteenth-century literature is Sterne's mocking preoccupation with tourist techniques throughout *A Sentimental Journey through France and Italy*. But Johnson treated these techniques seriously and attempted to synthesize old and new standards of geographical inquiry during his tour. Anyone curious about the traditions of Renaissance and Georgian travel can look to the *Journey* for a concise embodiment of both.

His travel book combines the humanistic studies of early grand touring and the scientific principles of contemporary exploration. Johnson followed the prescriptions of Howell's *Instructions for Forreine Travell* in emphasizing foreign manners and examining the moral and sociological significance of cultural data for the benefit of the public at home. But he also supported the aims of the new science in travel and showed a modern care for thoroughness and precision often missing in Renaissance tourism. He tried to avoid the untested prejudices and blind patriotism of seventeenth-century tourists by turning his journey into a fact-finding mission to grasp the true character of the Highlanders. As a consequence he revised his erroneous preconceptions of Scotland as a pastoral Arcadia and earned the right to praise England only after pondering the realities of Highland poverty. Where early grand tourists tended to concentrate on aristocratic sights confirming their prejudices, Johnson attended to particulars in domestic scenes correcting his parochial notions. He rejected the superficial coverage of courts and universities so typical of Renaissance narratives and dedicated himself to an intensive review of common life in the Hebrides: "The great mass of nations is neither rich nor gay: they whose aggregate constitutes the people, are found in the streets and the villages, in the shops and farms; and from them collectively considered must the measure of general prosperity be taken" (p. 22). So rigorous were Johnson's standards of scientific inquiry that he worried about the accuracy of his findings on the tour and even after the publication of his travel book. However unwarranted his fears, he would nevertheless tell Boswell later that the *Journey* dealt more with notions than with facts. The principal difference between Johnson and Renaissance tourists was that the Highland expedition was a true empirical education, during which subjective assumptions gave way to objective evidence abroad.

If a humanist of the old school, Johnson was scrupulous about observing the newer professional norms of geographical study on the trip. In the *Journey* he candidly admits that he is a neophyte traveler, intrigued as much by the empirical learning process as by the lessons learned in the Highlands. The first chapter commences his study of Scotland and the techniques employed to survey it. He notes the need for a companion to verify observations, ignores Edinburgh to gather new information on Inch Keith, and launches into a comparative analysis of Scottish and English islands to better convey the backward economic state of north Britain. At Saint Andrews he introduces his theme of social decay in religion, learning, and commerce. Here the evidence of a desecrated cathedral, a declining college, and urban blight gives rise to his earliest remarks on the ruins of time. His melancholy theme is further validated by the abbey ruins of Aberbrothick, where visitors "may from some parts yet standing conjecture its general form, and perhaps by comparing it with other buildings of the same kind and the same age, attain an idea very near to truth" (p. 11). This passage epitomizes the mode of inductive and comparative inquiry pursued during the tour. His mind worked from facts to produce conjectural hypotheses, and by comparing initial impressions with later findings, arrived at tentative truths about the Highlanders. What could be done with abbey ruins was accomplished throughout the *Journey*.

In subsequent chapters Johnson subjects his theme and investigative procedures to careful scrutiny. His exploration of the northeast coast of Scotland demonstrates both the universal devastation of the countryside and the importance of scientific observation. There is harsh criticism of careless Renaissance geographers: "The first race of scholars, in the fifteenth century, and some time after, were, for the most part, learning to speak, rather than to think, and were therefore more studious of elegance than of truth" (p. 15). In attacking the unenlightened geographers of the past, he was defining his own role as a modern scientific traveler following and examining the rules of accurate empirical research. What seems to be an overly detailed study of window frames at Bamff was integral to his professed reliance on the most minute data to form a valid portrait of the people. True conclusions in geography were to be reached only by thorough investigation of all the facts that revealed the daily pleasures and pains, hopes and fears, of the entire populace: "The true state of every nation is the state of common life" (p. 22). His apology for the "diminutive observations" at Bamff was really a declaration of his scientific approach to touring that placed severe restrictions on his reporting thereafter. He refuses to discuss Fort George at length for lack of precise information and frequently warns readers about the conjectural nature of his comments. At Lough Ness, for example, he isolates three major causes of inaccurate description—hearsay evidence, superficial study, and the exaggerations of the falsifying imagination—before noting his own hypothetical considerations. He attempts to explain by a characteristic process of induction and analogy the admittedly unproven notion that Lough Ness never freezes. But his deliberations end with an honest confession of guessing and an appeal to higher authority: let the natural philosophers of Scotland decide this moot question. The skeptical tendency of his inquiries mirrored the most advanced methods of geographical study in eighteenth-century travel.

The first third of the *Journey* clarifies his allegiance to enlightened principles of empirical investigation in preparation for his arrival at the Hebrides. He purposely advertises his credentials as a scientific traveler before undertaking his systematic survey of the real *terra incognita* of the trip. Before entering Sky, he paused at Anoch to discuss the prime educational value of travel that motivated his expedition and the wanderlust of his age. In his view any journey amplified the mind with new ideas for comparison with untested notions and stimulated the inductive powers of reason with factual information for developing general theories about phenomena. His defense of travel was prophetic of his own intellectual procedure during the ensuing examination of the isles. At Sky he refined his research techniques by enumerating the difficulties that hampered an accurate evaluation of the Highlanders. Their recent cultural upheaval prevented him from adequately gauging past traditions and confidently predicting future economic trends in the region. The most reliable evidence of ancient manners, extant ceremonies and well-preserved buildings, was far too scanty in the Hebrides. Uncertain oral tradition was a poor substitute for the concrete proof that Johnson desired. The natives often guessed and sometimes lied about their traditions; what they honestly remembered, they inevitably embellished. His review of the problems plaguing his study left him noticeably more cautious about accepting hearsay information and all the more determined to sift fact from fancy on the rest of the tour.

A conscientious regard for accurate research continues to the end of the *Journey*. Wherever his findings are inexact or incomplete, he honestly points out the deficiencies and usually mentions remedies for his faulty reporting. Tourists should carry measuring instruments, keep their journal entries up-to-date, and devote sufficient time to exploring sites in detail. The occasional flaws in his inquiries suggested useful solutions for succeeding travelers to practice. His demand for the utmost precision in description left him unduly sensitive to his few failures in investigation. For he closes his narrative with a self-effacing admission of his limitations as a tourist: "Novelty and ignorance must always be reciprocal, and I cannot but be conscious that my thoughts on national manners, are the thoughts of one who has seen but little" (p. 164). Yet, his nagging sense of being an apprentice traveler was largely responsible for his analysis of efficient tourist techniques that made the *Journey* a masterful case history of cultural revolution.

To ensure a comprehensive coverage of the Hebrides, Johnson made use of the exhaustive topics of inquiry recommended by the Royal Society. The *Philosophical Transactions* had long ago publicized an encyclopedic checklist of subjects embracing all "supraterraneous, terrestrial, and subterraneous" phenomena to encourage a full-scale examination of foreign countries.[9] Like many other eighteenth-century travelers, Johnson followed the Royal Society's directives and pursued his inductive survey with this checklist in mind to better assist the Baconian advancement of the sciences. The prescribed topics and subtopics of inquiry in geography, natural history, and anthropology organize his descriptions of the Highlands, Raasay, the Hebrides, and Coll. His lengthy account of the Hebrides, for example, ranges through their size and situation and their diverse flora and fauna before proceeding to the inhabitants. The Hebrideans, in turn, are intensively analyzed according to the categories of stature, temperament, government, religion, traditions, customs,

and literature. Johnson's inductive investigation of the Scottish mainland precedes his systematic treatment of the isles. The sight of
fallen cathedrals near Edinburgh leads to general conjectures about
a fallen culture at Elgin and a disarming recognition of life's universal pain in the Highlands. Later chapters contain his summary
findings on the Hebrides and his final views on the fate of a once
proud people conquered by modernity. Throughout the *Journey*,
current scientific conventions in travel dictated the direction and organization of his studies.

Guided by authorized rules for effective research, Johnson
brought his full powers of observation and reflection to bear upon
his Highland experience. His travel book offers readers an exceptional opportunity to follow the operations of his mind in digesting
information derived directly from the environment before him. His
morality exhorted all men to study life at first hand, and the *Journey*
is a striking testimony to his own expert skill in empirical observation. He prided himself on needing no assistance from other writings
to compose his narrative: "it was his wish and endeavour not to
make a single quotation."[10] While not strictly true, his boasted independence from literary influences was far greater in this book than
in most of his prose and poetry. He relied on the evidence of his
senses for his appraisal of Highlands manners and was relatively
unrestricted by the demands of sources shaping moral literature like
Rasselas. His travel book, letters, and conversations in Boswell's *Tour
to the Hebrides* show an inexhaustible curiosity about every aspect
of the Scottish culture. Little escaped his notice despite the dangers
and difficulties of exploration. He crawled through caves and castles,
climbed flooded glens and treacherous ocean cliffs, looked into libraries and forts, and tasted new food and drink. For all his former
mockery· of Scottish eating habits, he began to enjoy a steady diet
of oatmeal cakes and other favorite native dishes. He even inter-
rupted his total fast from liquor to test the virtues of Scotch whiskey
and, while preferring it to English brandy, refused to investigate
its manufacture on moral grounds: "nor do I wish to improve the art

of making poison pleasant" (p. 56). He repeatedly questioned his hosts about native superstitions and Erse literature and lamented the "laxity of Highland conversation" regarding oral tradition and ancient poetry. When disagreements arose over the construction of a ruined fortress, he returned to the site for a closer look to settle the dispute. At all times he searched for irrefutable facts to end conjecture and dispel error.

His preoccupation with factual evidence caused his trip to be a valuable learning experience. Perhaps the most significant development on the tour was the radical reduction of his lifelong prejudices against the Scots. Although Boswell noted a change in his friend's attitude toward Scotland, critics of the *Journey* have ever since tended to assume a pronounced insularity in his treatment of the nation. However, Johnson's prejudices did perceptibly diminish as his expedition approached the Hebrides. He distinguished between Highlanders and Lowlanders and grew to respect the former even if he continued to attack the latter for their partisan defense of *Ossian*. Not only were his romantic notions of the Hebrides completely changed, but also his sympathy for Highland customs increased to a marked degree. He had expected to see a pastoral wilderness of savage tribes needing the blessings of English civilization. Indeed, only a few years before the tour when contributing Vinerian Law lectures to Robert Chambers, he expressed contempt for Scotland's political independence and lauded the benefits of the British Union with all the smugness of an English Whig: "By this union which had been long wished and often projected, Scotland gained an immediate admission to that commerce which had been established over the world by English industry and English power, and became entitled to the benefits of trade in its advanced state, without partaking the dangers or suffering the losses of the first adventurers. They have since gained likewise an increase of liberty, and a deliverance from the oppression of old feudal establishments and of incommodiousness and vexatious tenures. The advantage to England is, that the whole island is united in one interest, . . . that intestine ravages are now at an end, and that no enemy of our king can now weaken or embarrass him by inciting one part of his subjects against the other."[11]

However, the opportunity of exploring Scotland on his own proved to be an illuminating education in qualifying such assumptions and appreciating, without exaggerating, the virtues of clan society. The *Journey* vividly shows him gradually modifying his endorsement of English reforms once the actual examination of the people begins at Lough Ness. There he first confronts the primitive inhabitants and enjoys the hospitality of a Highland lady. His report of her humble life-style demonstrates a care for ordering details around an understood hierarchy of human necessities. He describes the sturdy construction of her hut, then her manner of subsistence, and finally her devout religious principles: "She is religious, and though the kirk is four miles off, probably eight English miles, she goes thither every Sunday" (p. 33). His initial glimpse of a self-sufficient and pious way of life pleased him greatly. Further exposure to the inhabitants reinforced his favorable impression of their customs. Sharing a meal with the community of Glensheals had the quality of a culture shock as this civilized Londoner faced barbarian Highlanders with both fear and curiosity: "The villagers gathered about us in considerable numbers, I believe without any evil intention, but with a very savage wildness of aspect and manner. . . . Yet I have been since told, that the people are not indigent; and when we mentioned them afterwards as needy and pitiable, a Highland lady let us know, that we might spare our commiseration; for the dame whose milk we drank had probably more than a dozen milk-cows" (p. 42). Johnson's empirical inquiries continued to correct his misconceptions in the remainder of the tour. His adventures displayed a readiness to explore the unknown in comprehensive detail for factual proof of his later generalizations about the country. Through successive encounters with the Highlanders, he learned to revise his previous feelings about the culture: pity and condescension evolved into a manifest admiration for pastoral simplicity.

His long sojourn in the Hebrides completed the transformation of his outlook on the people. In the isles he could relive the ancient life-style and relish his nostalgic journey into a feudal past made vividly immediate by his generous hosts. The Laird of Raasay treated his visitors to an elaborate ball in the old Highland fashion. Toasts were pronounced, a regal dinner was served, and music and dancing enlivened the evening. The feast so overwhelmed Johnson that he had to pause from conversation and soothe his excited nerves by reading in the midst of the noisy entertainment: "Such a seat of hospitality, amidst the winds and waters, fills the imagination with a delightful contrariety of images" (p. 66). The pleasures of Highland travel intensified for him in later chapters of the *Journey*. He would salute the Jacobite patriot, Flora Macdonald, and be caressed by other charming hostesses in the Hebrides. At Kingsburgh he slept in Bonnie Prince Charlie's bed but "had no ambitious thoughts in it."[12] The Laird of Macleod would offer him an isle and a new title, "*Island Isay*, your health!," and captivate his imagination with dreams of ruling clans. By the end of the tour, Johnson's mind was filled with bittersweet memories of a rich and passing heritage. He would eventually don the headdress of a chieftan to dramatize his loyalty to ancient traditions: "His age, his size, and his bushy grey wig with this covering on it, presented the image of a venerable *sennachie*; and, however unfavourable to the Lowland Scots, he seemed much pleased to assume the appearance of an ancient Caledonian."[13] Whatever prejudices that Johnson had formerly cherished were to soften considerably by the time that he returned home.

The cumulative effect of his experiences abroad was a heightened veneration for Highland society. The tour had taught him that Arcadia had deserted the Hebrides but that the remaining ceremonies of the past deserved preservation in the present. His empirical survey had converted his early faith in social reforms into troubling doubts about the impact of commercial innovations upon an admirable way of life. The *Journey* registers the reversal in his sentiments; confidence succeeds to worry over the future welfare of the Highlands. As a scientist and humanist in his habits of travel, Johnson strove to study foreign manners objectively and learned to feel a compassionate empathy with the plight of the oppressed nation. A moralist who was a parochial city dweller at the start of the trip ended a cosmopolitan tourist fully receptive to unusual customs. His travel book stands beside the best of Georgian travel literature for its perceptive and appreciative observations. His integrated moral vision of the culture and his scientific standards of inquiry inspired a great work of philosophic art and travel illustrating personal growth and sociological discovery.

Johnson depended upon direct observation to substantiate his findings. But his reading in previous travel literature on Scotland affected his format and treatment of the Highlands in the *Journey*. Although his friends heard him assert his freedom from sources, he actually consulted numerous descriptions before publishing his own. He knew that such preparation was a prerequisite for the most effective and instructive touring: "So it is in travelling; a man must carry knowledge with him, if he would bring home knowledge."[14] He was not the first to report on the progressive disruption of the culture in the eighteenth century. The travel books of Martin Martin, William Sacheverell, and Thomas Pennant all told the same sad story of fading feudal traditions, albeit without the same unified perspective that gives the *Journey* a controlling theme. To his credit Johnson tried to avoid describing places and phenomena authoritatively covered by other authors and concentrated on unfamiliar sights. The better-known territory of the Scottish mainland takes up only a third of the narrative while the less accessible Hebrides receive the greatest attention: "To write of the cities of our own island with the solemnity of geographical description, as if we had been cast upon a newly discovered coast, has the appearance of very frivolous ostentation" (p. 13). Similarly, he made Highland manners his primary object of remark because his major sources and rival geographers, Martin and Pennant, had stressed natural history and romantic scenery. His familiarity with previous accounts had deepened his understanding of the region and indicated a neglected area of human interest worthy of the public's attention.

To write his travel book, Johnson depended upon a now missing "book of remarks" compiled during the tour, his letters to Mrs. Thrale, and his considerable research in the geography of Scotland. The lost notebook probably contained the kind of cryptic commentary found in his Welsh and French diaries and served to jog his memories of the trip. The series of letters, copied over by Mrs. Thrale for his later consultation, condensed much of the raw material of the *Journey* in a more vivid and spontaneous style. Using both of these primary sources, he deleted references to the Highland uprising to protect his Jacobite hosts and added moral reflections, technical information, and a travel book format influenced by previous accounts of Scotland. Besides consulting Martin's *Description* and Pennant's *Tour in Scotland* during the trip, he read the descriptions of Hector Boece, John Leslie, William Sacheverell, Kenneth Macaulay, and John Campbell. Beyond these seven narratives, there were a few histories of northern Britain that contributed to his general knowledge of the area.[15] However, the seven geographical accounts comprised his major secondary sources and offer a useful historical perspective for gauging Johnson's achievement in travel literature.

His study of these works did more than whet his curiosity and increase his knowledge about Scotland. They also introduced him to a history of Highland travel, spanning two centuries, that helped to determine his outlook and interests in the *Journey*. The political importance and scenic beauty of Scotland resulted in an unprecedented outpouring of travel literature on the country in the eighteenth century. The records in the British Museum and Advocates Library in Edinburgh list more than one hundred accounts of northern Britain published in the period. No comparable number of travel books appeared earlier; only a few descriptions, short and limited in scope, existed before 1700. The scarcity of geographical reports suggests the centuries of widespread ignorance about the

nation's topography and culture. As late as the Restoration, some
Europeans still considered Scotland a half-mythical island separated
from the English mainland.[16] For lack of dependable maps, the Renaissance historians Hector Boece and John Leslie had to substitute
written descriptions in their prefaces. Moreover, what they reported
was a romantic fable of primitive virtues and supernatural wonders.
Their tall tales about noble Highland savages and geographical marvels did, however, set a precedent for the primitivism permeating
later travel books. Even the *Journey* recounts an abortive search for
"savage virtues and barbarous grandeur" that no longer existed in
1773.

In his *Scotorum Historiae* (1527) Boece left posterity one of the
oldest and falsest surveys of Scotland. Leslie's account in *De Origine
Moribus et Rebus Gestis Scotorum* (1578) plagiarized the earlier
description and inserted a few more falsehoods for Johnson to
criticize. Their superstitions and patent errors violated his exacting
standards of scientific inquiry: "The contemporaries of Boethius
thought it sufficient to know what the ancients had delivered. The
examination of tenets and of facts was reserved for another generation" (p. 15). Notwithstanding his disapproval of their pre-Baconian
outlook on learning, he transformed their contrast between ancient
and modern manners into the major thesis of his travel book. Their
conception of a hardy race of innocent barbarians endangered by
the corruptions of English civilization foreshadowed his own vision
of a pastoral nation threatened by economic reforms. He sought the
golden world of Boece's romantic imagination: "This perfection of
life cumes to thaim onlie throw thair simplicitie; and followis, be
the samin, the futsteppis of Crist."[17] But he saw instead a displaced
culture, half savage and half civilized, that Boece and Leslie had
fearfully predicted: "There was perhaps never any change of national manners so quick, so great, and so general, as that which has
operated in the Highlands, by the last conquest, and the subsequent
laws" (p. 57).

Except for Donald Monro's cursory catalog of islands in 1549, no trustworthy description of the Hebrides appeared until Martin's *Description of the Western Islands of Scotland* in 1703. Occasionally Martin could be as credulous and primitivistic as Boece and Leslie, but his account followed the current trends of scientific travel that endeared the book to Johnson all the more. The work remains today the authoritative record of the isles before the cultural revolution occurred in the eighteenth century. More than any other source, this description filled Johnson's mind with romantic ideas about the Highlands and romantic dreams of one day going there. His father had given him the book in his youth, and ever after he was curious to see this bleak and lonely outpost of Great Britain. Martin combined romance with a scientific method, codified topics of inquiry, and simple style advocated by the Royal Society. He criticized Donald Monro's unenlightened era and emphasized the modern study of natural history: "Natural experimental philosophy has been much improved since his days; and therefore descriptions of countries, without the natural history of them, are now justly reckoned to be defective."[18] Johnson's early exposure to the work originally inspired his tour and profoundly affected his format and analysis of primitive manners, superstitions, and bardic poetry in the *Journey*.

The very similarity in the titles of the two travel books underscores their close relationship. The *Journey* possesses the same narrative blend of sequential description and summary discourses found in the *Description*. Martin's "Account of the Second Sight" directly anticipates Johnson's own presentation of supernatural occurrences, arguments, and objections to this marvelous phenomenon. Both travelers shared a scientific approach to investigation although Johnson was noticeably more rigorous in his pursuit of truth. Yet, despite common procedures of exploration, their accounts significantly differ in literary and intellectual quality. Johnson aspired to an elegance of style, a wealth of moral reflections, and a complete accuracy of observation missing in Martin's narrative. If anything, Johnson was far more skeptical about native superstitions and bardic poetry.

Unlike his predecessor, he witheld belief in second sight and rejected *Ossian*. He would have liked to witness the bards and Gaelic poetry reported by Martin but found no convincing evidence to support James Macpherson's claims in *The Poems of Ossian* that an ancient epic poem existed in manuscript. Having promoted an Erse translation of the Bible, he was deeply interested in preserving any records of a language that would help to clarify the linguistic history of Great Britain. However, he challenged Macpherson's bogus translation of a poem supposedly written in an illiterate age and correctly surmised that *Ossian* was only a new and poor elaboration of some old Highland tales.

Macpherson's forgeries angered him into a controversy raging between Scottish and Irish antiquaries over the national origins of the Celtic myths worked over in *Ossian*. The Irish had Johnson on their side and considered his refutation of Macpherson further evidence that Ireland was the birthplace of Celtic literature and legends. His Irish friend, Thomas Campbell, gladly cited his authority to debunk Scottish pretensions and Macpherson's assertions: "there not only were no such manuscripts in existence, but it was impossible there should be any such."[19] Doubtless, Johnson was right in denying the existence of *Ossian* manuscripts but wrong in minimizing the vitality of an oral tradition of Scottish poetry that inspired the counterfeit epic. Boswell heard him declare that "except a few passages, there is nothing truly ancient but the names and some vague traditions. Mr. Macqueen alleged that Homer was made up of detached fragments. Mr. Johnson denied it; said that it had been one work originally; and that you could not put one book of the *Iliad* out of its place; and he believed the same might be said of the *Odyssey*."[20] Johnson had too little faith in the power of oral tradition or the possibility of an oral formulaic theory of poetry that was responsible for the development of a rich literary heritage in Scotland. Some Gaelic poems and songs have survived orally from the sixteenth century, and the Gaelic original of *Ossian* appeared in

1807 without achieving the popularity of Macpherson's apocryphal version.

What most fascinated Johnson about Martin's *Description* was not its detailed report of natural history but its relatively short study of bardic traditions and ancient manners. Its recital of old Highland customs had prepared him to see a feudal society that had largely disappeared by 1773. Hence, he wished that Martin had chronicled more of the ancient culture when it still flourished in an uncorrupted state: "He might therefore have displayed a series of subordination and a form of government, which in more luminous and improved regions, have been long forgotten, and have delighted his readers with many uncouth customs that are now disused, and wild opinions that prevail no longer. . . . What he has neglected cannot now be performed" (p. 65). Aware of Martin's irretrievable omissions, he could at least stress the modern manners of the people without duplicating stale information for public consumption. Martin had actually cared little about preserving the memory of the Highland past and even supported economic reforms for turning the Hebrides into a trading community. Johnson, by contrast, wanted to document the last vestiges of a bygone culture and worried about modern progress in the isles. Where Martin wrote unemotionally about Iona, "anciently a seminary for learning famous for the severe sanctity of Columbus," Johnson saw the island as a culminating symbol of cultural ruin in the *Journey*. While the *Description* was a key influence upon his travel book, Johnson's moral focus on manners, his skeptical attitude, and somber conclusions were all his own.

Martin's account would be one of many Highland descriptions to appear in the eighteenth century. Tourists were drawn to the area by improved roads, the legislative union of England and Scotland in 1707, the Highland uprisings of 1715 and 1745, and the growing fame of the country's romantic scenery. Travelers brought a variety of viewpoints to their descriptions. Some indulged in political propaganda, economic schemes, or sociological inventories of national resources. Others chose to concentrate on antiquarian research, scientific investigation, or nature study. But one theme was fairly constant in these diverse documents, namely, the rapid changes transforming the Highland economy and society. Even before Scotland became a popular tourist attraction, Daniel Defoe had isolated the recurring concern of travel books throughout the century: "This alteration affords abundance of useful observations, and is a subject which none have yet meddled with, so we believe it will not be less acceptable for its novelty."[21] What began as a novel subject soon developed into a conventional topic for intensive investigation.

Just a year or so before Martin's *Description* was published, there appeared two accounts already preoccupied with the subject of cultural alteration. Thomas Morer's *Short Account of Scotland* (1702) endorsed economic innovations, whereas William Sacheverell's *Account of the Isle of Man* (1701) mourned the loss of the old Highland heritage. Johnson read the latter book long before his tour took place and sympathized with its nostalgic treatment of the Hebrides. His chapter on Iona virtually amplifies the following description of Sacheverell's angry survey of the island: "The vexation and disappointment I found was such, that I quitted the Abbey with indignation, to see so many noble monuments of virtue and piety of these great and holy men buried in their own ruins, and so celebrated a seminary of learning and religion sacrificed to zeal, avarice, and ignorance."[22] Not all the travel books at Johnson's disposal showed Sacheverell's abhorrence of cultural decay. An intelligent tourist like Thomas Pennant would later empathize with the Highland past as nostalgically as Sacheverell and as enthusiastically as Boece and Leslie. However, Johnson's other sources sided with the moderns in their scientific attitude toward exploration and in their support of social progress in the Hebrides. Martin Martin, Kenneth Macaulay, and John Campbell were all, according to Johnson's terminology, decidedly "Whig" topographers interested in the social reconstruction of the nation. Both groups are represented in

the *Journey*. The narrative reflects the division of opinion in its
ambivalent considerations of Scotland's future welfare.

Johnson judged Kenneth Macaulay's *History of St. Kilda* (1764)
"a very pretty piece of topography" but had serious reservations
about some of its material. Its uncritical report of supernatural wonders made Johnson laugh, and its advocacy of Whig reforms was
not completely consonant with Johnson's more conservative views.
The description is a contradictory mixture of primitivism and reform, superstition and science, and veneration for "these our domestic Indians" qualified by criticism of the same lairds and clans.
Johnson would have appreciated Macaulay's mixed feelings since
he himself vacillated between a Tory sympathy for the agrarian
values of clan society and a moderate Whig support of necessary
economic improvements in the Highlands. He probably found in
John Campbell's *Political Survey of Britain* (1774) a helpful summary of the required economic remedies. This encyclopedic review
of natural resources recommended programs reluctantly advertised
in the *Journey:* the growth of trade and industry, the introduction
of local courts and schools, and the suppression of emigration. Johnson disavowed Campbell's extreme solutions but shared his well-
meaning desire to alleviate the poverty of the Hebrides. For Campbell had already hoped for a more prosperous future in places like
Iona, "that even in its present miserable State it remains an indu-
bitable Monument of the former flourishing Condition of the Isles,
and . . . that the People who formerly inhabited them, were not
in a low, wretched, barbarous State, without Commerce or
Communication."[23]

Sensitive to the need for change but sympathetic to clan traditions, Johnson sought a compromise solution that would permit
the survival of the old life-style upon a more stable economic base
of modern commerce. Adumbrations of his conservative position on
reform had recently appeared in Thomas Pennant's *Tour in Scotland*
(1771) and its continuation, *A Tour in Scotland and Voyage to the*

Hebrides (1774, 1776). These two works, next to Martin's *Descrip-tion*, probably have the greatest bearing on the studies in the *Journey*. Johnson went so far as to rate Pennant "the best traveller I ever read" for having observed "more things than any one else does."[24] Perhaps his praise of Pennant, uttered during a heated argument with Bishop Percy, was merely a generous concession to a rival geog-rapher, renowned as a zoologist and antiquarian in his time. There is indeed a greater variety of inquiry in natural history, Scottish lore, and romantic scenery in Pennant's accounts than Johnson attempted on his tour. Yet, Pennant's description lacks the thematic unity and moral reflections that make the *Journey* a superior travel book. His thick volumes present one of the first complete surveys of Scotland without devoting too much attention to Highland manners. There-fore, Johnson could stress his favorite moral study of human life in his narrative and avoid needless repetition. The publication of Pen-nant's continuation dealing with the Hebrides in the same period might have proved embarrassing to Johnson. Fortunately, critics tended to consider the *Journey* an elegant supplement to Pennant's works with a different moral emphasis. In contrast to Johnson, Bos-well justifiably criticized Pennant for producing a "heap of frittered fragments" in no way comparable to his friend's well-told story of their tour.

What Pennant lost in superficial comprehensiveness, Johnson gained in style, depth of moral analysis, and thematic focus that raised the *Journey* above an artless journal. Political allegiances as well as literary abilities separated the two travelers. Pennant's attack on the clans and lairds in his *Tour in Scotland* had forced Johnson to concede that "He's a *Whig*, Sir, a *sad dog*."[25] However, Pennant's hostility to Highland traditions had considerably mitigated in his *Tour of Scotland and Voyage to the Hebrides*, published at Chester in 1774. There was now a more balanced appreciation of ancient customs and modern progress, not far removed from Johnson's own outlook: "The noxious part of the feudal reign is now abolished; the delegated rod of power is now no more. But let not the good part be lost with the bad: the tender relation that *patriarchal* government experiences should still be retained: and that mutual inclination to beneficence preserved. The chieftan should not lose with the power of doing harm, the disposition of doing good."[26] This new moderation in proposing reforms would surely have appealed to Johnson. The *Journey*, in fact, extols Pennant's accurate measurements, if not his belief in *Ossian*, and offers a comparable interpretation of the Highland problem. Few travel books before Pennant's descriptions made more of the ravages of modern commercialism and Highland poverty or more nearly approximated Johnson's troubled vision of cultural decay. The moralist replaced Pennant's intermittent Whig sympathies with an unwavering compassion and concern for the people and published a more integrated travel book.

Johnson's research in the travel literature of Scotland had prepared him well for the writing of the *Journey*. All seven sources had acquainted him with a representative sampling of changing historical attitudes toward the Highlanders for a new formulation in his travel book. He adopted Martin's scientific format and, with an unprecedented artistry, resumed the study of cultural upheaval initiated by Boece and Leslie and continued by Sacheverell, Macaulay, and Pennant. Most eighteenth-century descriptions promoted the social reforms cataloged in Campbell's treatise and carefully evaluated by Johnson. Martin's account was most responsible for suggesting the tour and the topics of inquiry, while Pennant's survey came closest to expressing the ambivalent sociological assessment in the *Journey*. Because his sources failed to concentrate on Highland manners, Johnson chose to execute an original and unified analysis of this complex subject. As travel literature, the *Journey* surpasses them all in literary merit and intellectual quality. His contemporaries judged the work to be an integral part of his moral writings, and posterity has honored their verdict. Its only real rival of enduring literary interest is its companion piece, Boswell's *Tour to the Hebrides* (1785), which records the manners of a moralist intent on reviewing the manners of a nation. Boswell was writing biography,

not topographical description. Where he looks inward into the mind
of his subject, Johnson looks outward to appraise the intellectual
history of a people.

In the history of Highland travel, the *Journey* stands midway between earlier scientific and political studies of the region and later
romantic and antiquarian surveys of its scenery and folklore. The
travel literature of the century documents a gradual shift in the
tastes and interests of tourists in Scotland. Former prejudices against
a primitive race and barren terrain in need of civilizing reforms
slowly yielded to a growing enthusiasm for wild people and places
uncontaminated by civilization. If Daniel Defoe felt disgust before
Highland mountains in 1726, Thomas Gray experienced religious
ecstasy there in 1765: "the Lowlands are worth seeing once, but
the mountains are ecstatic, and ought to be visited in pilgrimage
once a year. None but those monstrous creatures of God know how
to join so much beauty with so much horror."[27] So many tourists
would repeat this romantic pilgrimage that by the end of the century
John Stoddart added picturesque travelers to his list of scientists and
men of learning who had originally explored the area. While Stoddart's categories of tourists in his *Remarks on Local Scenery and
Manners in Scotland* (1801) are not all-inclusive, they do suggest
the changing trends of travel evident in the *Journey*.

Johnson certainly qualifies as one of Stoddart's men of learning,
who employed older scientific research techniques and exhibited
newer romantic tastes for the Highland heritage. Empirical investigation validated his astute moral analysis of a romantic realm made
famous in Scott's novels and Burns's poetry. Johnson shared with
later tourists a nostalgia for a vanished medieval civilization in the
presence of ruined fortresses that verified the "fictions of Gothic
romance." His imagination even transported the feudal past into
the present: "These castles afford another evidence that the fictions
of romantick chivalry had for their basis the real manners of the
feudal times, when every lord of a seignory lived in his hold lawless
and unaccountable, with all the licentiousness and insolence of un-

contested superiority and unprincipled power" (p. 155). The tour
had a time-tunnel effect upon his mind and allowed him to empathize with the ancient glories in the process of analyzing the
modern problems. An emotional escape into the remote history of
Scotland went hand in hand with a rational evaluation of the immediate environment. He could respond to sublime scenery as strongly
as any nature enthusiast but preferred an admixture of elegance and
sublimity on moral and psychological grounds. Sublime landscapes
implied sturdy virtues but also suggested poverty, chaos, and human helplessness: "An eye accustomed to flowery pastures and wav-
ing forests is astonished and repelled by this wide extent of hopeless sterility" (p. 39). Elegance connoted civilization, and Johnson
wanted to tame the Highland wilderness and improve the depressing
lot of the people by reforestation and agriculture. In his own life
and in the lives of others, he always championed the rational values
of civilization over the irrational depravities of an undisciplined
mind or an undeveloped society. The savagery and destitution pervading Highland scenery was an uncomfortable objective correla-
tive to the disturbed subjective landscape of his psyche and the
spirit of a nation. To replace chaos with stability was a supreme personal and moral imperative.

Nature study bore directly on morality, on the study of man
since the habitat molded and mirrored the character of the inhabitants. In fact, he tended to envision the country as a beggarly ado-
lescent, not yet arrived at the stage of prosperous maturity: "Sir . . .
your country consists of two things: stone and water. There is indeed a little earth above the stone in some places, but a very little;
and the stone is always appearing. It is like a man in rags; the naked
skin is always peeping out."[28] Despite the abundant evidence of his
fascination with wild scenery and manners, romantic tourists found
him wanting in proper aesthetic appreciation. William Gilpin, the
leader of picturesque travelers, considered him blind to the "great
and sublime in nature" and all those spectacular sights that later observers would reverently record and paint. However, picturesque

tourists favored a wholly different approach to nature and to travel. They stressed scenery and manipulated descriptions of landscapes to conform to an artistic ideal popularized by the paintings of Claude Lorrain and Salvator Rosa and by the nature poetry of Thomson and Dyer. They abstracted from the observed reality of nature to create sentimental pictures of melancholy lights and shades, powder puff clouds and sleepy hamlets, artificial vistas and purling streams. As Gilpin described the process, "floating, unconscious ideas become a kind of waking dream; and are often wrought by the fancy into more pleasing pictures than they in fact appear to be."[29] Ironically, Gilpin's criticism that Johnson's unappreciative eye tried to "bring every thing to its own model" more justly applied to his falsifying picturesque spectators.

However myopic, Johnson aimed to describe the scenes as he saw them. Obviously he was not a sentimentalist of sublime scenery nor a Wordsworthian devotee of primitive rustics, but he did examine wild nature and "barbarous manners" with a care for scientific accuracy and with a romantic feeling for Scotland's storied past. With the passing years, the picturesque tourist would replace the scientist, the political economist, and the moralist in the Highlands. Travel books would increasingly discard the codified format and geographical research of earlier descriptions to record rambling rhapsodies of personal feeling and charming prospects. The new concern of accounts like Stoddart's *Remarks*, John Bristed's *Pedestrian Tour through the Highlands* (1803), and Robert Forsyth's *Beauties of Scotland* (1805) was gathering verbal pictures of landscapes and documenting the psychology of feeling in an often consciously Wordsworthian vein.[30] None of them ever plumbed the ineffable mystery of Wordsworth's nature poetry or had the literary importance of the *Journey*. By the time that Robert Southey visited the region in 1819, picturesque tourism had already degenerated to a worn-out convention held up for ridicule in his *Journal of a Tour in Scotland*. The heady emotional thrills of romantic prospect hunting would eventually grow stale.

To Johnson the spectacle of romantic glens and ruins was a telling symbol of social impoverishment and human misery. He saw a country in cultural transition and composed a book indicative of a historical transition in travel literature between objective scientific reports and subjective romantic accounts of the primitive Highlands. The tensions in his treatment of past and present Scotland betrayed the cultural tensions of a changing society. His economic views hang fire between the gains and losses of introducing reforms and yield only tentative solutions, mingled with hope and fear, for the future: "The state of life, which has hitherto been purely pastoral, begins now to be a little variegated with commerce; but ... till one mode of life has fully prevailed over the other, no settled notion can be formed" (p. 89). The recent history of Scotland made a decisive appraisal of the situation almost impossible. The suppression of the Highland uprising of 1745 preceded the worst economic depression in the region in modern times. The English ministry pursued a policy of complete cultural assimilation to crush the clans forever and channel confiscated capital into improving roads, commerce, and agriculture. Harsh penal laws forbade the use of arms and Tartan dress and required loyalty oaths, immediate payments of mortgages, and forfeitures of rebel estates. To offset their loss of feudal authority, many lairds became oppressive landlords imposing high rents, short-term leases, and enclosures upon tenants to drive them away and build a lucrative sheep industry. Poverty and injustice increased as the population expanded and landholdings decreased.

When Johnson visited Scotland, the Highlanders desperately needed constructive reforms, Whig or otherwise, cried up by travelers since the beginning of the century. Understandably, most tourists supported a more diversified economy but often overlooked the trials and traditions of the people. There were many Britons who saw none of the golden age and good old days that Johnson associated with the colorful era of Stuart monarchy and clan community before the debacles of Sherriffmuir and Culloden. These were the Whig topographers who looked to Britain's future prosperity rather than Scotland's past glory and championed modern progress, trade, and industry. An anonymous anti-Stuart tract, *The Highlands of Scotland in 1750*, suggests the prevailing climate of opinion among the more extreme Whig propagandists. Its author launches into a bitter attack against the rebels and Catholic heritage of the Highlands before singing the praises of the British Union: "as it has freed the Scots from all . . . Tyranny as was often Exercised in Scotland; as it has given their Ecclesiastical Constitution as firm a Sanction as Humane Laws can give; as it has open'd a Trade with England, . . . as we have the Inestimable Blessing of a Protestant King and a British Parliament."[31] Johnson, however, was not quite so convinced about the benefits of British interference in Scotland.

The *Journey* does defend the monarchal and legislative union for spreading English civilization among the backward Highlanders. Johnson was a mercantilist concerned for the prosperity and integrity of Great Britain and the empire. Yet, humanitarian motives more than patriotic feelings accounted for his desire to unite the welfare of the Highlands with the commercial interests of England. Moral priorities in his economic theory dictated his appeal for some innovations in a substandard social system. In his view all societies evolved through successive stages of destitution, convenience, and luxury; but the middle state of convenience best served the ultimate human needs of virtue and religion (*Idler* 37). Thus, he reluctantly endorsed reforms for raising Scotland's depressed economy to this ideal middle state of civilized convenience, moderate wealth, and class mobility: "They are a Nation just rising from barbarity, long contented with necessaries, now somewhat studious of convenience, but not arrived at delicate discriminations."[32] Moral duty demanded the alleviation of poverty, the worst of human evils for inhibiting the intellectual and ethical development of individuals and producing the worst national misfortune, emigration. The terrible effects of emigration had haunted him as early as his *Life of Savage* and made any policy of Whig reform more palatable than the continual depletion of Britain's manpower: "The great business of insular policy is now to keep the people in their own country" (p. 131). In Sky alone almost four hundred inhabitants migrated in 1771, and possibly more than twenty thousand Highlanders drifted to America or industrial centers to the south between 1750 and 1800 even though the census records actually show a population growth of thirteen thousand Scots during the period.[33]

However, while aware of the need for economic changes, Johnson resisted radical measures for overturning clan traditions and valuable communal ties in a stable patriarchal society. There were equally important advantages to preserving a feudal culture that money and modern progress, with their antihumanistic and irreligious tendencies, could not buy. The old religious, social, and ethical values represented by the native life-style strongly appealed to Johnson's conservative temperament. Somehow the dilemma had to be reconciled by an economic program that would safeguard the Highland heritage while advancing national prosperity. One way of resolving the problem was to hope for the rise of more enlightened lairds like Donald Maclean of Coll, who retained his patriarchal authority and kept his clan at home by introducing commercial and agricultural improvements: "By such acquisitions as these, the Hebrides may in time rise above their annual distress" (p. 124). Throughout the tour Johnson's mind was disturbed by the perplexing issues revolving around the distressing state of a society that he had learned to admire. Because of the poverty and mass emigration, the whole matter finally boiled down to whether the Highlands could survive with enough of a population to move into the modern world with ancient traditions intact.

For Johnson the only hope, however faint, lay in a compromise solution engrafting the old onto the new through the efforts of responsible chieftans prepared to preserve and improve. After sadly documenting the plight of the Highlanders, the *Journey* ends on a slightly optimistic note with a description of a progressive school for the deaf and dumb that boded well for Scotland's future: "It was pleasing to see one of the most desperate of human calamities capable of so much help: whatever enlarges hope, will exalt courage; after having seen the deaf taught arithmetick, who would be afraid to cultivate the Hebrides?" (p. 164). History would frustrate that final hope. The young Laird of Coll drowned while the *Journey* was in preparation, and few enlightened lairds afterward appeared to follow his enterprising example. At the end of the century John Knox would report the failure of Whig reforms to remedy the national problems or assist in the survival of the ancient traditions: "With a quicker pace the feudal system vanished; property fluctuated; new laws and new customs stepped in, . . . and all this with such sudden and such violent convulsions, as may well account for the shaking of a fabric, which before seemed to defy time, and stood the wonder and delight of ages."[34] The tragic destiny of the Highlands fully justified Johnson's somber tone and dark presentiments.

Vindictive Scottish reviewers of the *Journey* missed the humanitarian sympathy and cosmopolitan objectivity of his survey. Instead they denounced his supposed prejudices, poor eyesight, elegant style, and fears of depopulation even though their own periodicals contained alarming notices of growing emigration. The *Weekly Magazine* carried at least six abusive critiques over a three-month period, and Donald M'Nicol's *Remarks on Dr. Samuel Johnson's Journey to the Hebrides* presented a scurrilous attack, longer than the travel book itself, indicting everything of value in the narrative. With an eye to sales and profits Johnson welcomed the notoriety given his work by the reviewers. The book was sufficiently popular to run through two editions amounting to four thousand copies in 1775 and at least twenty-three more authorized and pirated editions, including abridgements and foreign translations, by 1824.[35] During the bicentennial anniversary of Johnson's tour, the *Journey* has deservedly received renewed critical attention culminating in Mary Lascelles's excellent Yale edition of the text. The travel book chronicles one of the happiest experiences in Johnson's career when the process of moral discovery in *Rasselas* became an actual experiment in eighteenth-century travel. What Johnson said of the best travelers could certainly apply to himself: "He, who would bring home the wealth of the Indies, must carry the wealth of the Indies with him."[36] So it was with the writing of the *Journey*, a peerless work of art and travel that Johnson enriched with a wealth of compelling moral insights and erudite observations.

Dr. Johnson in His Hebridean Costume, adapted from Thomas Trotter's engraving, *Dr. Johnson in His Travelling Dress* (1786) and appearing as an attached frontispiece to *A Journey to the Western Islands of Scotland* (1775). Courtesy of the Harvard College Library.

THE END OF A JOURNEY

If God delights so much in variety, as all things animate and inanimate sufficiently prove, no wonder that man should do so
too: and I have now been so accustomed to move, though
slowly, that I intend to creep on to my *journey's end*, by which
means I may live to have been an inhabitant of every town almost in Europe, and die . . . a free citizen of the world, slave to
no sect, nor subject to any King.   Philip Thicknesse,
A Year's Journey through France and Part of Spain

THE FINAL YEARS of Johnson's life marked the realization of
many early ambitions to travel, first conceived in his youth and then
mirrored in the writings of his middle age. The Rambler began his
moral rambles in earnest in the 1770s and ceased from touring only
when heart disease sapped his vigor and the deathbed irrevocably
arrested his life's journey. The Highland tour of 1773 had transformed a novice traveler notorious for his insularity into an expert
explorer eager to undertake further trips with Boswell to "some
part of Europe, Asia, or Africa."[1] Boswell, however, could not
escape his domestic responsibilities, and Johnson had to content
himself with more modest jaunts to Wales and France (1774–1775),
Bristol and Essex (1776–1778), Sussex and Stonehenge (1782–
1783), and, lastly, Oxford and Lichfield (1784). Year by year the
range of his travels perceptibly diminished as his energy decreased
in the final decade. Still, an irrepressible wanderlust distinguished
his old age and kept him alive to geographical developments in an
epoch of discovery. To the end he remained a representative eighteenth-century tourist, whose principles and literary uses of travel
were symptomatic of the interests of fellow English writers. As in so
much else that he thought about and wrote, his views and habits of
travel were an expression of his age.

Johnson's touring in later life often became a desperate attempt to recover one last burst of good health and one more glimpse of human life in the little time remaining: "My friend's Chariot is always ready. We have run this morning twenty four miles and could run forty eight more. *But who can run the race with death?*"[2] Since a journey offered him the very elixir of vitality invigorating his mind and body, he contemplated many far-flung expeditions around the globe. His curiosity about foreign manners encompassed the complete geographical spectrum of the earth's arts and sciences that James Howell had encouraged him to see: "They *budded* first amongst the *Brachmins* and *Gymnosophists* in India, then they blossom'd amongst the Chaldeans and Priests of *Egypt*, whence they came down the *Nile*, and crossed over to *Greece*. . . . Afterwards they found the way to *Italy*, and thence they clammer'd over the Alpian hils to visit *Germany* and *France*, whence the *Britaines* with other North-west *Nations* . . . fetch'd them over; and it is not improbable that the next Flight . . . will be to the Savages of the new discovered World, and so turne round, and by this circular perambulation visit the *Levantines* again."[3] English navigators had opened up this world of cultures for Johnson's consideration, and he looked to many places from China to Peru as future sites for exploration. America and Africa were the least desirable destinations because they were a barren wilderness of either political rebels or savage Hottentots lacking sufficient human interest to make a trip worthwhile. Conversely, the more civilized areas in Europe, around the Mediterranean basin, and in Asia strongly appealed to a moralist usually preoccupied with human life in advanced societies.

For a time even the newly discovered regions of the South Pacific had captured his imagination. Johnson confessed to a momentary desire for joining Cook's second voyage. Boswell found to his surprise that his friend had once considered the idea of a tropical cruise: "Why, yes, but I soon laid it aside. Sir, there is very little of intellectual, in the course. Besides, I see but at a small distance. So it was not worth my while to go see birds fly, which I should not have seen fly; and fishes swim, which I should not have seen swim."[4] If Johnson had gone, his geographical research for writing *Thoughts on the Late Transactions respecting Falkland's Islands* (1771) would have prepared him to be a brilliant historian of Pacific exploration. He once speculated on the classic document that Sir Philip Sidney might have composed from the adventures of Drake's voyages. He himself would have produced an equally elegant and learned travel book in the company of Cook. When he returned from Scotland in 1773, his mind was on recent geographical exploits that made his Highland tour seem negligible by comparison: "They congratulate our return as if we had been with Phipps or Banks; I am ashamed of their salutations."[5] Old as he was he had to satisfy his curiosity by reading all the official accounts of Cook's voyages and leave to other associates the honor of exploring the South Seas with the great navigator. He conversed with Joseph Banks and Charles Solander about the first Pacific voyage and followed the rising career of his friend's son, Capt. James Burney, on the second and third expeditions.

Had Johnson been willing or able to sail with Cook, he would have befriended a renowned explorer with a passion for truth in travel equal to his own. Boswell stood in awe of this sailor's zeal for precise evidence during an interview that left him hero-worshiping Cook and wishing for a berth on the next voyage: "Cook . . . was a plain, sensible man with an uncommon attention to veracity. My metaphor was that he had a balance in his mind for truth as nice as scales for weighing a guinea."[6] Johnson obviously missed a great opportunity when he rejected the idea of accompanying Cook on the second Pacific voyage. While he toured the Hebrides, Cook explored the New Hebrides and exploded the myth of a temperate southern continent in the Antarctic. However, the achievement of penetrating the Antarctic Circle entailed severe trials at sea that would probably have killed Johnson. For on the trip he would have been a true Ancient Mariner subjected to the Coleridgean perils of fog and cracking ice, stormy oceans and iridescent skies, and a nightmarish polar region of eternal snow and cold. There were even friendly albatrosses shot by the voyagers for no other motive than sport: "We began to see those birds about the time of our first falling in with the ice islands, and some have accompanied us ever since."[7] Johnson would also have seen a Polynesian paradise and have heartily agreed with Cook about the need to civilize the repulsive cannibals of New Zealand. As the navigator reported, "Curiosity . . . got the better of my indignation, and being desirous of becoming an eye-witness of a fact which many doubted, I ordered a piece of flesh to be broiled and brought to the quarter-deck, where one of the natives ate it with a surprising avidity. This had such an effect on some of our people as to make them sick. . . . An intercourse with foreigners would reform their manners and polish their savage minds."[8]

No doubt, the gruesome experiences of this voyage would have made Johnson proclaim the blessings of civilization all the louder and have confirmed his hatred of sailing. Fortunately, he could assess the value of Cook's discoveries and the validity of the noble savage concept at home in the company of James Burney and Omai the Tahitian. Since the age of ten, "Jemmy" Burney (1750–1821) had spent most of his early years at sea and through his father's friendship with Lord Sandwich, First Lord of the Admiralty, was commissioned to serve on Cook's second voyage as second lieutenant in the *Adventure* under the command of Captain Furneaux. Cook had previously been a visitor to the Burney home in 1772 and came to respect James's abilities on the cruise. Having learned the Tahitian dialect, young Burney was assigned to escort Omai around England upon their return and treated his family to colorful tales of Polynesian life, trials at sea, and the "horrid massacre" of ten crew members by cannibals. More naval service followed off the coast of a rebellious Boston in 1775 before James joined Cook's last voyage into the north Pacific a year later. Although he rose to the rank of commander of the *Discovery*, the tragic finale of this exploration would have given him little cause for happiness over the promotion for through his telescope he had the sad duty of witnessing the great navigator being clubbed and stabbed to death in the waters of Keala-kekua Bay, Hawaii. Johnson and Henry Thrale visited his ship at dock in 1780 and invited him to Streatham to display his specimens and recount his adventures. As Fanny Burney proudly noted, John-son instantly liked this plain and open-hearted sailor and "pro-nounced an actual eulogium upon Captain Burney to his listeners—how amiable he was and how gentle in his manners, tho' he lived so many years with sailors and savages."[9] Afterward, James's fortunes surprisingly declined in the Royal Navy, but his fame was assured with the publication of *A Chronological History of the Discoveries in the South Sea or Pacific Ocean* (1803–1817), still one of the stan-dard studies of the subject.

Johnson was grateful for what must have been stimulating con-versation about newly discovered areas of the South Seas: "I ques-tion if any ship upon the ocean goes out attended with more good wishes than that which carries the fate of Burney."[10] His acquaint-ance with Burney, Banks, and Solander brought him into close con-tact with the most recent exploits in Pacific navigation. But another personage, Omai the Tahitian, offered him a unique opportunity to examine the noble savage at first hand. Captain Furneaux had brought this brown and stocky native of the Friendly Islands to England in 1774. George III granted the savage an audience, and Sir Joshua Reynolds painted his portrait. Four years before, Bougain-ville had already transported to Europe a Polynesian who died of smallpox in France. Omai was consequently inoculated and properly fitted out to meet an enthusiastic English gentry in the company of Banks and Constantine Phipps. Johnson studied this curiosity with the Thrales at Streatham: "Sir, he had passed his time, while in En-gland, only in the best company; so that all he had acquired of our manners was genteel. As a proof of this, Sir, Lord Mulgrave and he dined one day at Streatham; they sat with their backs to the light fronting me, so that I could not see distinctly; and there was so little of the savage in Omai, that I was afraid to speak to either, lest

I should mistake one for the other."[11] Omai amazed other Britons far more and helped to spawn a romantic literary interest in Polynesia that would inspire later writers from Byron and Melville to Twain and Stevenson. Already in Johnson's time the Pacific voyages had resulted in poetry satirizing Polynesian sexuality, mourning Cook's untimely death, and eulogizing Omai. In *The Task* William Cowper would ask this "gentle savage" if his visit had shown "With what superior skill we can abuse / The gifts of Providence, and squander life."

Omai, however, loved the civilized caresses of English society and fulfilled Cook's prophecy that the pampering would eventually harm him back in the islands. His honors and his arrogance made him enemies among the Polynesians, and he died soon after his return in the same year, 1779, that Hawaiians massacred Cook. Johnson remained skeptical about Omai's innate virtues and increasingly criticized the achievements of Cook's explorations. From his conversations with Banks, he probably formed the notion that the data collected by the voyagers lay mainly in the field of natural history. What really mattered to him was the study of manners, and, to his chagrin, the explorers had admittedly investigated Polynesian anthropology inadequately. He shared with Cook a devotion to accurate facts and despised the premature theories that idealized the islanders. Boswell's excitement over the new noble savages only intensified Johnson's hostility to the popular contemporary cult of primitivism: "Don't cant in defence of Savages."[12] Yet, while he opposed such romantic idolatry at home, he staunchly defended backward cultures against the injustices of European discoverers. He knew the commercial and political advantages of Pacific exploration to England, but the spread of European diseases and the possibility of colonial abuses in Polynesia appalled him. When the accounts of Cook's ill-fated third voyage appeared in 1784, he shrugged at reading another report of European cruelty and savage virtue: "A man had better work his way before the mast, than read them through."[13] His last published writing would refer to the

Pacific territories as "lands of unprovided wretchedness." They came to represent one more chapter in the sorry history of imperialism that he had criticized throughout his career: "Much knowledge has been acquired, and much cruelty been committed; the belief of religion has been very little propagated, and its laws have been outrageously and enormously violated."[14]

Too old and too reluctant to join a Pacific expedition, he did discuss the possibility of voyaging to the northern countries of Europe on the Highland tour. James Gregory, the future Professor of Medicine at Edinburgh University, even suggested a trip to Iceland. Mrs. Thrale gave mocking approval to the idea: "Well! 'tis better talk of Iceland. Gregory challenges you for an Iceland expedition; but I trust there is no need; I suppose good eyes might reach it from some of the places you have been in" (*Life*, 3:455). Mrs. Thrale was probably unaware that Johnson had long been seriously interested in Iceland and other northern countries. His preface to *Lobo's Voyage* (1735) already revealed a fascination with incredible reports of "irremediable barrenness" and "perpetual gloom" in polar regions. He accepted the classical theory of geographical compensations and believed that no nation, however poor its climate, lacked God-given natural advantages to support life. Yet travel books at his disposal sometimes refuted this theory and whetted his curiosity to see at least one area of the globe seemingly devoid of the barest human necessities. Political and antiquarian concerns also marked his investigations of northern geography. His early contributions to the *Gentleman's Magazine* included monthly summaries of current affairs in Scandinavia and Russia as well as reviews of foreign books occasionally dealing with northern Europe. In an anonymous notice of Ludovico Muratori's *Antiquitates Italicae* in 1742, there is an eloquent defense of the study of medieval Norse antiquities that explains his own avid interest in feudal history and anticipates his brilliant analysis of medieval British jurisprudence in the Vinerian Law Lectures of 1766–1768: "But if it be considered that by the Conquests of the *Northern* Nations the whole Face of

Europe was changed, and that new Laws and Customs were established and new Languages produced by them, which remain at this Day among us, it will appear not useless to attend to the Customs and Transactions of those Times, from which, however they are censured for Barbarity, many excellent laws are derived; and to examine the Manners of those Men who have at least some Right to our Regard as our Ancestors, and from this Nation a particular Title to Veneration as the Authors of our Constitution and the Fathers of Liberty."[15]

Reading descriptions of northern countries probably stimulated an imaginative empathy with a primitive feudal past that served to clarify the obscure origins of British culture. By the early 1750s he had composed a Greenland tale in *Ramblers* 186 and 187 based on Hans Egede's *Description of Greenland* (1745) and was apparently thinking of touring Iceland with a London apothecary at the time of his wife's death. The Horatian motto of this tale hints at his desire to visit polar regions, and his introductory remarks suggest possible motives for taking the proposed trip: "A native of England, pinched with the frosts of December, may . . . if he turns his thoughts towards the polar regions, and considers the nations to whom a great portion of the year is darkness, and who are condemned to pass weeks and months amidst mountains of snow, . . . reflect how much he owes to providence, that he is not placed in Greenland or Siberia." The harsh northern countries would disclose to Johnson a "pure" state of nature forcibly confirming the superior benefits of civilization while illuminating the basic human traits and aspirations from which civilization sprang. Here would be truly something new to see. But nothing came of these plans for an Iceland expedition. Work on the *Dictionary* and continuing financial hardship would have kept him firmly anchored in London.

Although much of his personal life in this period is unknown, there are indications of a persistent curiosity about the Arctic. In his preface to the *Preceptor*, he had especially recommended the study of polar geography because of the remarkable climatic conditions that made travel so perilous in places like Greenland. Later, in 1756 he extracted a brief account of Greenland for special notice in his review of Thomas Birch's *History of the Royal Society of London*. Like his preface to the *Preceptor* (1748), this article testifies to his abiding fascination with the sterile geography of the Arctic as well as with adventure stories of human survival recounted by travelers: "their poor companions were left behind, but [were] found alive at their next return; having lived upon fowl and deer, and saved themselves from being frozen by the coals they found there."[16] In 1758 he seems again to have considered an Iceland voyage and may have first read Niels Horrebov's *Natural History of Iceland* (1758) at the time. Horrebov's book, which Johnson quoted from memory years later, cataloged a succession of physical and political miseries that must have seized the moralist's attention. The inhabitants suffered grievously under a Danish commercial monopoly, destructive volcanoes, famine, and plague. Here was a country that apparently defied any theory of geographical compensations by possessing few of the natural resources that made life bearable and even possible. Iceland would be worth a close examination because its absolute barrenness would provide important evidence of what unassisted human nature could endure and perform in a savage environment and why civilization best served the greatest human needs.

At the end of 1758 Johnson was certainly discussing a tour of Iceland with the wife of Christopher Smart. He became acquainted with Anna Maria Smart around 1755 when he was closely associated with her husband and her stepfather, the publisher John Newbery. The poet's periodic confinements in mad houses left his wife depressingly poor and alone. In November, 1758 she had to migrate to Ireland without her two children for a livelihood and, with the assistance of the Falkiner family, set up shop in Dublin. Johnson sent her a sympathetic letter of consolation over her forced exile from England. The letter indicates how seriously he wanted to see Iceland for the express purpose of more fully appreciating the comparative advantages of his own civilized climate and culture: "To one that has passed so many years in the pleasures and opulence of London, there are few places that can give much delight. . . . I think, Madam, you may look upon your expedition as a proper preparation to the voyage which we have often talked of. Dublin, though a place much worse than London, is not so bad as Iceland. You will now be hardened to all from the sight of poverty, and will be qualified to lead us forward, when we shrink at rueful spectacles of smoky cottages and ragged inhabitants. One advantage is also to be gained from the sight of poor countries; we learn to know the comforts of our own."[17] This Iceland scheme also failed to materialize. Johnson's mother died a few weeks later, and the expenses of her funeral required him to concentrate on writing *Rasselas*. Anna Maria Smart would return to England in 1761, but a rupture in her friendship with Johnson ended any hope of their touring Iceland together.

In later years English explorations of the Arctic would keep Iceland and other countries vividly in Johnson's mind. Captain Constantine Phipps sailed for the North Pole in 1773 to seek a northeast passage to the Indies. He had previously investigated Labrador and Newfoundland with Joseph Banks in 1766 and accepted the command of this polar expedition after Daines Barrington persuaded the Royal Society to finance the trip. Barrington (1727–1800) was a typical eighteenth-century virtuoso who dabbled in law, natural history, antiquities, and geography and grew friendly enough with Johnson to become a member of the Essex Head Club. Although he knew of the many failures to find the fabled northwest passage to India, he argued the possibility of an ice-free Arctic ocean to the northeast. The financial rewards of a successful voyage would have been great because Parliament had instituted a cash prize of £20,000 for just such a discovery in 1745. Johnson wisely disputed his friend's theory on the Highland tour: "Talking of Phipps's voyage to the North Pole, Dr. Johnson observed, that it 'was conjectured that our navigators have kept too near land, and so have found the sea frozen far north, because the land hinders the free motion of the tide; but, in the wide ocean, where the waves tumble at their full convenience,

it is imagined that the frost does not take full effect.' "[18] He would
have found his doubts vindicated after reading the short voyage
account of Phipps's foolhardy venture in 1774. The navigator
reached the impenetrable ice north of Spitzenbergen and was forced
to execute a speedy return to England. Barrington, however, was not
a man to be daunted by failure. He would devise a new plan for the
Royal Society's consideration a year later and see it become a part
of Captain Cook's design on the third voyage to chart a northeast
passage to Europe from the Pacific ocean. This plan proved equally
erroneous but had helped to spur a momentous exploration that led
to the discovery of Hawaii.

Johnson was friendly with two other polar geographers who
recently revived interest in Iceland. Joseph Banks and Charles Solander toured the country in 1772 after losing their chance to sail on
Cook's second Pacific voyage. Their expedition accomplished what
Johnson had probably projected over the years. Banks was the first
Englishman to climb Mount Hecla and complete a scientific survey
of the island. He would see the forbidding terrain that Johnson could
only imagine, collect curiosities and Norse manuscripts that Johnson
would have examined, and champion Icelandic liberties that Johnson
might well have defended. In the moralist's case, the Highland tour
of 1773 proved to be a worthy substitute for the polar expedition
that never took place. The *Journey to the Western Islands of Scotland* alludes to Bank's recent survey and displays that keen curiosity
about primitive manners and places which had originally motivated
Johnson's study of northern geography. The more accessible Hebrides would be the *Ultima Thule*, that northernmost frontier for
Johnson to investigate savage virtues and medieval traditions, weigh
the geographical compensations of backward nations, and validate
the superiority of British civilization. As Boswell makes clear, the
Highland experience was enough of an education in the privations of
primitive habitats and the blessings of London society: "Our satisfaction of finding ourselves again in a comfortable carriage was very
great. We had a pleasing conviction of the commodiousness of

civilization, and heartily laughed at the ravings of those absurd visionaries who have attempted to persuade us of the superior advantages of a *state of nature*."[19] Others had shared the trials and triumphs of penetrating the Arctic. But Johnson had to content himself with the lowlier role of being an avid student of polar exploration.

After the success of his journey to the Highlands, he dreamed of traveling to the more civilized areas of the globe. There were at least two discussions with Boswell about making a tour of Asia between 1778 and 1780: "He expressed a particular enthusiasm with respect to visiting the wall of China. I catched it for the moment, and said that I really believed I should go and see the wall of China, had I not children, of whom it was my duty to take care. 'Sir, (said he,) by doing so, you would do what would be of importance in raising your children to eminence. . . . I am serious, Sir.' "[20] His desire to explore Asia had probably existed for years. *Rasselas* had celebrated the Chinese wall twenty years before, and his review of Du Halde's *Description of the Empire of China* in 1742 evinces more than a routine interest in the East: "As the vast Empire of *China* has for a long time been in *Europe* the Subject of Enquiry and Admiration, it cannot be doubted but the Publick will set a high value on a Book that will satisfy that Curiosity which the Relations hitherto exhibited have only raised."[21] In advertising the culture to his countrymen, he bestowed special praise on the durable political system and ingenuity of the Chinese. As a moralist, he naturally paid close attention to their religion and traditions and esteemed their exemplary pursuit of virtue, "a Practice which it is astonishing to see so little followed by Protestants with Respect to those Books from which the Way to eternal Happiness is to be learned."[22] Although he never regarded the East as fully civilized as the West, he did express his respect for Chinese law and the Confucian code of ethics and hoped one day to personally investigate the country's unrivaled architectural wonders. Only a year before his death, he would dine with the Duc de Chaulnes and, though sick and in bodily pain, was

eager to hear this French scientist recount his travels to China.
While his own hopes of Asian travel went unrealized, his curiosity
about Cathay expressed a pioneer knowledge of the East that Europeans would strive to perfect in the next century.

A fascinating and little-known episode of Johnson's life concerns
his serious intentions to migrate to India midway in his writing
career. Robert Clive had conquered the country for the British
Empire, and the East India Company enjoyed almost absolute commercial and political privileges in the colony. With a little luck,
much courage, and the right connections, any adventurer might
amass a huge fortune and lucrative posts quickly. The lure of easy
riches and advancement seems to have strongly appealed to Johnson
during his struggling years in Grubstreet. At a crucial turning point
in his life, he prepared to leave his beloved London for the Orient.
Sometime between 1755 and 1762 after completing the *Dictionary*
in a dispirited and impoverished state, he decided to seek his fortune
in India with Joseph Fowke. Fowke had returned from India in
1752 and, afterward befriending Johnson, probably filled the moralist's head with dreams of instant wealth: "He resolved to go out
again to the East-Indies, and make his fortune anew. He got a considerable appointment, and I had some intention of accompanying
him. Had I thought then as I do now, I should have gone: but at the
time, I had objections to quitting England."[23] Fortunately for English literature, Johnson discarded a scheme that might have cost
him his life and almost certainly would have prevented the publication of *Rasselas*, the *Plays of William Shakespeare*, the *Journey*, the
Lives of the English Poets, and Boswell's *Life of Johnson*. As events
turned out, Fowke was later charged with conspiracy against Warren Hastings after returning to India in 1771 and would ask Johnson
to publish a defense on his behalf in England. Johnson refused because of his friendship with Hastings but would loyally promote
Fowke's career among colonial officials thereafter. The award of a
government pension in 1762 saved Johnson from a possibly tragic

fate in India and allowed him to continue on in London as the presiding Cham of English letters.

Nevertheless, he paid close attention to Indian affairs for the rest of his life. *Rasselas* probably reflects his frustrated curiosity about the Orient in its portrayal of Imlac's passion for travel and survey of the great Mogul's dominions. Fiction became a surrogate vehicle for Johnson's disappointed hopes of exploring India. Yet those hopes definitely revived in the two decades that followed the appearance of the tale. During that period his career displayed a strong political and legal orientation with far less emphasis upon the moral and literary concerns that had made him famous, if not wealthy. After 1765 he would collaborate with Robert Chambers, Boswell, and William Gerard Hamilton in matters of law and politics, campaign for Henry Thrale and compose propagandist pamphlets for the ministry, publish a sociological survey of Scotland, and lament his failure to have become renowned as a lawyer and statesman. India had an important place in his political interests and, perhaps, in his suppressed ambitions for political fame and fortune. By the end of 1766 he was writing to Robert Chambers for help in defending the East India Company from the ministry's attempt to appropriate the administration and revenues of the colony: "If you could get me any information about the East Indian affairs, you may promise that if it is used at all, it shall be used in favour of the Company."[24] A parliamentary committee was investigating the company's finances and commercial policies and early in 1767 heard legal counsel concerning the propriety of governmental interference in a trading company's operations. Although Johnson could be very critical of English commerce in India, he apparently sympathized with the cause of the company.

His role in this quarrel is not precisely known, but his support of the East India Company would have strengthened his ties with colonial officials who helped to interest him again in visiting India. At the time he requested information from Chambers possibly because their association with Robert Vansittart at Oxford could have provided a direct access to the papers of his brother, Henry Vansittart, who was deeply involved in the affairs of the company and testified in the inquiry of 1767. The Vansittart brothers descended from a family of merchant-adventurers and were both profligate members of the notorious Hell-Fire Club before Johnson came to know them. Robert channeled his restless energies into a teaching career in law at Oxford, where he and his younger colleague, Chambers, originally met Johnson in the mid-1750s. During that period Henry Vansittart (1732–1769) had returned to India to recover his depleted fortunes and eventually succeeded Clive as governor of Bengal from 1761 to 1764. He was a man of some leadership ability and shared with his loyal assistant, Warren Hastings, a taste for oriental scholarship and a sincere intention to reform trading abuses against the natives. Unfortunately, mutinous subordinates paralyzed his efforts and forced his recall with Hastings under suspicion of maladministration.

Back in England, Governor Vansittart published two collections of official documents, *A Narrative of the Transactions in Bengal* (1766) and *A Letter to the Proprietors of East-India Stock* (1767). Both writings vindicate his regime. Johnson shared his contempt for Vansittart's rival, Baron Clive, "a man who had acquired his fortunes by such crimes, that his consciousness of them impelled him to cut his own throat."[25] Moreover, the friendship with Robert Vansittart seems to have become sufficiently cordial to allow Johnson to think of traveling to India with him in the late 1760s. There may be some truth to this report, which first appeared in 1784: "Twenty years ago he offered to attend his friend Vansittart to India, who was invited there to make a fortune; but it did not take place."[26] If this claim has any validity, Johnson was surely fortunate that he stayed home. The ship carrying Vansittart was lost at sea in December 1769, and none of its passengers survived.

So ended what may have been Johnson's last real hope of a voyage to India. Henceforth, other friends in the Vansittart circle would tour the country for him and realize his dream of recording its exotic natural and cultural history. Robert Chambers eventually resigned his post as Vinerian Professor of Law at Oxford for a more lucrative appointment to the Supreme Court of Bengal in 1774. He would collect a large library of oriental manuscripts at Johnson's prodding and cap a successful career as chief justice in India by assuming the presidency of the Asiatic Society of Bengal in 1797. His younger and greater Oxford colleague at University College, William Jones, would leave his mark on English history as the most distinguished student of Indian law and literature. Happily, Johnson played a part in promoting their careers and foreign studies by recommending them both to another celebrated friend, Warren Hastings, the central figure in the growth of the British Empire in India. Over the course of twenty years a mutual admiration developed between these two men to the degree that Hastings would entrust personal papers perhaps for the defense of his administration to Johnson for criticism and possible publication in 1784. Johnson apparently refused the responsibility, but his political support of the man who ensured a commanding British presence in India for almost two centuries was unwavering: "I wish you a prosperous government, a safe return, and a long enjoyment of plenty and tranquillity."[27]

Hastings was a poor and relatively obscure subordinate of Vansittart when he first visited Johnson's lodgings in the late 1760s. Their meeting produced a lasting attachment and significantly occurred when Johnson was perhaps intimate with other members of the Vansittart circle and was championing the cause of the East India Company. An active proponent of oriental studies, Hastings was at the time pondering the foundation of a college to educate Indian civilians and approached Johnson for help in establishing a professorship of Persian at Oxford to be financed by the East India Company. Although Johnson promised to draft a code of regulations, nothing came of the proposal, and Hastings soon returned to India to begin the empire-building career that would make him famous. His public defense of the company before the House of Commons and the grudging assistance of Lord Clive during his lean years in London helped to hasten his career advancement in the colony after his arrival in 1769. His success as governor of Bengal earned him the supreme post of governor general of India, which Lord North's Regulating Act of 1773 created to increase the government's control over the company's dominions. The same act also established the Supreme Court of Bengal to extend British law to Indian subjects and ultimately caused Johnson to start a noteworthy correspondence with Hastings that had some impact on the direction of oriental studies in India.

Johnson wrote the first letter in 1774 primarily to recommend Robert Chambers, one of the new Indian judges authorized by Lord North's bill. However, the most significant aspect of this farsighted epistle was his eloquent appeal for volumes of data about the country to improve oriental scholarship at home: "Of the natural productions animate and inanimate we yet have so little intelligence that our books are filled, I fear, with conjectures about things which an Indian peasant knows by his senses. Many of those things my first wish is to see; my second to know by such accounts as a Man like You will be able to give."[28] His letter not only documents his regret over never going to India but also calls attention to the *Grammar of the Persian Language* (1771) by William Jones, who would one day accomplish the requested research. Hastings treasured the correspondence and never forgot the advice. A year later while resisting a conspiracy of assistants and just after defeating native princes, the indefatigable governor general paused from the strife of war to compose a thoughtful reply for cultivating the arts of peace: "Although the situation in which I have been placed has, by a peculiarity of circumstances attending it, precluded me from gratifying my curiosity by researches of my own into the history, traditions, arts, or natural productions of this country, yet I have not been inattentive to them, having esteemed it among the duties of my station to direct and encourage the pursuits of others to these discoveries, who were better qualified by their talents or leisure for the attainments of them, nor I hope altogether without success."[29] Hastings followed through with his promise of patronizing oriental studies by encouraging the scholarly labors of Chambers, Jones, Wilkins, and other brilliant associates in his government. In return for sending the *Journey*, Johnson received one of the first English accounts of Tibet by George Bogle and would later read Nathaniel Halhed's *Code of Gentoo Laws* (1776), published under Hastings's supervision.

The current renaissance in Indian scholarship went hand in hand with increasing British dominance in the country. In the decade before Johnson's death, Hastings proved to be an enthusiastic student of the native culture and a bold imperialist intent on expanding England's supremacy over French and native forces. Johnson must have recognized this leader's paradoxical attitude of calculated aggression against the very civilization that he so much admired and wanted others to appreciate. Naturally he always endorsed Hastings's aims as a scholar even though he expressed a growing uneasiness about his rumored transgressions as a military commander. He would have welcomed Hastings's political reforms and many services on behalf of oriental research. A college and printing press would be founded at Calcutta, and the Asiatic Society of Bengal would be formed by Hastings and his learned colleagues for the systematic study of Indian language, literature, philosophy, history, science, and law. In view of all the exciting developments and his friendship with the forward-looking governor general, no wonder Johnson spoke often of exploring India between 1774 and 1779. At the age of sixty-six he would playfully suggest a repeat performance of Imlac's youthful tour in *Rasselas* to Mrs. Thrale: "If I had money enough, what would I do? Perhaps, if you and master did not hold me, I might go to Cairo, and down the Red Sea to Bengal, and take a ramble in India. . . . Half fourteen thousand would send me out to see other forms of existence, and bring me back to describe them."[30]

As usual, limited finances and failing health stood in the way of distant voyaging. Perhaps the memory of his own frustrated dreams of Indian wealth had some influence upon his later criticism of fortune hunting in the East. Boswell heard him remark that making a modest fortune in England was better than accumulating the vast riches of India: "a man who has lived ten years in India, has given up ten years of social comfort and all those advantages which arise from living in England."[31] Johnson genuinely loved his British lifestyle and London comforts. But if he remembered his lost opportunities in India and his years of poverty in London, his boast of superior English advantages would have been peculiarly pathetic. While Hastings grew wealthy in the Indies, Johnson had scarcely been able to afford his Highland tour. Even his faith in British civilization afterward suffered a severe blow by what appeared to be the last tragic act in the rise and fall of the modern Augustan Empire. Although Hastings virtually completed Clive's conquest of India by 1783, a hostile Whig ministry tried to disgrace his administration in preparation for impeachment proceedings that would not exonerate him of personal corruption until 1795. At the end of his life, Johnson was understandably depressed not only by the success of the American Revolution but also by the scandals surrounding his friends in India. To make matters worse, Burke had recently drafted a bill introduced by Fox in Parliament to curtail drastically those very powers of the East India Company that Johnson had years ago defended: "The tumult in government is, I believe, excessive . . . at a time when we have all the world for our enemies, when the King and parliament have lost even the titular dominion of America, and the real power of Government every where else. . . . Mr Burke has just sent me his speech upon the affairs of India. . . . I will look into it; but my thoughts now seldom travel to great distances."[32] By 1784 Johnson could no longer feel so curious about the globe when the worldwide dominions of the British Empire seemed doomed to decay by new barbarians abroad and blind politicians at home.

Previously his curiosity had exhibited a truly imperial range of geographical interests. Wherever the destination in the East or the West, he was usually eager to make a journey of human inquiry despite his advanced age. Of all the places on his global itinerary, the Mediterranean countries had always stood uppermost in his mind. For a moralist who reverenced his heritage of Hebraic wisdom and Graeco-Roman values, a trip to the birthplace of Western civilization seemed an imperative course of action: "A man who has not been in Italy, is always conscious of an inferiority, from his not having seen what it is expected a man should see. The grand object of travelling is to see the shores of the Mediterranean. On those shores were the four great Empires of the world; the Assyrian, the Persian, the Grecian, and the Roman.—All our religion, almost all our law, almost all our arts, almost all that sets us above savages, has come to us from the shores of the Mediterranean."[33] In this area Johnson located the seat of Christianity and classical learning, all the civilizing arts and sciences that made the West culturally superior to the East. His preferences in places to visit were symbolic of his national prejudices and pride of European birth. For after having completed his patriotic tour of Britain, the most civilized spot on earth in his eyes, he then wanted to undertake a pilgrimage to the source of European piety and culture in Italy and around the Mediterranean basin.

Italy, more than any other country, singularly appealed to Englishmen in an era of empire building which rivaled the great age of Augustus. Here Addison and Gibbon contemplated its ancient magnificence while Smollett and Sharp showed typical English contempt for its modern decadence. Johnson dreamed of visiting its universities from his earliest years and, when touring France with the Thrales in 1775, dearly wanted to include Italy on the itinerary. After his return from France, he immediately began studying Italian and discussed with Boswell the possibility of writing a travel book on the country. While he planned to see "Rome, Naples, Florence, and Venice, and as much more as we can," Giuseppe Baretti was secretly arranging a different route through southern Italy and Sicily

to force Johnson into meeting his relatives.[34] But the sudden death of
Thrale's son canceled the trip, and Johnson's repeated urgings never
persuaded the despondent brewer to resume the project. By 1784
Johnson's failing health made an Italian tour increasingly necessary.
Fielding and Smollett had convalesced on the Continent, and Johnson hoped to follow suit in order to keep his curiosity and body alive.
Sir Joshua Reynolds vainly petitioned Lord Thurlow for a larger
pension to cover the costs of the proposed trip. There were offers
of loans by Thurlow and Dr. Brocklesby that met with polite re-
fusals. Too poor and yet too proud to accept charity from friends,
Johnson at any rate preferred to sit out his last years in London
unable to run the race with death. The final decade of his life witnessed successive hopes of travel doomed to repeated disappointments. His lifelong desire to see the world never really materialized
in old age and constituted one more disillusioning lesson in the
vanity of human wishes.

His life and writings repeatedly demonstrate his love of travel and
preoccupation with the learning process of a journey. He was a
practical moralist who equated the art of living wisely with the act
of traveling well. All men were born to the roles of empirical travelers in need of release from the subjective prison of self-delusion and
melancholy introspection by the discovery of a corrective realm
of objective truths. Their quest for happiness followed an inductive
moral course of exposure to life's limitations for a glimpse of the
limitless satisfactions promised in paradise. To perfect the art of
living, an individual had to know and practice the proper rules for
exploring and penetrating the varied mysteries of human nature and
the ultimate meaning of human existence. Johnson's theory of travel
expounded all those principles to help moral travelers on the road
and throughout their journey of life. His fascination with touring
was more than a happy pastime of reading travel books and riding
in coaches. The "motion of going forward" defined the very means
by which men achieved psychological health, moral virtue, and
spiritual growth. Travel remained a central theme of his writings

because clear-sighted traveling was a central duty of human life.

Since all kinds of journeys had a consummate symbolic importance for man, no wonder his theory of travel was so carefully
reasoned from a time-tested heritage of ideas. A Renaissance philosophy of travel, summed up in Howell's *Instructions for Forreine
Travell*, profoundly influenced Johnson's preoccupation with the
cultural data and moral ends of foreign inquiry. Thus Johnson's
journeys in life and literature had a pronounced humanistic tendency; be it in the Highlands of the *Journey* or the Cairo of *Rasselas*,
the major topic of investigation is the intellectual and ethical history
of mankind. For the sake of accurate appraisals of the human condition, he also adopted the rigorous standards of scientific research in
contemporary travel. John Locke had taught him the necessity of a
careful empirical search for factual truths clarifying the state of
nations and human nature in geography and morality. Johnson's
protagonists normally act out the *Essay concerning Human Understanding* during their harried pursuit of elusive hopes. Beyond the
ethical and scientific traditions of travel, there were newer fashions
of romantic tourism affecting his emotional response to people and
places. Touring the geography of Great Britain became an imaginative excursion into his island's glorious history: "Far from me and
from my friends, be such frigid philosophy as may conduct us indifferent and unmoved over any ground which has been dignified
by wisdom, bravery, or virtue."[35] Perhaps the distinguishing feature
in his treatment of travel was an overriding religious outlook on the
vanity of the human quest for happiness. Travel was an inevitably
disillusioning experience correcting the undisciplined imagination
and disclosing the need for spiritual aspirations in a world of predominant unhappiness. All in all, the Johnsonian journey was a scientific education in moral realities that chastened the tourist's romantic or nostalgic conceptions during an antiromantic survey of
mankind.

Johnson's enjoyment of travel literature matched his fondness
for touring. His wide reading in travel books reflected an abiding

literary interest of his age and his varied career as a journalist, moralist, historian, and geographer. His literary criticism set forth a most comprehensive review of travel book principles to improve the intellectual and artistic quality of genre that would, with many notable exceptions, tend to degenerate in the next two centuries. In 1792 Arthur Young's call for simple guidebooks of tourist sights was prophetic of the often inferior descriptions coming later: "The only traveller's guide that would be worth a farthing would be a *little* book that gave a catalogue of the best articles to be seen in every town, in the order of merit."[36] Young wisely chose to ignore his own advice when he wrote his celebrated travel books. Georgian readers would have rejected mediocre publications like *Europe on Five Dollars a Day* insulting the intelligence of travelers today. They demanded writings of serious geographical research and sufficient artistic merit to stimulate the mind and stir the imagination.

From the evidence of his habits of travel and his one fine travel book, Johnson was eminently qualified to produce numerous masterpieces of geographical description if only more opportunities to ramble had existed. His boast to his well-traveled biographer, Boswell, "I have more spirit of adventure than you," was true enough insofar as his boundless curiosity about the globe was concerned. Unfortunately, financial pressures and poor health too often confined him to the role of a fireside traveler, forced to study mankind from China to Peru in the accounts of others. His one major expedition to Scotland left him supremely happy and showed him what he might gain from future touring in more remote lands: "I got an acquisition of more ideas by it than by any thing that I remember. I saw quite a different system of life."[37] He was afterward anxious to appease his hunger for the new and the unknown by more ambitious excursions around the world. Although all his later schemes of travel ended in disappointment, his Highland tour was ample proof of his expertise in research techniques promulgated and practiced by the best geographers of his day. He belongs in the company of those distinguished polymath explorers whose enthusiasm for inquiry, devotion to fact, and inexhaustible interest in the earth's miscellaneous phenomena opened European eyes to a larger and more diversified world picture. He was a moralist bent on studying manners and a scientist intent on gathering precise data on every aspect of a country's habitat and culture. Above all he could cast prejudice aside and broaden his understanding and appreciation of human differences. He truly learned from his travels.

Certainly the greatest travelers of the century, from Dampier to Cook, exhibited the same disciplined curiosity about the world to a high degree. Their application of scientific principles to global research ushered in a geographical revolution affecting the lives and letters of contemporary Englishmen. As John Hawkesworth proudly affirmed, Georgian explorers were making more accurate and sympathetic assessments of foreign nations than ever achieved on previous voyages and travels: "The adventurers in such expeditions have generally looked only upon the great outline of Nature, without attending to the variety of shades within, which give life and beauty to the piece."[38] The careful empirical explorations in the age of Johnson helped to undermine notions of moral uniformity and foster a cosmopolitan spirit that even allowed Europeans to use distant nations as models of utopian virtues. The reduction of home-bred prejudices was a significant development in the social history of the times and prepared for the intensified receptivity to exotic cultures in the Romantic period. The brilliant travel poems of the English Romantics would often transform the cosmopolitan outlook of Georgian travelers into a total imaginative empathy with foreign places and societies.

Romantic tourists were frequently far less impersonal than their predecessors in surveying global phenomena. The rigorous scientific approach of former exploration evolved into a more emotional, imaginative, and self-centered study of foreign topography. However, the Romantics preserved the older standards of objective empirical inquiry and strove to ground their personal preoccupations in the carefully observed data of the physical world. Keats equated

his trip to Scotland with an initiation rite of escape from the burdens
of parochial sensations into the liberating realities of a new environment: "I purpose within a Month to put my knapsack at my back
and make a pedestrian tour through the North of England, and part
of Scotland—to make a sort of Prologue to the Life I intend to pursue—that is to write, to study and to see all Europe at the lowest
expence. I will clamber through the Clouds and exist. I will get such
an accumulation of stupendous recollolections that as I walk through
the suburbs of London I may not see them."[39] True revelations about
the self proceeded from a cosmopolitan identification with foreign
sights. Hence, the wanderer of Wordsworth's *Excursion* becomes
a modern Ulysses surveying the manners of many other men to complete a subjective journey of self-discovery:

> From his native hills
> He wandered far; much did he see of men,
> Their manners, their enjoyments, and pursuits
> Their passions and their feelings; chiefly those
> Essential and eternal in the heart

The majority of Romantic travel narratives display a creative interaction of subjective feeling and objective observation ultimately
inherited from the sympathetic and scientific studies of Georgian
explorers.

The Georgians shared with the Romantics an unqualified enthusiasm for travel literature of all kinds and all countries. Most eighteenth-century Englishmen regarded voyages and travels as essential intellectual documents for improving the arts and sciences and
entertaining the mind with the romance of discovery. Otherwise,
Johnson and his fellow writers would not so often have exploited
or parodied the conventions of the genre in their masterpieces. One
measure of Johnson's representative position among eighteenth-
century authors is his mastery of journey themes and travel motifs
pervading contemporary English literature. A random sampling of

works by Fielding, Goldsmith, Smollett, Sterne, and Boswell only confirms the central importance of Johnson's writings in an age of travel. For these authors as well as for Johnson, the typical hero is a modern tourist renewing the archetypal quest of Quixote, Ulysses, and the Christian pilgrim for wisdom and happiness abroad.

Fielding's writings express a humanistic perspective on travel governing Johnson's outlook on the subject. The two authors treated a journey as an ethical education in human life by a pilgrim-Ulysses of Quixotic travel. Their tales and travel books reveal common assumptions: a concern with manners surveyed with moral insight and rhetorical eloquence; a faith in moral universals acquired from comparative study of human differences; and a Christian-classical concept of spiritual growth on the road.[40] Just as Johnson's *Journey* and *Rasselas* possess close structural ties, so also Fielding's *Voyage to Lisbon* (1755) and *Tom Jones* (1748) have similar thematic interests. What begins in Fielding's travel book as simply a sick man's search for health develops into a pilgrimage of life burlesquing the *Odyssey* and recalling *Don Quixote:* "the first man was a traveller, and . . . he and his family were scarce settled in Paradise, before they disliked their own home, and became passengers to another place. Hence it appears, that the humour of travelling is as old as the human race, and that it was their curse from the beginning."[41] So Fielding accounts for his own impulse to sail under his "Captain Ulysses" on a Quixotic odyssey to recover his spirits abroad. The same metaphorical strategy obtains in *Tom Jones*, an epic odyssey in prose presenting a Quixotic pilgrimage from Paradise Hall: "*The World*, as *Milton* phrases it, *lay all before him*; and *Jones* no more than *Adam*, had any Man to whom he might resort for Comfort or Assistance."[42] Fielding and Johnson may differ in their opinions about human nature and human happiness, but their vision of travel has common roots in the Bible, the classics, and Cervantic antiromance.

Goldsmith's poetry and prose reflect another side of Johnson's philosophy of travel. *The Traveller* (1764) is an echo of *Rasselas* albeit in a more topical and political form. The poem similarly affirms the futility of searching for perfect happiness in a world everywhere allotted an equal portion of partial evil and partial good. Even *The Citizen of the World* (1762) merits comparison with *Rasselas* in its portrayal of another "Discontented Traveller" on a global survey of human limitations correcting his idealistic preconceptions about mankind: "The superstition and erroneous delicacy of Italy, the formality of Spain, the cruelty of Portugal, the fears of Austria, the confidence of Prussia, the levity of France, the avarice of Holland, the pride of England, the absurdity of Ireland, and the national partiality of Scotland, are all conspicuous in those diurnal publications."[43] Goldsmith's citizen of the world also assumes scientific and psychological principles of travel advocated by Johnson. He considers himself an experimental philosopher of foreign manners (letter 7) and employs codified topics of scientific inquiry (letter 2) to execute an accurate moral survey (letter 30) and inculcate cosmopolitan values (letter 4) by objective exploration (letter 108). Psychologically, his imagination and curiosity set his journey in motion (letter 3); the former thrives on the romance of new sights while the latter attends to the universal moral realities. Johnson practiced such scientific methods and so theorized about the psychological propellants of travel. If less satirical and more reverential toward tradition than Goldsmith, he did make use of the same disillusioning journey theme and enlightened approach to moral discovery in his tales and travels.

Johnson's prejudices against foreigners were indicative of the residual English insularity that distinguished a fellow tourist like Tobias Smollett. Johnson did indeed support a cosmopolitan view of life and criticized Smollett's contemptuous tour of the Continent: "There has been, of late, a strange turn in travellers to be displeased."[44] But, ironically, on his own French tour, he recorded his complete displeasure with the nation in a few devastating couplets:

A Calais
Trop de frais
St. Omer
Tout est cher
Arras
Helas!
A Amiens
On n'a rien
Au Mouton
Rien de Bon.[45]

Smollett's *Travels though France and Italy* (1766) had amplified this peevish theme with enough irascible force to become renowned as the most prejudiced British tourist of his day. His account illustrates the literary possibilities of travel books in the fiction of Johnson's age. Smollett's last novel *Humphry Clinker* (1771) clearly elaborates many adventures in his travel book in a new setting and with a different cast of characters. The novel presents the same epistolary format, circular journey, and querulous valetudinarian enduring filth, ignorance, and mishaps abroad. Matthew Bramble makes his peace with mankind upon his return home, and Smollett himself had recovered his love of life at the end of his Continental travels: "As my disorder at first arose from a sedentary life, producing ... indolence, and dejection of spirits, I am convinced that this hard exercise of mind and body, co-operated with the change of air and objects, to brace up the relaxed constitution, and promote a more vigorous circulation of the juices, which had long languished even almost to stagnation."[46] Like Johnson, Smollett made the truths of travel serve the ends of literary creation.

Both writers agreed about the therapeutic value of travel in reviving the depressed spirits and enriching the empty mind. In this respect at least, Johnson was also in accord with Laurence Sterne, whose exuberant love of travel equaled the moralist's own. In fact, Sterne's novels rest on a dynamic conception of vital human motion for psychological health and intellectual growth that was funda-

mental to Johnson's moral vision of man. However, their adherence
to a common moral principle resulted in radically different writings
that place them in opposite schools of travel. Where Johnson sought
rational order, objectivity, and general truths authenticated by experience and tradition, Sterne reveled in the emotional chaos of dis-
crete sensations, subjectivity, and ever new revelations of personal
meaning. Tristram Shandy is an iconoclast of travel who discards
all the conventional tourist inquiries to speed his race with death
and follow the impulse of feeling (*Tristram Shandy*, volume 7).
Similarly, *A Sentimental Journey through France and Italy* (1768)
irreverently burlesques the spleenish travels of Smollett ("Smel-
fungus") and Samuel Sharp ("Mundungus") and abandons the usual
travel book format and topics. Yorick emerges as a Don Quixote of
fine feelings brought low by his prurient appetites; his is a hilarious
quest for benevolent sensations in the solipsistic empire of spiritual
love and natural emotion.[47] If Johnson shared Sterne's feeling for
man's dynamic nature, the Shandean break with traditional travel
was foreign to the moralist's sentiments.

Ironically, the Georgian traveler most closely approximating the
Shandean tourist in life was none other than Johnson's great friend
and biographer. On his grand tour of Europe Boswell felt smitten
with a "Don Quixote humour" to travel and explore the "workings
of sensibility" in himself and others. His journals as well as his *Tour
to Corsica* (published in the same year as Sterne's *Sentimental Journey*) chronicle a subjective approach to travel strikingly like Yorick's own. Boswell similarly minimizes the usual tourist inquiries
to study personal feelings, ponder his sensations and impressions,
find release from the melancholy self by identifying with the lives
of celebrities, and glorify liberty and natural virtue in Corsica. The
Shandean comic irony is missing in Boswell's confessional reports,
but otherwise his trip had the quality of a sentimental journey adum-
brating the subjective preoccupations of Romantic tourism. Johnson's very different view of travel did not prevent him from enjoying
the emotional, impressionistic dimension of Boswell's *Tour to Cor-*

sica: "You express images which operated strongly upon yourself, and you have impressed them with great force upon your readers. I know not whether I could name any narrative by which curiosity is better excited, or better gratified."[48] From Johnson's standpoint the whole episode of Boswell's grand touring could have been reminiscent of *Rasselas*. When they first met in 1763, just before Boswell's Continental travels, the moralist inculcated Imlac's advice to study mankind abroad, fix upon a choice of life ("choose and pursue your choice"), and return home matured by the knowledge of life's limitations. These directives Johnson's real life Rasselas spent the rest of his life trying to carry out.

As the works of his contemporaries testify, Johnson's diverse interests in travel were, for the most part, consistent with the literary tendencies of his times. His writings gather together the major trends and literary uses of travel prevalent in eighteenth-century prose and poetry. *Rasselas* is his classic statement of the pervasive journey theme in his morality and magnificently commemorates the dynamic and disillusioning process of all human development. His tale assimilated numerous traditions of travel in history and literature to teach, with a compelling authority, the inconclusive nature of man's perennial quest for happiness. Subsequent generations of writers would long remember and reverence its lessons. Goldsmith would allegorize the story in *The Citizen of the World* (letter 37), and a sentimental continuation would appear in the form of a novel. The oriental romance was a special favorite with the late eighteenth-century public, safe reading for moralistic Evangelical families and a formative influence upon the rebellious minds of Romantic poets. Authors in the next century would sometimes dispute its teachings but pay high tribute to its exotic Abyssinian setting and provoking moral ideas.

Romantic literature would glorify a happy valley myth of transcendent imaginative joy even though Johnson had intended to disprove the possibility of earthly utopias in his Abyssinian paradise. Coleridge in *Kubla Khan* would dream of total imaginative bliss on

Mount Amhara: "It was an Abyssinian maid / . . . Singing of Mount Abora." In his *Guide through the District of the Lakes* Wordsworth would seek communion with nature among majestic Cumberland vales "like the Abyssinian recess of Rasselas." *The Prelude* would record another epiphany in the happy valley of Lake Como "confined as in a depth / Of Abyssinian privacy." Shelley too would model the paradise of *Alastor* and his utopia of love and reason in *The Assassins* on the happy valley: "The mountains of Lebanon had been divided to their base to form this happy valley. . . . And they . . . idolized nature and the God of nature, to whom love and lofty thoughts and the apprehensions of an uncorrupted spirit were sustenance and life." American authors would also cherish Johnson's myth of Mount Amhara. In *Fanshawe* Hawthorne would recall his happy valley youth at Bowdoin College, and in *A Week on the Concord and Merrimack Rivers* Thoreau would climb the happy valley mountains of New Hampshire with Yankee reservations about his spiritual epiphanies: "At length, like Rasselas and other inhabitants of happy valleys, we had resolved to scale the blue wall . . . not without misgivings that thereafter no visible fairy-land would exist for us." Most of these writers would sadly come to realize the lesson that Rasselas had already learned. Fairyland was a doubtful dream, a momentary apprehension and extension of man's spiritual hopes for eternal happiness. We read these great Romantic writings to recapture our youthful intimations of immortality; we ponder Johnson's sturdy wisdom to learn the mature art of living, hoping, and enduring in the world.

Johnson's far-reaching influence and enduring appeal can be partly explained by the sheer honesty of his moral insight into life, his robust refusal to despair, and his catholic interests in human affairs. If troubled by the cultural stresses in his milieu, he yet remained open to old and new ideas, Renaissance traditions and modern progress, in his transitional age of science, industry, and geographical discovery. His *Journey to the Western Islands of Scotland* is both an elegy to a vanishing past and a qualified eulogy of that

Georgian zeal for inquiry hastening the advent of the modern world. While respecting an intellectual heritage of Western wisdom, he applauded and defended free inquiry and future improvements in the quality of European civilization: "Many that presume to laugh at projectors, would consider a flight through the air in a winged chariot, and the movement of a mighty engine by the steam of water, as equally the dreams of mechanic lunacy" (*Adventurer* 99). The experimenters and explorers could all expect support from a man who promoted Lewis Paul's spinning jenny, Zachariah Williams's marine chronometer, and the Society for the Encouragement of Arts, Manufactures, and Commerce. By the end of his life in 1784 he foresaw and championed revolutionary developments in travel as he witnessed the aeronautical wonders of Vincent Lunardi's balloon: "I have however continued my connection with the world so far as to subscribe to a new ballon which is [to] sustain five hundredweight, and by which, I suppose, some Americo Vespucci, for a new Columbus he cannot now be, will bring us what intelligence he can gather from the clouds."[49]

Throughout his life Johnson's restless curiosity never waned. Poverty, poor health, and the inevitable ravages of old age successively defeated his hopes of distant travel. Nevertheless, his modest trips and grandiose schemes of touring expressed an irrepressible drive to see the diverse human family and better understand the nature and destiny of man: "He had often in his mouth this line of Pope, 'the proper study of mankind is man.' He was desirous of surveying life in all its modes and forms, and in all climates."[50] His love of travel and travel literature mirrored a geographical epoch of exploration and discovery when English literature proclaimed a cosmopolitan interest in the worldwide community of mankind. His moral vision of man as a perpetual wanderer, a pilgrim-Ulysses of Quixotic travel, permeates his writings and captures the questing energies of his inquisitive age. His protagonists betray the wanderlust of their creator on his tours, in his reading of travel books, and in his search for a synthesis of old values and modern views in the intellectual wilderness of his century. His noble life of disciplined exploration and ceaseless discovery was its own metaphor of travel circumscribing a tireless pursuit of truth and peace in a changing world of limited satisfactions. As death approached, he concluded his moral pilgrimage with hopes of permanent happiness, true to the principles of his art and travel: "I have taken my viaticum: I hope I shall arrive safe at the end of my journey, and be accepted at last."[51] After traversing moral paths for posterity to follow, he forever shut his eyes to human life in preparation for everlasting rest in the final choice of eternity.

NOTES

ABBREVIATIONS AND SHORT TITLES

Diaries   *Samuel Johnson: Diaries, Prayers, and Annals*, ed. E. L. McAdam, Jr., with Donald and Mary Hyde (New Haven, Conn.: Yale University Press, 1958).

GM   *Gentleman's Magazine.*

Howell   James Howell, *Instructions for Forreine Travell, 1642*, ed. Edward Arber (London, 1869).

Idler   *Samuel Johnson: The Idler and the Adventurer*, ed. W. J. Bate, J. M. Bullitt, and L. F. Powell (New Haven, Conn.: Yale University Press, 1963).

Journey   *Samuel Johnson: A Journey to the Western Islands of Scotland*, ed. Mary Lascelles (New Haven, Conn.: Yale University Press, 1971).

Letters   *The Letters of Samuel Johnson*, ed. R. W. Chapman, 3 vols. (Oxford: Clarendon Press, 1952).

Life   *Boswell's Life of Johnson*, ed. George Birbeck Hill and L. F. Powell, 6 vols. (Oxford: Clarendon Press, 1934–1950).

Miscellanies   *Johnsonian Miscellanies*, ed. George Birbeck Hill, 2 vols. (New York: Barnes and Noble, 1966).

Piozzi   Hester Lynch Piozzi, *Anecdotes of the Late Samuel Johnson, LL.D.* (Cambridge, Mass.: Harvard University Press, 1932).

Poems   *Samuel Johnson: Poems*, ed. E. L. McAdam, Jr., with George Milne (New Haven, Conn.: Yale University Press, 1964).

Rambler   *Samuel Johnson: The Rambler*, ed. W. J. Bate and Albrecht B. Strauss, 3 vols. (New Haven, Conn.: Yale University Press, 1969).

Works   *The Works of Samuel Johnson, LL.D.*, 9 vols. (Oxford, 1825).

INTRODUCTION

1. *Miscellanies*, 2:287.
2. *Letters*, no. 880.
3. *Life*, 2:361.
4. Howell, p. 13.
5. *Works*, 5:238.
6. *Letters*, no. 409.
7. *Letters*, no. 329.
8. *Life*, 5:248.

1 · JOHNSON'S LIFETIME, 1709–1784: THE AGE OF TRAVEL

1. Sir William Temple, *An Essay upon the Ancient and Modern Learning*, in *Five Miscellaneous Essays by Sir William Temple*, ed. Samuel Holt Monk (Ann Arbor: University of Michigan Press, 1963), p. 60. See also Edward Heawood, *A History of Geographical Discovery in the Seventeenth and Eighteenth Centuries* (New York: Octagon Books, 1965), on contemporary knowledge of geography.

2. David Hume, *An Enquiry concerning Human Understanding*, sec. 8, pt. 1, par. 65. For the belief in uniformitarian principles among English empiricists, see Meyrick Carré, *Phases of Thought in England* (London: Oxford University Press, 1949).

3. Henry Fielding, *Tom Jones*, 8.15.

4. Jean Gailhard, *The Compleat Gentleman* (London, 1678), p. 179.

5. Père J. B. Du Halde, *A Description of the Empire of China* (London: Edward Cave, 1738), 1:1.

6. [John Douglas] ed., Preface to *A Voyage to the Pacific Ocean . . . for making Discoveries in the Northern Hemisphere* (London: W. Strahan, 1784).

7. Johnson, Dedication for George Adams's *Treatise on the Globes* (1766).

8. *Life*, 4:250.

9. *Poems*, 6:302.

10. Oliver Goldsmith, *The Citizen of the World*, *Works*, ed. J. W. M. Gibbs (London: George Bell and Sons, 1885), 3:292.

11. John Locke, *An Essay concerning Human Understanding*, bk. 1, chap. 3, par. 8. For the spread of moral relativism, see James Sutherland, *English Literature of the Late Seventeenth Century* (New York: Oxford University Press, 1969), pp. 294–296, and Ernst Cassirer, "The Mind of

the Enlightenment," in *Backgrounds to Eighteenth-Century Literature*, ed. Kathleen Williams (Scranton: Chandler, 1971).

12. Patrick Brydone, *A Tour through Sicily and Malta* (London: Strahan, 1773), 2:312.

13. John Hawkesworth, ed., *An Account of the Voyages . . . for Making Discoveries in the Southern Hemisphere* (London: Strahan, 1773), 3:128.

14. Arthur Young, *Travels in France and Italy during the Years 1787, 1788, and 1789* (London: J. M. Dent, 1927), p. 325.

15. Johnson, Preface to *Father Lobo's Voyage to Abyssinia* (London [Birmingham], 1735). For the dual influence of moral relativism and moral uniformity upon the minds of writers, see Bonamy Dobrée, *English Literature in the Early Eighteenth Century* (Oxford: Clarendon Press, 1959), p. 16.

16. Boswell, *Boswell on the Grand Tour, Germany and Switzerland, 1764*, ed. Frederick Pottle (New York: McGraw-Hill, 1953), p. 102.

17. See Chapter VII below and Arthur Sherbo, "The Making of *Ramblers* 186 and 187," *PMLA* 67 (1952): 575–580.

18. According to the preface of the 1820 edition of David Cranz's *History of Greenland*, Johnson greatly admired the book and the Moravian mission. His library contained the 1767 edition of the travel book in two volumes.

19. *Letters*, no. 299.

20. *Works*, 5:228.

21. Richard Savage, *Of Public Spirit in Regard to Public Works* (1737), ll. 291–292.

22. Johnson, *Lives of the English Poets*, ed. George Birbeck Hill (New York: Octagon Books, 1967), 2:393.

23. *Miscellanies*, 2:51.

24. Johnson, Review of Lewis Evans's *Geographical . . . Map of the Middle British Colonies in America*, *Literary Magazine* 1 (January 1756): 454–455.

25. For further information on Johnson's anti-imperialistic views on the American conflict, see Donald J. Greene, "Samuel Johnson and the Great War for Empire," in *English Writers of the Eighteenth Century*, ed. John H. Middendorf (New York: Columbia University Press, 1971), pp. 37–68.

26. Preface to *Father Lobo's Voyage to Abysinnia.*

27. Lady Mary Wortley Montagu, *The Letters and Works of Lady*

Mary Wortley Montagu (Paris: Baudry's European Library, 1837), 1:301–302.

28. Johnson, *Rasselas*, chap. 11, ed. J. P. Hardy (New York: Oxford University Press, 1968). All further references to this tale are to this edition. For tourist interest in Greece and the Orient, see James Osborn, "Travel Literature and the Rise of Neo-Hellenism in England," in *Literature as a Mode of Travel*, ed. Warner Rice (New York: New York Public Library, 1963).

29. *Letters*, no. 834.

30. *Journey*, p. 26.

31. For the part that Hastings's circle of friends in India played in promoting Oriental studies, see Alfred Mervyn Davies, *Strange Destiny: A Biography of Warren Hastings* (New York: Putnam, 1935).

32. *Letters*, no. 353.

33. Sir William Jones, *The Third Anniversary Discourse for the Asiatick Society of Bengal* (1786).

34. Johnson, Review of Du Halde's *Description of the Empire of China*, *GM* 12 (1742): 357.

35. Preface to William Chambers's *Designs of Chinese Buildings* (1757).

36. *Letters*, no. 645.1.

37. *Rambler* 150. See also *Rambler* 103, the dedication of *Lobo's Voyage to Abyssinia*, and the *Life of Drake*.

38. William Dampier, *A New Voyage Round the World*, ed. Sir Albert Gray and Percy G. Adams (New York: Dover, 1968), p. 312.

39. George Anson, *Anson's Voyage round the World by Richard Walter*, ed. G. S. Laird Clowes (London: M. Hopkinson Ltd., 1928), p. 71.

40. See Appendix A, *Letters*, I:439. Johnson has also been suspected of writing at least the introductory paragraph of "Abridgement of a Voyage round the World, in the Years 1740–41–42–43–44, by *George Anson*, Esq.," *GM* 19 (1749): 393. See C. Linnart Carlson, *The First Magazine: A History of the Gentleman's Magazine*, vol. 4 (Providence: Brown University Studies, 1938).

41. Hawkesworth, ed., *An Account of the Voyages . . . for making Discoveries in the Southern Hemisphere*, vol. 3, chap. 10.

42. Hawkesworth, vol. 3, chap. 30. For an excellent biography, consult J. C. Beaglehole, *The Life of Captain James Cook* (Stanford: Stanford University Press, 1974).

43. *Life*, 5:511. See also Hector Charles Cameron, *Sir Joseph Banks, the Autocrat of the Philosophers* (London: Belchworth Press, 1952).

44. Boswell, *Boswell: The Ominous Years, 1774–1776*, ed. Charles Ryskamp and Frederick A. Pottle (New York: McGraw-Hill, 1963), p. 341.

45. *Life*, 3:50.

46. *Letters*, no. 707.

47. G. R. Crone and R. A. Skelton, "English Collections of Voyages and Travels, 1625–1846," in *Richard Hakluyt and His Successors*, ed. Edward Lynan, no. 2 (London, 1946), 93:78.

48. *Letters*, no. 369.2.

49. Preface to *Sir John Narbrough's Voyage to the South-Sea*, in *An Account of Several Late Voyages and Discoveries* (London, 1711).

50. Johnson, introduction to *Debates in the Senate of Lilliput, GM* (1738): 283. For information on bogus voyages and travels, see Percy G. Adams, *Travelers and Travel Liars: 1660–1800* (Berkeley: University of California Press, 1962).

51. Jonathan Swift, *Gulliver's Travels*, 2.1.

52. Johnson, *Rasselas*, chap. 12. For the *Odyssey* archetype in literature, see William B. Stanford, *The Ulysses Theme: A Study in the Adaptability of a Traditional Hero* (Oxford: Blackwell, 1963), and Ethel Thornbury, *Henry Fielding's Theory of the Comic Prose Epic* (Madison: University of Wisconsin Press, 1931).

53. See respectively John Loofbourow, *Thackeray and the Form of Fiction* (Princeton, N.J.: Princeton University Press, 1964); Martin Battestin, *The Moral Basis of Fielding's Art: A Study of Joseph Andrews* (Middletown, Conn.: Wesleyan University Press, 1959); James Sutherland, *Daniel Defoe, A Critical Study* (London: Methuen, 1970); and Goldsmith's "Advertisement" to *The Vicar of Wakefield*.

54. Samuel Purchas, *Hakluytus Posthumous or Purchas His Pilgrimes* (Glasgow: J. MacLehose and Sons, 1905–1907), 1:138.

55. *Johnson's Lives of the English Poets*, 1:209. For the *Don Quixote* archetype in the early English novel, see Ronald Paulson, *Satire and the Novel in Eighteenth-Century England* (New Haven, Conn.: Yale University Press, 1968).

56. See Paul Fussell, *The Rhetorical World of Augustan Humanism* (Oxford: Clarendon Press, 1965), pp. 262–282, and Northrop Frye, *Anatomy of Criticism* (Princeton, N.J.: Princeton University Press, 1957), pp. 52–62.

57. Henry David Thoreau, *A Week on the Concord and Merrimack Rivers* (New York: Holt, Rinehart, and Winston, 1963), pp. 259–260.

58. John Livingston Lowes, *The Road to Xanadu* (Boston: Houghton Mifflin, 1927), pp. 295–339. For the treatment of travel themes and geography in Romantic literature, see also Georg Roppen and Richard Sommer, *Strangers and Pilgrims* (New York: Humanities Press, 1964); Bernard Blackstone, *The Lost Travellers* (London: Longmans, 1962); and Charles Norton Coe, *Wordsworth and the Literature of Travel* (New York: Bookman Associates, 1953).

59. William Hazlitt, *On Going a Journey*. For the changing conventions of travel, see Herbert Barrows, "Convention and Novelty in the Romantic Generation's Experience of Italy," in *Literature as a Mode of Travel*, pp. 70ff. and G. R. Crone, *Modern Geographers* (London: Royal Geographical Society, 1970).

60. Piozzi, p. 171.

61. *Letters*, no. 929.2.

2 · JOHNSON AND THE TRADITION OF TRAVEL LITERATURE

1. So Johnson wrote in *Idler* 97 in the process of demanding and suggesting higher literary standards in travel literature.

2. Fussell, "Patrick Brydone: The Eighteenth-Century Traveler as Representative Man," in *Literature as a Mode of Travel*, pp. 54–55.

3. *Letters*, no. 326.

4. Renaissance commentators on the grand tour, from Roger Ascham to James Howell, so conceived the biblical journey pattern in actual travel. Novelists like Defoe, Fielding, and Smollett explicitly allude to this religious motif in their travel plots.

5. Johnson, Advertisement to John Newbery's *The World Displayed* (1759) in *Life* 1:546.

6. John Bunyan, *The Pilgrim's Progress*, ed. James Wharey and Roger Sharrock (Oxford: Clarendon Press, 1960), p. 8.

7. Bishop Simon Patrick, *The Parable of the Pilgrim* (London, 1667), pp. 324–325.

8. Hawkesworth, ed., Preface to *An Account of the Voyages . . . for making Discoveries in the Southern Hemisphere*.

9. Johnson, Review of James Grainger's *Sugar Cane*, *Critical Review* (October 1764).

10. See the appendix of Thurston M. Moore, "Samuel Johnson and

the Literature of Travel" (Ph.D. diss., University of Michigan, 1966), for a comprehensive, if incomplete, list of Johnson's readings in travel literature.

11. Isaac Watts, "The Improvement of the Mind," in *The Works of Isaac Watts* (Leeds, 1813), 8:37–38. Compare with *Life*, 1:57.

12. See Crone and Skelton, "English Collections of Voyages and Travels, 1625–1846," 93:66–80.

13. *Life*, 1:345.

14. Johnson, Dedication to *Father Lobo's Voyage to Abyssinia.*

15. Review of Lewis Evans's *Geographical . . . Map of the Middle British Colonies in America, Literary Magazine* 1 (January 1756): 454.

16. Giuseppe Baretti, Preface to *A Journey from London to Genoa* (London, 1770).

17. Brydone, *A Tour through Sicily and Malta*, 1:107–108.

18. Johnson, Review of Du Halde's *Description of China*, GM 8 (1738): 365.

19. Jean Hagstrum, *Samuel Johnson's Literary Criticism* (Chicago: University of Chicago Press, 1967), pp. 155–158.

20. See Joel Gold, "Johnson's Translation of Lobo," *PMLA* 80 (1965): 51–61.

21. *Life*, 4:381n1.

22. Johnson, Review of Abbé Guyon's *Dissertation on the Amazons*, *GM* 11 (1741): 208.

23. For the identification of the source materials by Nicholas Bourne and Nathaniel Crouch, see E. L. McAdam, "Johnson's Lives of Sarpi, Blake, and Drake," *PMLA* 58 (1943): 466–476. A third undocumented source on the Thomas Doughty conspiracy in the biography is Richard Hakluyt's "Two Famous Voyages . . . by Sir Francis Drake and M. Thomas Candish," in *The Principal Navigations, Voyages, and Discoveries of the English Nation* (Glasgow, 1903), 11:101–133. This identification constitutes perhaps the most definite evidence that Johnson had read Hakluyt's great collection of travels.

24. For the identification of the source materials by Joseph Lafitau and Manuel de Faria y Sousa, see Allen J. Hazen, *Samuel Johnson's Prefaces and Dedications* (New Haven, Conn.: Yale University Press, 1937), pp. 216–221. A third undocumented source for Johnson's opening comments on primitive navigation is John Locke's *History of Navigation*, which prefaces Awnsham Churchill's *Collection of Voyages and Travels* (1704–1745).

25. Johnson, *Introduction to the Political State of Great Britain*, in *Works*, 6:124.

26. *Introduction to the World Displayed*, in *Works*, 5:221.

27. *Life of Drake*, in *Works*, 6:326.

28. *Introduction to the Political State of Great Britain*, in *Works*, 6:138.

29. Purchas, *Hakluytus Posthumous or Purchas His Pilgrimes*, 1:xl. For further information on travel in the Enlightenment period, see R. W. Frantz, "The English Traveller and the Movement of Ideas, 1660–1732," *Nebraska University Studies* 32–33 (1932–1933): 3–160.

30. *Life*, 4:308.

31. *Life*, 5:209.

32. Preface to *Sir John Narbrough's Voyage to the South-Sea*, in *An Account of Several Late Voyages and Discoveries* (London, 1711).

33. Johnson, Review of Du Halde's *Description of China*, *GM* 12 (1742): 320.

34. George B. Parks, "Travel as Education," in *The Seventeenth Century*, ed. Richard Foster Jones et al. (Stanford, Calif.: Stanford University Press, 1951), pp. 264–290.

35. Robert Devereux, Earl of Essex, *Profitable Instructions* (London: Benjamin Fisher, 1633), pp. 1–24.

36. John Evelyn, Prefatory letter to *The State of France* (London, 1652). For the grand tour, see Clare Howard, *English Travellers of the Renaissance* (New York: John Lane, 1914); Constantia Maxwell, *The English Traveller in France, 1689–1815* (London: G. Routledge and Sons, 1932); and William Mead, *The Grand Tour in the Eighteenth Century* (Boston: Houghton Mifflin, 1914).

37. *Life*, 1:431.

38. *Works*, 6:493.

39. *Letters*, no. 419.a. See also Thomas Jemielity, "Dr. Johnson and the Uses of Travel," *PQ* 51 (1972): 448–459, for the humanistic dimension of Johnson's approach to travel.

40. In his *Life of Thomas Browne*, Johnson slightly misquotes Howell's analysis of language; he also uses Howell's information on the Patuecos of Spain in *Rambler* 169.

41. Howell, p. 13. All future references to the guidebook are to the 1869 edition of the text.

42. Johnson, Preface to *Father Lobo's Voyage to Abyssinia*.

43. *Rasselas*, chap. 11.

44. See chap. 5 below. The fifth paragraph of *Idler* 97 parodies an exciting passage from another source important to the creation of *Rasselas* —his own translation of *Lobo's Voyage*.

45. *Life*, 3:356.

46. Johnson, Review of Du Halde's *Description of China*, GM 12 (1742): 320–322.

47. *Life*, 3:7–8.

48. *Letters*, no. 236.

49. Henry Fielding, Preface to *The Journal of a Voyage to Lisbon* (1755).

50. *Life*, 2:345–346.

51. *Johnson's Lives of the English Poets*, 2:86–87.

52. Brydone, 1:24. See also Fussell, "Patrick Brydone: The Eighteenth-Century Traveler as Representative Man."

<h2 style="text-align:center">3 · HABITS OF TRAVEL IN
WALES AND FRANCE WITH THE THRALES</h2>

1. Thomas Macaulay, Review of Croker's Edition of Boswell's *Life of Johnson*, in *Edinburgh Review* (September 1831).

2. Laurence Sterne, *Tristram Shandy*, 7.13.

3. Daniel Defoe, *A Tour through the Whole Island of Great Britain*, ed. Pat Rogers (Harmondsworth, Middlesex: Penguin Books, 1971), p. 401.

4. Howell, p. 13.

5. *Life*, 1:73.

6. *Letters*, no. 555.

7. *Life*, 3:269.

8. *Life*, 1:367.

9. *Johnson on Shakespeare*, ed. Arthur Sherbo (New Haven, Conn.: Yale University Press, 1968), 7:407–408.

10. *Life*, 4:27–28.

11. *Letters*, no. 440.

12. *Letters*, no. 409.

13. *Letters*, no. 140.

14. Fielding, Preface to *The Journal of a Voyage to Lisbon*.

15. *Life*, 4:199.

16. Macaulay, *History of England* (New York: Houghton Mifflin, 1900), 2:91–92.

17. Locke, *An Essay concerning Human Understanding*, bk. 2, chap.

21, par. 52. For Locke's influence upon Johnson, consult Paul Alkon, *Samuel Johnson and Moral Discipline* (Evanston, Ill.: Northwestern University Press, 1967).

18. *Letters*, no. 528.

19. Locke, "Epistle to the Reader," *An Essay concerning Human Understanding.*

20. *Letters*, no. 409.

21. Francis Bacon, *The Great Instauration*, in *English Prose: 1600–1660*, ed. Victor Harris and Itrat Husain (New York: Holt, Rinehart and Winston, 1965), p. 16.

22. *Letters*, no. 892.

23. *Letters*, no. 877.

24. Piozzi, p. 177.

25. *Letters*, no. 256.

26. Arthur Murphy, *Life of Samuel Johnson*, in *Works*, 1:23.

27. Young, *The Farmer's Letters to the People of England* (London, 1767), p. 34.

28. Piozzi, p. 34.

29. *Letters*, no. 142.

30. *Letters*, no. 772.

31. *Letters*, no. 163.

32. *Letters*, no. 110.

33. *Miscellanies*, 1:329.

34. *Letters*, no. 431.

35. *Letters*, no. 190.

36. *Johnson's Lives of the English Poets*, 3:351.

37. *Letters*, no. 560.

38. *Life*, 2:451. For the improved traveling conditions of the time, see H. L. Beales, "Travel and Communications," in *Johnson's England*, ed. A. S. Turberville (Oxford: Clarendon Press, 1933), 1:125ff.

39. *Letters*, no. 431.

40. *Letters*, no. 360.

41. Piozzi, "Journal of a Welsh Tour," *Dr. Johnson and Mrs. Thrale*, ed. A. M. Broadley (New York: J. Lane, 1910), p. 189.

42. *Life*, 2:285.

43. Piozzi, *Anecdotes*, p. 66.

44. *Diaries*, 1:208.

45. Piozzi, "Journal," p. 179.

46. Defoe, *A Tour through the Whole Island of Great Britain*, pp. 387–388.

47. George Lyttelton, "An Account of a Journey into Wales," in *The Works of Lord Lyttelton* (London, 1776).

48. For further information on the growing romantic vogue in tourism, see George B. Parks, "The Turn to the Romantic in the Travel Literature of the Eighteenth Century," *MLQ* 25 (1964): 22–33. Other works related to the subject are Marjorie Hope Nicolson's *Mountain Gloom and Mountain Glory* and Myra Reynolds's *The Treatment of Nature in English Poetry between Pope and Wordsworth*.

49. Piozzi, "Journal," p. 205.

50. *Life*, 2:285.

51. *Diaries*, 1:203.

52. Piozzi, *Anecdotes*, pp. 169–170.

53. *Letters*, no. 360.1.

54. *Life*, 3:352.

55. *Journey*, 9:44.

56. Hector Saint John de Crèvecoeur, *Letters from an American Farmer* (New York: New American Library, 1963), p. 65. See also Crone, *Modern Geographers*, pp. 10–22.

57. Gilbert Burnet, *Some Letters Containing an Account of . . . Switzerland, Italy, and some Parts of Germany, . . . 1685 and 1686* (London, 1708), pp. 42–43.

58. Montagu, *The Letters and Works of Lady Mary Wortley Montagu*, 1:333.

59. Tobias Smollett, *Travels through France and Italy* (London: John Lehmann, 1949), p. 64. See also Adams, *Travelers and Travel Liars: 1660–1800*, pp. 178–79.

60. Young, *Travels in France and Italy during the Years 1787, 1788, and 1789*, pp. 74–75.

61. Sterne, *A Sentimental Journey through France and Italy*, ed. Ian Jack (New York: Oxford University Press, 1972), p. 50.

62. *Life*, 3:352.

63. *Diaries*, 1:238.

64. *Letters*, no. 438.

65. *Life*, 3:300.

66. *Diaries*, 1:255–256.

4 · MORALITY AND THE METAPHOR OF TRAVEL

1. *Life*, 3:162.

2. Howell, p. 15.

3. William Wimsatt, *The Prose Style of Samuel Johnson* (New Haven, Conn.: Yale University Press, 1963), p. 10. An excellent study of Johnson's moral dynamism is Walter Jackson Bate's *The Achievement of Samuel Johnson* (New York: Oxford University Press, 1955).

4. *Johnson's Lives of the English Poets*, 3:230.

5. *Introduction to the Political State of Great Britain*, in *Works*, 6:127.

6. *Essay on the Origin and Importance of Fugitive Pieces*, in *Works*, 5:191.

7. *Johnson on Shakespeare*, ed, Arthur Sherbo (New Haven, Conn.: Yale University Press, 1968), 7:109.

8. John Hawkins, *The Life of Samuel Johnson* (Dublin, 1787), p. 45.

9. *Works*, 8:99.

10. See Donald Greene, *Samuel Johnson* (New York: Twayne Publishers, 1970), p. 61. Morris Golden notes Johnson's preoccupation with the journey theme in morality and fiction in *The Self Observed* (Baltimore: Johns Hopkins Press, 1972).

11. Robert Burton, *The Anatomy of Melancholy* (New York: Dutton, 1965), 1:305–306. However autobiographical, Johnson's portrait of the scholar seems to have been influenced by the catalog and order of academic trials enumerated in Burton's well-known "Digression of the Melancholy of Scholars." Johnson was a devoted fan of Burton's book. For the influence of Ecclesiastes and William Law's *A Serious Call to the Devout and Holy Life* upon Johnson's writings in general, see Bate, *The Achievement of Samuel Johnson*.

12. Johnson, Sermon 15, in *Works*, 9:424.

13. *Diaries*, 1:43.

14. Sermon 10, in *Works*, 9:379.

15. *Introduction to the World Displayed*, in *Works*, 5:227.

16. Sermon 20, in *Works*, 9:471.

17. John Hughes, "An Essay on Allegorical Poetry," in *The Works of Spenser* (London, 1750), 1:23. Johnson knew and criticized the essay in his *Life of Hughes*.

18. See Stanford, *The Ulysses Theme: A Study in the Adaptability of a Traditional Hero*. Of relevance to Johnson's Spenserian imitation of the *Odyssey* in *Rambler* 102 is his use of *The Faerie Queene* (2.12) to illustrate the moral meaning of the word "voyage" in the *Dictionary*.

19. These classical allegories on the choice of life theme, with female personifications of education and reason, merit comparison with *The Vision of Theodore*. However, missing in both these analogues is a religious dimension present in *The Pilgrim's Progress* and Johnson's adaptation of Bunyan's Hill Difficulty episode in his own story.

20. Sometimes the very language of *The Pilgrim's Progress* carries over into Johnson's allegory. In fact, the guardians in both stories ask their pilgrims the same question, "whither art thou going?," before demonstrating the perils of idleness afflicting Christian and Theodore.

21. *Rambler* 67 also bears a close resemblance to *The Tablet of Cebes* in Xenophon's *Memorabilia*, 2.1.21–33.

22. Bunyan, *The Pilgrim's Progress*, ed. James Wharey and Roger Sharrock, pp. 110–113.

23. See Hagstrum, *Samuel Johnson's Literary Criticism*, p. 7, and compare with *Johnson on Shakespeare*, 7:61–62: "but the pleasures of sudden wonder are soon exhausted, and the mind can only repose on the stability of truth."

24. Hughes, 1:35.

25. *Lives of the English Poets*, 3:233.

26. Piozzi, p. 180. For the archetypal plot patterns in eighteenth-century prose fiction, see Paulson, *Satire and the Novel in Eighteenth-Century England*, pp. 41ff.

27. Paulson analyzes the Cervantic strategy in *The Fictions of Satire* (Baltimore: Johns Hopkins Press, 1967), pp. 100ff. An excellent and exhaustive study of Johnson's approach to fiction is Carey McIntosh, *The Choice of Life, Samuel Johnson and the World of Fiction* (New Haven, Conn.: Yale University Press, 1973).

28. *Lives of the English Poets*, 1:209–210.

29. *Rasselas*, chap. 4.

30. See *Ramblers* 158, 23, and 104.

31. Johnson quotes this remark by Soame Jenyns with complete approval in his review of Jenyns's *A Free Inquiry into the Nature and Origin of Evil*, in *Works*, 6:69.

32. *Lives of the English Poets*, 1:99.

33. *Life*, 2:351–352.

34. Johnson, bk. 9, chap. 11, in Charlotte Lennox's *The Female Quixote* (1752). See also *Rambler* 4.

35. Piozzi, p. 13.

36. Johnson, bk. 9, chap. 11, in Charlotte Lennox's *The Female Qui-*

xote. According to Thomas Percy, " 'when a boy he was immoderately fond of reading romances of chivalry. . . . Yet I have heard him attribute to these extravagant fictions that unsettled turn of mind which prevented his ever fixing in any profession.' "

37. *Preface to Shakespeare*, in *Works*, 5:126.

38. *Rasselas*, chap. 29.

5 · MYTHIC AND HISTORIC TRAVEL IN THE CREATION OF *RASSELAS*

1. *Life*, 1:341.

2. Johnson, Preface to *An Essay on Milton's Paradise Lost*, in *Works*, 5:268.

3. See Donald Lockhart, " 'The Fourth Son of the Mighty Emperour': The Ethiopian Background of Johnson's *Rasselas*," *PMLA* 78 (1963): 516–528, and Arthur Weitzman, "More Light on *Rasselas*: The Background of the Egyptian Episodes," *PQ* 48 (1969): 42–58.

4. See Fussell, *The Rhetorical World of Augustan Humanism*, pp. 262 ff., and Northrop Frye, *Anatomy of Criticism*, pp. 52–62.

5. Johnson, *Preface to Shakespeare*, in *Works*, 5:123. See also *Life*, 4:218, for Johnson's special fondness for the *Odyssey*.

6. Roger Ascham, *The Schoolmaster*, in *The Renaissance in England*, ed. Hyder E. Rollins and Herschel Baker (Boston: D. C. Heath, 1954), p. 831. Eighteenth-century authors, like Pope and Fielding, lauded the domestic focus on "common life" in the *Odyssey* and translated the epic episodes into contemporary moral equivalents in their writings. See "The Postscript" to *Pope's Odyssey* and Fielding's *Journal of a Voyage to Lisbon*. By the same token, Johnson's *Rambler* 102 converted the *Odyssey* adventures into a modern voyage of life that basically condenses the meaning and movement of Rasselas's moral odyssey. From the standpoint of *Rambler* 102, the plot of *Rasselas* is reducible to an allegorical framework that Renaissance writers had associated with the kind of traveling performed by Rasselas.

7. For a detailed study of Bunyan's influence upon Johnson's story, see Thomas M. Curley, "The Spiritual Journey Moralized in *Rasselas*," *Anglia* 91 (1973): 35–55. John Loofbourow notes the relationship between the two works in *Thackeray and the Form of Fiction*, pp. 99–100.

8. Plato, *Republic*, trans. Paul Shorey (Cambridge, Mass.: Harvard University Press, 1963), 2.10.618. Johnson venerated Socrates as the most

"Christian" of pagan philosophers and praised his moral wisdom (see the *Life of Milton*) even though his own moral viewpoint was often radically different. For comparisons between Johnson and Socrates, see Boswell's *Tour to the Hebrides* and Percy Hazen Houston, *Dr. Johnson: A Study in Eighteenth-Century Humanism* (Cambridge, Mass: Harvard University Press, 1923).

9. Gwin Kolb, "The Structure of *Rasselas*," *PMLA* 66 (1951): 698–717. Geoffrey Tillotson doubtfully argues that *Rasselas* has a direct antecedent in the *Persian Tales* in " 'Rasselas' and the 'Persian Tales,' " *Essays in Criticism and Research* (New York: Macmillan, 1942), pp. 111–116.

10. Johnson, *Preface to the English Dictionary*, in *Works*, 5:47ff.

11. Thomas Preston, "The Biblical Context of Johnson's *Rasselas*," *PMLA* 84 (1969): 274–283. Recent studies of *Rasselas* are demonstrating that successive chapters of the tale assimilated a wide variety of source materials, some of which are mentioned below.

12. *Diaries*, 1:66.

13. See Fussell, *Samuel Johnson and the Life of Writing* (New York: Harcourt, Brace and Jovanovich, 1971), chaps. 4 and 5.

14. Johnson, Advertisement to John Newbery's *The World Displayed* (1759).

15. Howell, p. 88.

16. For the scholarship on the travel book sources of *Rasselas*, consult the following: J. R. Moore, "*Rasselas* and the Early Travellers to Abyssinia," *MLQ* 15 (1954): 36–41; Ellen Leyburn, " 'No Romantick Absurdities or Incredible Fictions': The Relation of Johnson's *Rasselas* to Lobo's *Voyage to Abyssinia*," *PMLA* 70 (1955): 1059–1067; Gwin Kolb, "The 'Paradise' in Abyssinia and the 'Happy Valley' in *Rasselas*," *MP* 56 (1958): 10–16; Donald Lockhart, " 'The Fourth Son of the Mighty Emperour': The Ethiopian Background of Johnson's *Rasselas*," *PMLA* 78 (1963): 516–528; and Arthur Weitzman, "More Light on *Rasselas*: The Background of the Egyptian Episodes," *PQ* 48 (1969): 42–58.

17. See John Livingston Lowes, *The Road to Xanadu*, for what is yet one of the best studies of Coleridge's creative process.

18. So inconclusive is Lobo's narrative that Johnson, following Le Grand's text, appended the accounts of later travelers to round out the story of the abortive Jesuit mission in Abyssinia.

19. Alvarez mentions the inundating rains flooding Seged's retreat; Tellez pointedly denies that Lake Dambea possesses crocodiles which

frighten Seged's attendants; and Poncet records an Abyssinian emperor's river chase for hippopotami and thus suggested Seged's prowess at hunting. See the articles listed in n. 16 above.

20. Job Ludolf, *A New History of Ethiopia* (London: S. Smith, 1682), pp. 191, 210, 350.

21. For the influence of Ecclesiastes upon *Rasselas*, see Preston, "The Biblical Context of Johnson's *Rasselas*," Ian Jack, " 'The choice of life' in Johnson and Matthew Prior," *JEGP* 49 (1950): 523–530, and J. W. Johnson, "Rasselas and his Ancestors," *N&Q* 204 (1959): 185–188. Johnson considered Solomon the author of Ecclesiastes even though modern Bible scholars doubt this attribution. To avoid confusion, I have similarly equated the anonymous "Preacher" of Ecclesiastes with Solomon in this chapter.

22. Balthazar Tellez, *The Travels of the Jesuits in Ethiopia* (London: Knapton and Bell, 1711), p. 189.

23. Ludolf, pp. 195ff.

24. *Lobo's Voyage* briefly refers to an Abyssinian merchant-philosopher, Meropius, who wandered around India with two kinsmen and was killed upon his return home. See Johnson, *A Voyage to Abyssinia by Father Jerome Lobo* (London: Elliot and Kay, 1789), pp. 294–295.

25. Ludolf, p. 3.

26. John Hawkins, *The Life of Samuel Johnson*, pp. 329ff.

27. Johnson, *A Voyage to Abyssinia by Father Jerome Lobo*, p. 113.

28. See Lockhart, pp. 516–528, for the influence of the bogus reports by Urreta and Baratti upon the happy valley description. Urreta associates Mount Amhara with Solomon's concubine, Sheba.

29. John Bermudez, *Voyage to Abyssinia*, in Purchas, 11:358.

30. William Lithgow, *Rare Adventures and Painefull Peregrinations* (Glasgow, 1906), p. 269.

31. George Sandys, *A Relation of a Journey, ... 1610* (London, 1621), pp. 122, 125.

32. Richard Pococke, *Description of the East and Some Other Countries* (London, 1743–1745), 1:169–170.

33. Sandys, pp. 128–129. See Weitzman, "More Light on *Rasselas*: The Background of the Egyptian Episodes," for John Greaves's influence upon Imlac's dissertation in *Rasselas*, chap. 31 as well as other contributions by Aaron Hill, Pococke, and Sandys to Johnson's description of the pyramid.

34. Pococke, 1:116–120.

35. See also Weitzman for the influence of Alexander Russell's *Natural History of Aleppo* and Johnson's own *Irene* upon the harem episode.

36. *Works*, 6:480.

37. Johnson, *A Voyage to Abyssinia by Father Jerome Lobo*, p. 118.

38. *Life*, 4:427–428.

6 · PHILOSOPHIC ART AND TRAVEL IN THE HIGHLANDS

1. Boswell, *Boswell's Journal of a Tour to the Hebrides*, ed. Frederick A. Pottle and Charles A. Bennett (New York: Viking, 1936), p. 372.

2. *Boswell's Journal*, p. 3.

3. *Letters*, no. 323.

4. *Boswell's Journal*, p. 383.

5. *Journey*, 9:164. All further references to the travel book are to Mary Lascelles's standard edition of the text.

6. For the recent debate concerning the *Journey*, consult the following: Jeffrey Hart, "Johnson's *A Journey to the Western Islands of Scotland:* History as Art," *EIC* 10 (1960): 44–59; Mary Lascelles, "Some Reflections on Johnson's Hebridean Journey," *New Rambler*, June 1961, pp. 2–13; Arthur Sherbo, "Johnson's Intent in the *Journey to the Western Islands of Scotland*," *EIC* 16 (1966): 382–397; Donald Greene, "Johnsonian Critics," *EIC* 10 (1960): 476–480; T. K. Meir, "Pattern in Johnson's *Journey to the Western Islands of Scotland*," *Studies in Scottish Literature* 5 (1968): 185–193; Clarence Tracy, "Johnson's *A Journey to the Western Islands of Scotland:* A Reconsideration," *Studies on Voltaire and the Eighteenth Century* 58 (1967): 1593–1606; and Arthur Schwartz, "Johnson's *Journey*," *JEGP* 69 (1970): 292–303.

7. *Letters*, no. 318.

8. Griffiths's review appeared in both the *Scots Magazine* 37 (January 1775), and the *Monthly Review* 52 (January-February 1775).

9. Robert Boyle, "General Heads for a Natural History of a Country," *Philosophical Transactions of the Royal Society*, ed. Charles Hutton et al. (London, 1809), 1:63–65.

10. *Miscellanies*, 2:368.

11. Johnson, "Of Aliens, and of the Incorporation of England with Wales and its Union with Scotland," in E. L. McAdam, Jr., *Dr. Johnson and the English Law* (Syracuse, N.Y.: Syracuse University Press, 1951), pp. 104–105.

12. *Boswell's Journal*, p. 160.

13. *Boswell's Journal*, p. 314.

14. *Life*, 3:302.

15. Johnson refers to Sir John Davies's *Discoverie of the True Causes Why Ireland Was Never Entirely Subdued* (1612) in his travel book and knew, among other histories, William Robertson's *History of Scotland* (1759) and John Macpherson's *Dissertations on . . . the Ancient Caledonians, Picts, and British and Irish Scots* (1768). Thomas Jemielity notes the possibility of Johnson's familiarity with at least a *Gentleman's Magazine* review of Edward Burt's *Letters from a Gentleman in the North of Scotland* (1754) in *Philosophy as Art: A Study of the Intellectual Background of Samuel Johnson's Journey to the Western Islands of Scotland*, (Ph.D. diss., Cornell University, 1965). Despite Johnson's claim of having imitated Charles Burney's *Present State of Music in France and Italy* (1771) and his *Present State of Music in Germany, Netherlands, and the United Provinces* (1773), his comment must have been a compliment because their works have very little in common.

16. P. Hume Brown, ed. Preface to *Early Travellers in Scotland* (Edinburgh: D. Douglas, 1891).

17. Hector Boece, "Description," (an early English trans. of *Scotorum Historiae*), in Brown, p. 93.

18. Martin Martin, Preface to *A Description of the Western Islands of Scotland* (Glasgow: T. Morison, 1884).

19. Thomas Campbell, *A Philosophical Survey of the South of Ireland* (London: Strahan, 1777), p. 85.

20. *Boswell's Journal*, p. 129.

21. Defoe, *A Tour through the Whole Island of Great Britain* (London: Everyman, 1962), 2:138.

22. William Sacheverell, *An Account of the Isle of Man* (Douglas, Isle of Man: Manx Society, 1859), p. 107. According to *Life*, 5:336, Johnson declared that his expectations of Iona were based on his reading of this work.

23. John Campbell, *A Political Survey of Britain* (London, 1774), 1:606. Johnson refers to this work during his remarks on deforestation in the *Journey*.

24. *Life*, 3:274.

25. Ibid.

26. Thomas Pennant, *A Tour in Scotland and Voyage to the Hebrides* (London, 1776), 2:338.

27. Thomas Gray, letter 85, in *The Works of Thomas Gray*, ed. Ed-

mund Gosse (London, 1884), 2:223–224. For the growing romantic vogue in travel books, see Parks, "The Turn to the Romantic in Travel Literature of the Eighteenth Century," *MLQ* 25 (1964): 22–23.

28. *Boswell's Journal*, p. 341.

29. William Gilpin, *Observations, Relative Chiefly to Picturesque Beauty, . . . on Several Parts of England* (London, 1786), 2:19. See also Christopher Salvesen, *The Landscape of Memory: A Study of Wordsworth's Poetry* (Lincoln: University of Nebraska Press, 1965), chap. 1.

30. John Stoddart, in his *Remarks on Local Scenery and Manners of Scotland* (London: W. Miller, 1801), explicitly bases his psychology of feeling and observing on Wordsworth's *Preface to the Lyrical Ballads*.

31. *The Highlands of Scotland in 1750* (London, 1750), p. 141.

32. *Letters*, no. 329. For Johnson's economic principles, see John H. Middendorf, "Johnson on Wealth and Commerce," in *Johnson, Boswell, and Their Circle* (Oxford: Clarendon Press, 1965), pp. 47–64.

33. Bernard Kelly, *The "Children of the Mist"* (London: Virtue, 1946); Malcolm Gray, *The Highland Economy, 1750–1850* (Edinburgh and London, 1959). See also Alexander Irvine, *Inquiry into the Causes and Effects of Emigration from the Highlands and Western Islands of Scotland* (Edinburgh, 1802) and John Walker, *Economical History of the Hebrides* or the *Western Islands of Scotland* (Edinburgh and London, 1899).

34. John Knox, *A Tour through the Highlands and the Hebride Isles in 1786* in *Extracts from the Publications of Mr. Knox, Dr. Anderson, Mr. Pennant, and Dr. Johnson relative to the Northern and North-Western Coast of Great Britain* (London, 1787).

35. See Jemielity, "Philosophy as Art: A Study of the Intellectual Background of Samuel Johnson's *Journey to the Western Islands of Scotland*" (Ph.D. diss., Cornell University, 1965).

36. *Life*, 3:302.

7 · THE END OF A JOURNEY

1. *Letters*, no. 701.

2. *Letters*, no. 984.

3. Howell, pp. 13–14.

4. *Life*, 2:148.

5. *Letters*, no. 338.

6. *Boswell: The Ominous Years*, p. 308.

7. James Cook, *A Voyage towards the South Pole, and Round the World*, ed. John Douglas (London: Strahan, 1777), 2:5.

8. Cook, 2:5.

9. Fanny Burney, *Diary and Letters of Madame d'Arblay*, 1:454, in Percy A. Scholes, *The Great Dr. Burney* (New York: Oxford University Press, 1948), 2:25.

10. *Letters*, no. 749.

11. *Life*, 3:8.

12. *Life*, 4:308–309.

13. *Life*, 4:308.

14. Johnson, *Introduction to the World Displayed*, in *Works*, 5:219. For his final remarks on the miserable state of the Polynesians, see his dedication to Charles Burney's *Account of the Musical Performances in commemoration of Handel* (1785).

15. See the reviews of Foreign Books, *GM* (July, 1742) and compare with Johnson's endorsement of investigating northern countries in his *Account of the Harleian Library* (1742). For his part in reviewing foreign books in *GM*, consult Donald Greene, "Some Notes on Johnson and the *Gentleman's Magazine*," *PMLA* 74 (1959): 75–84; Gwin Kolb, "More Attributions to Dr. Johnson," *SEL* 1 (1961): 77–95; and Arthur Sherbo, "Samuel Johnson and the *Gentleman's Magazine*," in *Johnsonian Studies*, ed. Magdi Wahba (Cairo and London, 1962), pp. 133–159.

16. Johnson, Review of Thomas Birch's *History of the Royal Society of London*, *Literary Magazine* 1 (1756): 32. See Greene, "Johnson's Contributions to the *Literary Magazine*," *RES*, n.s. 7 (1956): 367–392.

17. *Letters*, no. 1154. For the dating of this letter and his association with Mrs. Smart, see Sherbo, *Christopher Smart: Scholar of the University* (East Lansing: Michigan State University Press, 1967), pp. 122–126.

18. *Life*, 5:236. For Barrington's part in the current search for a northern passage to India, see Beaglehole, *The Life of Captain James Cook*, chap. 19.

19. Boswell, *Journal of a Tour to the Hebrides*, p. 362.

20. *Life*, 3:269.

21. Johnson, Review of Du Halde's *Description of China*, *GM* 12 (1742):320.

22. Review of Du Halde's *Description of China*, *GM* 12 (1742): 354.

23. *Life*, 3:20.

24. *Letters*, no. 187.2. For a lucid account of Johnson's admittedly obscure part in the affairs of the East India Company, consult Donald

Greene, *The Politics of Samuel Johnson* (New Haven, Conn.: Yale University Press, 1960), chap. 7. See also Sir Arnold McNair, *Dr. Johnson and the Law* (Cambridge: Cambridge University Press, 1948) and Lucy Sutherland, *The East India Company in Eighteenth-Century Politics* (Oxford: Clarendon Press, 1952), chap. 7, for further information about Johnson's "Indian" associates and the complexities of the company's contemporary history.

25. *Life*, 3:350.

26. *Miscellanies*, 2:367. For his friendship with Vansittart and others in the circle, see n. 24 above and "Henry Vansittart," in *Dictionary of National Biography*. The *DNB* entry for "Robert Vansittart" repeats the claim that Johnson "was invited to visit India with [Robert Vansittart] by his brother Henry." Another close friend of Johnson, Sir Joshua Reynolds, painted Henry Vansittart's portrait in 1767, roughly the same period when Johnson was allegedly associated with the Indian governor.

27. *Letters*, no. 367.

28. *Letters*, no. 353.

29. Warren Hastings, letter to Dr. Johnson, 7 August 1775, in George R. Gleig, *Memoirs of the Right Honorable Warren Hastings* (London: Richard Bentley, 1841), 2:18. See also Davies, *Strange Destiny, A Biography of Warren Hastings*, pp. 338ff. for Hastings's role in Indian studies.

30. *Letters*, no. 417.

31. *Life*, 3:400.

32. *Letters*, no. 928.

33. *Life*, 3:36.

34. *Life*, 3:19, 470–471.

35. *Journey*, 9:148.

36. Young, *Travels in France and Italy during the Years 1787, 1788, and 1789*, p. 255.

37. *Life*, 4:199.

38. Hawkesworth, ed., Preface to *An Account of the Voyages ... for Making Discoveries in the Southern Hemisphere*. See also Crone, *Modern Geographers*, pp. 5–13.

39. John Keats, Letter to Benjamin Robert Haydon (8 April 1818), in *John Keats: Selected Poems and Letters*, ed. Douglas Bush (Boston: Houghton Mifflin, 1959), pp. 269–270. See also Barrows, "Convention and Novelty in the Romantic Generation's Experience of Italy," in *Literature as a Mode of Travel*, pp. 7off.

40. See the Man of the Hill's view of travel in *Tom Jones* (8.15) and the preface to *The Journal of a Voyage to Lisbon*. Fielding's two greatest novels are cast as moral journeys of inquiry into the manners of English society and exploit the Homeric, Cervantic, and Christian traditions of travel. See Martin Battestin, *The Moral Basis of Fielding's Art: A Study of Joseph Andrews* and Ethel Thornbury, *Henry Fielding's Theory of the Comic Prose Epic*.

41. Fielding, *The Journal of a Voyage to Lisbon*, in *The Complete Works of Henry Fielding*, ed. W. E. Henley (New York: Barnes and Noble, 1967), 3:203. Like his comic epic novels, Fielding's *Journal* parodied the *Odyssey* plot in a Cervantic fashion and presents contemporary moral equivalents of many epic adventures and personages.

42. *Tom Jones*, 7.2.

43. Goldsmith, *The Citizen of the World*, letter 5.

44. *Life*, 3:236.

45. *Poems*, 6:286.

46. Smollett, *Travels through France and Italy*, p. 272. See also Paulson, *Satire and the Novel in Eighteenth-Century England*, pp. 190–194.

47. See A. Alvarez, "The Delinquent Aesthetic," *Hudson Review* 19 (1966–1967): 590–600, and Morris Golden, "Sterne's Journeys and Sallies," *Studies in Burke and His Time* 16 (1974): 47–62.

48. *Letters*, no. 222. See also Northrop Frye, "Towards Defining an Age of Sensibility," in *Backgrounds to Eighteenth-Century Literature* (New York: Oxford University Press, 1959), pp. 312–322.

49. *Letters*, no. 929.1. See also Maurice Quinlan, "Balloons and the Awareness of a New Age," *Studies in Burke and His Time* 14 (1973): 221–238, and Richard Schwartz, *Samuel Johnson and the New Science* (Madison: University of Wisconsin Press, 1971).

50. *Miscellanies*, 2:367.

51. *Miscellanies*, 2:155.

INDEX

SJ = Samuel Johnson